Understanding Central Banks

Nils Herger

Understanding Central Banks

 Springer

Nils Herger
Department of Economics
University of Bern
Bern, Switzerland

Translation from the German language edition:
Wie funktionieren Zentralbanken? Geld- und Währungspolitik verstehen by Nils Herger
Copyright © Springer Fachmedien Wiesbaden GmbH, 2016
Springer Fachmedien Wiesbaden GmbH is part of Springer Nature.
All Rights Reserved.

ISBN 978-3-030-05161-7   ISBN 978-3-030-05162-4   (eBook)
https://doi.org/10.1007/978-3-030-05162-4

Library of Congress Control Number: 2019931850

This Springer imprint is published by the registered company Springer Nature Switzerland AG
The registered company address is: Gewerbestrasse 11, 6330 Cham, Switzerland

To Hua

Preface

Because central banks are responsible for setting monetary policy, they are regularly the subject of public debates. During serious economic crises, which can be manifested in, for example, high levels of inflation, turmoil in the international monetary system, or systemic financial instability, monetary issues can even dominate the economic-policy agenda. However, broader audiences may not always understand the mechanisms by which a central bank influences economic outcomes. For example, such readers may ask how a central bank adjusts the money supply? Via which channels does monetary policy affect key economic variables, such as inflation and employment? Why is a central bank's independence important? What are the advantages and disadvantages of common currencies? How can central banks deal with financial and banking crises? How do ancient metallic currencies and modern fiat-money systems differ? Were past monetary systems more stable than their modern counterparts? This book was written to answer such questions for a broad readership using nontechnical language.

This book is based on an earlier German version entitled *Wie funktionieren Zentralbanken?—Geld- und Währungspolitik verstehen* (ISBN: 978-3-658-07875-1). However, rather than providing a word-for-word translation of the original, I have decided to adapt and update the discussion and to use suitable examples for the international readership, for which *Understanding central banks* was written. In particular, Chap. 2 includes a more extensive discussion of the global financial crisis, Chap. 3 discusses the money-and-credit multiplication process in more detail, and Chap. 6 provides more background material on the differences and similarities between Keynesians and Monetarists regarding the role of central banks in the broad economy. Nevertheless, reflecting the positive feedback that *Wie funktionieren Zentralbanken?* received, the main structure of the text and the arrangement of the chapters have been preserved. In any case, I hope that the English edition of this book will help readers to better understand the world of central banking.

Gerzensee, Switzerland   Nils Herger
October 2018

Contents

1

Introduction

There have been three great inventions since the beginning of time: fire, the wheel, and central banking. Will Rogers (American comedian, 1879–1935)[1]

1.1 What Is a Central Bank?

Will Rogers, the speaker of the opening quote, was a widely adored comedian and successful Hollywood actor before he died in a tragic plane crash in 1935. To this day, his words ridiculing the historical significance of central banking amid the economic troubles of the 1930s have remained popular with the guardians of the currency, a group of men and women not otherwise known for their sense of humour. Nevertheless, regardless of whether we consider the Great Depression, or the current period, central banks indeed wield great influence over a country's monetary, financial, and economic conditions. Concretely, ordinary purchases are often made in cash, which includes banknotes issued by the central bank. Even as more and more economic transactions are settled electronically, they require a sophisticated payment infrastructure which is supervised, or even partly managed, by the central bank. In addition to organising the payment system, monetary authorities—to introduce an alternative expression for the central bank—are also responsible for setting monetary policy. In doing so, they have typically retained a remarkable degree of independence from direct government interference despite the broad

---

[1]Origin of quote unknown.

© Springer Nature Switzerland AG 2019
N. Herger, *Understanding Central Banks*, https://doi.org/10.1007/978-3-030-05162-4_1

economic effects that may result from their decisions and interventions. At first glance, monetary policy seems to be of minor importance to the average citizen. However, as with other triumphs of civilisation, such as the supply of electricity or the management of mass-transportation systems, the crucial role of a well-functioning monetary system is only clear in the case of failure, or an outright breakdown. In monetary affairs, such adverse events are manifested in various forms of crises, during which instability within the financial or banking system or pervasive levels of inflation can have far-reaching effects. In this regard, it is important to recognise that good monetary policy can prevent, or alleviate, such crises, but that bad monetary policy can also be the main culprit behind economic turmoil. History provides many examples for both scenarios.

In very rough terms, the economic importance of central banks is based on their privilege to issue currency, that is, officially recognised forms of money.[2] The way in which the currency is arranged in a given country has large implications for its monetary and financial system. In particular, the terms and conditions under which central-bank money is provided affects the domestic level of interest rates and, hence, the price of borrowing and lending, with profound effects on the total amount of money and credit in circulation. Ultimately, via these and other channels, the kind of monetary policy pursued by the central bank can affect macroeconomic outcomes such as the level of unemployment and inflation.

Given the crucial role of monetary policy in modern economies, it is not surprising that central banks are regularly in the headlines. Especially in times of economic and financial turmoil, the corresponding political debates can be fierce and sometimes become emotional or even hostile. Nevertheless, the broader public may often find it difficult to understand how the central bank's decisions affect economic outcomes. Instead of providing detailed explanations, the public debate often incorporates vague statements. For example, it is commonly said that the central bank is 'pumping liquidity into the system' or 'printing money' to describe expansionary monetary-policy interventions. Against this background, this book was written to shed light on the interactions between central banks and other parts of the economy. The reader is not expected to be familiar with the technical aspects of economic analysis, let alone macroeconomic models.

---

[2]Note that particularly in the United States, the term 'currency' is often used in the narrower sense of banknotes (or 'currency notes') and coins. The following discussion uses 'currency' in a broader sense that includes the reserves held by financial institutions in their accounts at the central bank. Physical forms of currency, e.g. banknotes and coins, are henceforth referred to as 'cash'.

As a first step towards understanding, note that the central banks of different countries are referred to by different names. In a few cases, such as the 'European Central Bank' (ECB) or the 'Hong Kong Monetary Authority', the terminologies introduced above appear directly in the names of central banks. However, owing to the historical significance of managing and providing reserves, the term 'reserve bank' is used in Australia, India, New Zealand, South Africa, and the United States with the 'Federal Reserve System' (or, briefly, the 'Fed'). In Germany, the 'Bundesbank' replaced the former 'Reichs-bank' after the Second World War. To this day, the Swedish central bank is called 'Riksbank'. Austria and Switzerland call their monetary authority the 'Nationalbank', or national bank. In England, France, Italy, and Japan, the authority responsible for the conduct of monetary policy uses the name of the country; these authorities are called the Bank of England, Banque de France, Banca d'Italia, and Bank of Japan, respectively. This naming is potentially confusing since the Bank of America, the Deutsche Bank, or the Bank of China are not central, but commercial banks. As you are probably about to ask yourself that question, the central bank of the Middle Kingdom is instead called the 'People's Bank of China'. Regardless of the terminology used, the term 'central bank' refers to a financial institution—nowadays often under the public law—with the preeminent responsibility of formulating and implementing the monetary policy of a currency area (typically a country). A central bank wields influence because it has been granted a monopoly over the issuance of currency, which implies that its main liabilities (banknotes and bank reserves) serve as the purest form of money. By managing these liabilities via monetary-policy instruments, such as repurchase agreements or open-market operations, central banks can regulate interest-rate levels and, in turn, control the amount of money and credit circulating through the economy. Modern central banks ultimately aim to ameliorate macroeconomic outcomes by, for example, keeping the price level stable (preserving the purchasing power of the currency) and smoothing the business cycle. Furthermore, central banks also play a leading role in safeguarding the stability of the financial system by traditionally acting as lenders of last resort for the banking sector. Finally, their miscellaneous activities can include acting as bankers for the government, issuing banknotes, managing a country's international reserves, supervising commercial banks and determining their capital requirements, supervising and managing parts of the payment system and the financial-market infrastructure, and providing consumer protection regarding monetary and financial matters.

To provide a rough overview of the topics covered in this book, the next section endeavours to highlight some of the major connections between the central bank and other parts of the economy.

1.2   The Central Bank, the Economy, and the Outline of This Book

As a monetary authority, the central bank is primarily connected with the wider economy via several classes of broad monetary transactions. Figure 1.1 depicts some of these transactions involving firms, households, commercial banks, financial markets, foreign countries, and the government. At this stage, it is unnecessary to go into the details; this illustration merely serves as preparation for the more in-depth discussions in the subsequent chapters of this book.

As shown in the bottom part of Fig. 1.1, economic transactions commonly result from private domestic consumption, that is households purchasing goods and services from firms (or companies) which, in turn, employ labour and capital within the production process. As compensation, firms pay incomes to households in the form of wages and disbursed profits. This interaction between households and firms represents a rudimentary version of the so-called 'circular flow of income and spending', which connects different parts of the economy. More sophisticated versions of this model account for additional aspects of the economy, such as the international sector. In

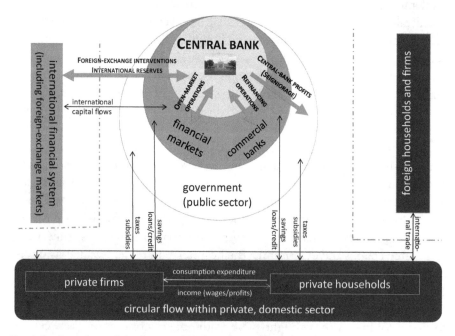

Fig. 1.1 Overview of the interactions between the central bank and the economy

particular, private consumption and production involve not only domestic markets but also foreign firms and households, which gives rise to exports and imports of goods and services. Furthermore, along with the private sector, the public sector accounts for a major share of modern economic activity. Governments collect taxes from firms and households to offer public services, and make financial transfers. Finally, the financial system in general, and commercial banks in particular, collect savings and provide various forms of loans and credit to households, firms, and the government. In doing so, financial firms typically adopt an intermediary position between lenders and borrowers. Financial transactions can also involve foreign countries leading to international flows of capital and money.

Figure 1.1 depicts income and spending in terms of monetary flows. However, just as, for example, the legal system and established business procedures underpin commercial contracts, pecuniary transactions rely on a set of formal rules and informal customs which shape the monetary framework. Thus, many questions arise. Should a country have its own currency? Is it sensible to fix the external value of a currency—that is, the exchange rate—to the value of a precious metal, such as gold? Should the currency be issued by several competing commercial banks, or by only one designated central bank? Should the central bank be a private or public institution? What are the main goals of monetary policy? Are restrictions on international capital flows necessary? Some of these questions may seem strange in the modern era, as almost all countries have their own central bank, precious metals have long been demonetised, monetary policy mainly aims to preserve the purchasing power of fiat money, and capital can move more or less freely across borders. It is therefore, perhaps, surprising to hear that these questions have been answered quite differently in the past. To understand the similarities and differences between current and former monetary frameworks, Chap. 2 of this book looks back on the historical development of central banking across the past centuries. Furthermore, most of the above-mentioned questions touch on an overarching topic, namely, the definition of money. It is immediately clear why this definition matters to the monetary authority, but the answer is anything but straightforward. Hence, Chap. 3 focuses on understanding what money really is.

It is impossible to maintain the purchasing power of a currency without controlling the amount of money in circulation. When private or public agents oversupply money, an economy will soon suffer from inflation and, in extreme cases, a currency collapse. Historical examples of severe monetary turmoil, which have occasionally resulted in episodes of hyperinflation, suggest that such a scenario is more than a mere theoretical possibility. Therefore, adequate management of the money supply lies at the heart of modern central banking. The bold arrows connecting the inner circles of Fig. 1.1 suggest that currency is not usually distributed directly to households and firms. Instead, central bank refinancing operations are typically conducted with commercial banks. In practice, this implies that they have central-bank accounts with so-called 'reserves'. Conversely, firms and households hold their accounts at commercial, or retail, banks. The private banking sector is also largely responsible for the final distribution of banknotes and coins via a network of branches and cash machines. Furthermore, by buying and selling government bonds or other securities, central banks undertake direct financial-market interventions. Since these transactions occur in the open market, they are called 'open-market operations'. Finally, direct interventions can also occur on the foreign-exchange market, as when a monetary authority buys or sells its own currency against foreign currency. Such interventions are typically made to influence the exchange rate. Taken together, these various transaction classes reflect the most commonly applied monetary-policy instruments (or tools). Chapter 4 discusses these instruments.

By its very name, a central bank adopts a central position within the financial system. Most importantly, changes in the so-called 'base interest rate' charged on bank-reserve holdings can send shock waves not only across the average level of interest rates, but also other terms and conditions on a broad range of loans and credit. Because cash and bank reserves serve as ultimate means of payment, the central bank holds a unique position to create 'liquidity'. This ability becomes crucial, when the trust in private alternatives to officially recognised forms of money, such as demand deposits (checkable accounts), has been undermined by scandals within the banking and financial industry. In this case, central banks traditionally act as lenders of last resort to commercial banks confronted with a liquidity shortages and, hence, preserve the stability of the financial system. Chapter 5 discusses these financial-stability issues in greater detail.

The effects of monetary interventions are by no means limited to the financial system. Rather, they can affect most parts of the economy. The above-mentioned connection between the base interest rate and the provision of loans and credit to the private sector already encapsulates this idea. It is easy to pursue this notion further, as the total amount of loans and credit impinges on aggregate investment and consumption levels. This mechanism is just one example of the effect of central-bank decisions on the real side of the economy, which includes, for example, the business cycle and unemployment. Of course, monetary policy matters even more for the nominal side, which represents economic phenomena in terms of monetary variables. It is indeed intuitive that the amount of money in circulation and the average price level have a close connection. When the money supply increases, but the output of goods and services remains constant, a monetary overhang arises. Firms eventually respond to this overhang with across-the-board price increases. Based on the same concept as filling up a balloon with air, an ongoing increase, or 'blowing up', of the average price level is called 'inflation', whereas the opposite is called 'deflation'. The manifold monetary effects on the economy provide the basis for using—and also abusing—the complex interrelationships between nominal and real economic variables for political purposes. The term 'monetary policy' refers to such efforts and actions by central banks and governments to influence macroeconomic outcomes (e.g. economic output, employment, inflation, etc.) by manipulating monetary variables, such as interest rates, the supply of money, credit conditions, and exchange rates. Chapter 6 deals with monetary policy.

Owing to their comprehensive role in stabilising the financial and economic environment, modern central banks form an integral part of the political system and, hence, are to some degree connected with their governments (see the outer circle of Fig. 1.1). As mentioned above, the public privilege to issue currency provides a stepping-stone for setting monetary policy. However, in exchange for this right to issue a country's currency, central banks have traditionally helped to raise funds for the government. To this day, the monopoly profits from issuing officially recognised forms of money provide a source of public revenue and, therefore, give rise to potential conflicts between fiscal and monetary authorities. The connection between fiscal and monetary policy is by no means one-sided, as, for example, excessive levels of public debt and even sovereign defaults have historically led to some of the most severe cases of monetary turmoil. Similarly, thorny interrelationships arise due to trade-offs between the short- and long-term effects of monetary policy. Since prices and wages typically do not react instantaneously to changes in the economic environment, it is plausible that monetary impulses exhibit only gradual effects on inflation. However, central-bank interventions tend to have short-lived, but rather instantaneous effects on real economic phenomena such as the level of employment. The interaction between fiscal and monetary policy as well as the different nominal and real effects of monetary policy across different time horizons pose major challenges for central banks wishing to preserve the purchasing power of the currency (in terms of keeping inflation low and stable). Chapter 7 discusses these challenges as well the role of central-bank independence as a potential remedy.

As illustrated by the left part of Fig. 1.1, central-bank interventions can also involve the international financial system and, specifically, take place on the foreign-exchange market. Although these interventions primarily affect the conditions of the international financial system—particularly the exchange rate—sooner or later they will also manifest themselves more broadly in cross-border flows of goods, services, and capital. To cite the best-known example, a currency devaluation tends to provide a temporary boost to the domestic economy because exports become relatively cheaper in terms of foreign currency units, whereas imports tend to become relatively more expensive in terms of domestic currency units. The importance of exchange-rate fluctuations depends crucially on the international monetary system and the exchange-rate regime adopted by a given country. Ignoring nuance for the moment, a country can essentially choose between a floating or fixed exchange-rate system. Under the former system, foreign-exchange interventions occur only occasionally, whereas, under the latter system, the central bank routinely buys and sells its currency against a foreign anchor currency at a preannounced rate. Chapter 8 describes the primary aspects of international monetary policy by discussing the economic effects of various exchange-rate regimes, the role of international reserves, and the advantages and disadvantages of a common currency.

Finally, Chap. 9 provides some concluding remarks and discusses the current and future roles of central banks.

Further Reading

Introductory textbooks on economics deal with the very basics of money and central banking. A widely popular example is Mankiw, N. Gregory, 2018: *Principles of Economics*, Cengage Learning.

Most central banks provide background material on their activities. These various web-resources and brochures focus on the monetary-policy framework of the corresponding country.

2

A Brief History of Central Banks

The bank hath benefit of interest on all moneys which it creates out of nothing.
William Paterson (Co-founder of the Bank of England, 1658–1719)[1]

2.1 Origins of Central Banks

Owing to the numerous innovations in money and banking as well as the political and economic developments over the last few centuries, the role of central banks has changed enormously throughout their history. Hence, to better understand the tools and goals of modern central banks, it is perhaps useful to look back on their history. Doing so not only provides some rather entertaining stories, but also reveals the sources of ongoing monetary-policy debates, broadens the understanding of the current interrelationships between central and commercial banks, and clarifies the similarities and differences between current and former monetary systems. In general, it is often difficult to appreciate the key issues in central banking when their historical background is ignored.

The oldest central banks arose from early European experiences with paper money during the seventeenth and eighteenth centuries. At that time, Europe not only developed innovative insurance products and established primitive versions of public bond and stock markets, but also experimented with various

---

[1]The origin of this quote is unclear. It is said to be from the prospectus for the Bank of England.

© Springer Nature Switzerland AG 2019
N. Herger, *Understanding Central Banks*, https://doi.org/10.1007/978-3-030-05162-4_2

schemes for issuing banknotes.[2] The aims of these schemes were to provide an alternative means of payment to coins, and to raise funds for the government. Whereas some schemes, such as the French 'Banque Royale', quickly ended in financial fiascos, others provided the nuclei for some of the oldest central banks in the world, including the Swedish Riksbank (founded in 1668) and the Bank of England (founded in 1694).[3] However, when these time-honoured institutions were founded, they had little in common with modern monetary authorities, but rather were established as private enterprises to obtain official charters to issue banknotes. As the introductory quote indicates, the privilege of issuing state-backed paper money was lucrative, as alternative means of payment, such as dispatching coins, could be costly, and the direct transfer of book money between bank accounts was only available to a small number of wealthy merchants. The state benefited from private note-issuing schemes by collecting taxes in exchange for granting this privilege. Since public indebtedness often became a pressing issue in times of military conflict, it is perhaps not surprising that the Riksbank and the Bank of England were founded shortly after the Second Northern War (1655–1660) involving Sweden and during the Nine Years' War (1688–1697) involving England, respectively.

In many places, note issuing was not monopolised by a publicly supported bank until well into the nineteenth century. In Europe, some embryonic versions of banknotes had instead emerged as by-products of private businesses dealing with precious metals or other pecuniary assets. Probably the best-known example of such a business is the goldsmiths, who had the knowledge, experience, and capacity to store gold and silverware. Some goldsmiths realised that they could offer the public the service to safeguard valuables. To confirm deposits, receipts promising to pay the bearer the amount of gold or silver that had been taken into custody were commonly issued. Eventually, these

---

[2]Note that paper money was not invented in Europe, but rather had already appeared centuries before in China (see Sect. 3.2).

[3]The Banque Royale is one of the earliest examples of a central note-issuing bank. In particular, in 1716, King Louis XV of France granted the Scottish economist and gambler John Law de Lauriston a charter to set up a bank, based on which he created an empire of merchant monopolies in France and overseas. A few years later, Law acquired also a monopoly to issue banknotes, which he used without restraint. Around the year 1720, the newly printed paper money created a massive bubble in the share prices of Laws' merchant society, the 'Mississippi Companie'. When this bubble burst, both the Banque Royale, under a massive amount of debt, and Law, under the psychological stress, collapsed. After the crash, the French economy was left with large amounts of worthless paper money. Arguably, due to this catastrophic experience with new forms of money, France became hostile towards financial modernisation for decades or even centuries. Indeed, the Banque de France was only founded in 1800 to restore monetary order, which had been undermined by another chaotic experiment with paper money, the so-called 'Assignats' issued during the aftermath of the French Revolution of 1789. For details see: Murphy, Antoin E., 1997: *John Law Economic Theorist and Policy-maker*, Clarendon Press.

'promissory notes' began to represent a convenient means for large payments, avoiding, for example, the hassle and risk of dispatching coins. After all, as long as these notes were fully convertible into a monetary metal that formed the backbone of the currency system, there was no reason to treat them differently from the same amount of coins. Some modern banknotes carry relics of their historical origins. For example, Fig. 2.1 illustrates that the inscription 'I promise to pay the bearer on demand the sum of ... pounds', which is still imprinted on modern sterling notes, originally referred to a claim on a certain amount of gold. Of course, under today's fiat-money system (see Chap. 3), the

Banknote of the Bank of England issued in 1811 with a nominal value of two pounds. The 'promise to pay on demand the sum of two pounds' is confirmed by the signature of the cashier.

Modern pound note whose inscription bears witness to the historical origin as 'promissory note'.

Signature of the treasurer on the US dollar. Banknotes are "legal tender".

Fig. 2.1 Banknotes now and then. Images: Bank of England and Federal Reserve System

corresponding promise is nothing more than a historical legacy. Furthermore, modern banknotes almost always bear the signature of a cashier or treasurer. In the past, these signatures confirmed that a certain amount of precious metal had been deposited.

2.2   The Two-Tiered Banking System Emerges

The increasing popularity of paper money during the nineteenth century led to a fierce debate as to whether banknotes merely represent a convenient alternative to gold and silver coins or, instead, serve as a completely new financial instrument. The corresponding discussion, which reflected Great Britain's rapid financial development, was partly academic, but also had concrete implications for the degree to which paper money should be backed by precious metal. Specifically, in numerous pamphlets, the representatives of the so-called 'currency school' (e.g. David Ricardo) called for a high, if not complete, level of gold backing. They argued that banknotes were just a novel form of money and, hence, needed to be convertible, on demand, into the currency of the time—that is precious metal—to inhibit banks from overissuing paper money. To support this view, the representatives of the currency school could point to bad experiences with several inconvertible paper-money schemes. Above all, the suspension of convertibility of Bank of England notes after 1797 to finance the military struggle against Napoleon had, arguably, caused a noticeable increase in inflation (see also Sect. 3.2).[4] In contrast, the representatives of the so-called 'banking school' (e.g. Thomas Tooke or John Fullarton) believed that banknotes constituted a path-breaking financial instrument that could broaden access to bank credit. According to this line of thought, for the benefit of the broad public, the development of the banknote business should not be hampered by strict rules as regards gold or silver convertibility. From today's perspective, this controversy may seem odd and outdated. However, it does touch on a number of important issues in central banking, such as the appropriate definition of money (see Sect. 3.1), methods to control inflation (see Sect. 6.2), and the benefits and risks of the

---

[4]To make their case, the currency school postulated a close connection between the money supply and inflation that would, in essence, resurface prominently with the Monetarists during the twentieth century. Because the stock of bullion should restrict the amount of money in circulation, the early supporters of strict control over the money supply were called 'bullionists'. The currency school and the bullionists had considerable overlap in terms of both substance and representatives.

creation of liquid liabilities by commercial banks to refinance bank loans (see Sects. 3.4 and 5.4).

Politically, the currency school eventually prevailed. In England, this success was manifested in two acts of Parliament named after Robert Peel (1788–1850), the home secretary and, later, prime minister. The first of Peel's bank acts (officially known as the 'Resumption of Cash Payments Act'), passed in 1819, marked the return to banknotes that could be converted into fixed quantities of gold. The second, and probably more revolutionary, of Peel's bank acts was passed in 1844. Under the official heading of 'Bank Charter Act', this piece of legislation obliged the Bank of England to hold substantial amounts of bullion and, hence, ensure that paper money was deemed as good as gold. Furthermore, the banknote business was henceforth monopolised by the Bank of England.[5] Bereft of the right to issue promissory notes, the competing commercial banks had to find alternative ways to refinance their bank loans. Offering interest-bearing bank accounts to the broad public turned out to be the primary solution to this problem. Taken together, these developments mark the beginning of today's two-tiered banking system, in which a central bank issues officially recognised forms of money, and commercial banks only offer money-like products (formerly cheques and bills of exchange, presently, various forms of current accounts) and are largely responsible for the allocation of credit and loans.

As mentioned above, the early central note-issuing banks were not the only proponents of paper money. Well into the nineteenth century, all sorts of financial firms could issue their own versions of non-interest-bearing promises to pay. The problem with having multiple banknotes was that they typically circulated only in small amounts. Conversely, assigning the right to issue paper money to one government-chartered financial institute allowed for the standardisation of banknotes, which was crucial for turning them into a widely recognised, and hence broadly accepted, means of payment. Moreover, rightly or wrongly, the official backing of a designated note-issuing bank was thought to foster the public's confidence that the promised amounts of monetary metal could indeed always be paid on demand. With the establishment of currency monopolies, and the granting of legal-tender status to officially backed banknotes, more and more commercial banks realised that they could

---

[5]Peel's Bank Act of 1844 did not apply to all parts of the British Isles. This fact is still evident today, as three retail banks in Scotland (Bank of Scotland, Clydesdale Bank, and the Royal Bank of Scotland) and four in Northern Ireland (Bank of Ireland, First Trust Bank, Danske Bank, and Ulster Bank) have retained the right to issue their own sterling banknotes (although they are now under the supervision of the Bank of England).

hold liquid reserves in the form of banknotes, rather than storing vast amounts of specie in their vaults. This realisation marked the beginning of a process that would eventually give note-issuing banks a central position within the financial system. Again, England was the leader in this development. In particular, during the second half of the nineteenth century, the Bank of England became an increasingly important provider of higher-ranking payment and deposit services to the banking system (i.e. it acted as the bank for bankers), and began to adopt the responsibility of storing the national bullion reserve. Given this background, it is perhaps not surprising that the term 'central bank' was arguably introduced during the 1870s by Walter Bagehot (1826–1877), the first editor of the newspaper 'The Economist'.[6] In contrast, large parts of continental Europe and the rest of the world lagged behind these developments. Hence, during the nineteenth century, innovative means of payment, such as banknotes, and new credit instruments, such as cheques, were far from omnipresent.

The special capabilities of central note-issuing banks became most evident during financial crises. Because central banks hold the privilege of issuing officially backed and, hence, broadly accepted money, they were, and still are, in a unique position to inject liquid reserves into financial firms on the brink of bankruptcy. In nineteenth-century Britain, country banks were typically at the mercy of the local agricultural sector and, without outside support, could quickly fall victim to an upsurge in credit defaults caused by a bad harvest. Moreover, on several occasions, more widespread cases of financial instability arose, including the panic of 1825, which was partly caused by large losses from risky investments in Latin America, and the panic of 1847, which involved a crash following speculative mania in railway stocks. Amid these recurrent episodes of financial turmoil, it became apparent that an increasingly interrelated banking system required some sort of lender of last resort (see also Sect. 5.5). The principles according to which a central bank should lend freely, at a high interest rate, to a struggling bank as long as that bank can pledge sound collateral (e.g. securities), which are still upheld today, were already put forward by the British economist Henry Thornton (1760–1815) in 1802.[7] However, examples of a central bank actually providing generous liquidity support to contain a financial crisis did not occur until much later. Again, the Bank of England pioneered such policies. In particular, during the financial

---

[6]See The Economist, A Survey of the World Economy, Monetary metamorphosis, 23 Sept. 1999.
[7]See Thornton, Henry, 1802: *An Enquiry into the Nature and the Effects of the Paper Credit of Great Britain*, Hatchard.

crises of the early nineteenth century, the Bank was primarily concerned with protecting its own bullion reserves.

Since aggravated levels of economic and political risk tended to initiate flights towards pure forms of money, such as gold coins, panics were typically associated with a massive demand for precious metal, which could occasionally lead to a suspension of the convertibility of banknotes. However, in his famous book on the London money market in 'Lombard Street', which was written following the devastating collapse of the leading London banking house Overend & Gurney in 1866, Walter Bagehot (1826–1877) argued that turning away anxious banks would precipitate a further loss of confidence and could end up aggravating a financial downturn. During the second half of the nineteenth century, the Bank of England—with other central banks soon following suit (see Table 2.1)—gradually learned the lessons of Thornton and Bagehot and began to act as the lender of last resort during a financial crisis. By the time of the so-called 'Baring Crisis' of 1890, the policy stance had changed. The Barings Bank suffered massive losses on risky investments in Argentina. To avoid a catastrophic collapse of one of the biggest London merchant banks, the Bank of England accepted its responsibility as the guardian of financial stability by arranging a consortium of banks and financiers that raised enough capital

Table 2.1 Central banking institutions founded before 1900

Bank	Established	Monopoly note issue	Lender of last resort (decade)
Sveriges Riksbank	1668	1897	1890
Bank of England	1694	1844	1870
Banque de France	1800	1848	1880
Bank of Finland	1800	1886	1890
Nederlandsche Bank	1814	1863	1870
Austrian National Bank	1816	1816	1870
Norges Bank	1816	1818	1890
Danmarks Nationalbank	1818	1818	1880
Banco de Portugal	1846	1888	1870
Belgian National Bank	1850	1850	1850
Banco de España	1874	1874	1910
German Reichsbank	1876	1876	1880
Bank of Japan	1882	1883	1880
Banca d'Italia	1893	1926	1880

Source: Capie, Forrest, Charles Goodhart, Stanley Fisher, and Norbert Schnadt, 1994: *The Future of Central Banking—The Tercentenary Symposium of the Bank of England*, Cambridge University Press, p. 6

to absorb the Barings Bank's losses.[8] The adoption of a lender-of-last-resort policy has served the British financial system rather well. From the middle of the nineteenth century until 2007, that is for around 150 years, no bank failures with catastrophic consequences occurred. However, the provision of emergency liquidity assistance has profound implications in the sense that, during a crisis, the central bank must be prepared to place the public goal of maintaining a stable financial system over more narrow commercial interests.

The centralisation of note issuing, and, as a result, the development of a two-tiered banking system with a lender-of-last-resort policy, did not happen everywhere at the same time. As summarised in Table 2.1, only around a dozen central banks had been founded before 1900. Conversely, throughout the nineteenth century, in countries such as the United States, and Switzerland, attempts to abolish the free-banking system, in which financial firms are allowed to issue their own banknotes, ran into fierce opposition. From today's perspective, it may be difficult to understand the controversy around central note issuing. However, at the time, forbidding commercial banks from issuing their own notes was widely seen as an unnecessary violation of the freedom of enterprise. Although some concerns regarding government intervention into monetary affairs are valid, and occasionally resurface today,[9] free-banking systems suffer from serious drawbacks. In particular, as some note-issuing banks are safer and better managed, the quality of the various forms of paper money can vary. This variation is not a problem per se, as long as commercial banks are able to cultivate banknote brands that allow the public to distinguish between different forms of paper money. Still, competing banknotes hinder the development of a uniform means of payment and, hence, undermine the well-known advantages of having a single, standardised type of money (see Sect. 3.2). The proponents of free banking would likely argue that such rivalry would subsequently eliminate all but the best form of money. However, this process would essentially lead to a situation, where the most successful private bank monopolises the market for banknotes and, hence, adopts an equally special position to that of a central note-issuing bank.

To make banknotes more uniform, the governments of free-banking countries typically imposed rules on the convertibility between banknotes and

---

[8]Ironically, around 100 years later, in 1995, the Barings Bank was ultimately brought down by again suffering massive losses on foreign investments. Specifically, Barings fell victim to one of their own employees crating a loss of around 1.4 billion US dollars through unauthorised speculation in Asian financial markets. Some parts of the bankrupt Barings Bank were sold to other commercial banks.

[9]A twentieth-century proponent of a free-banking system was Friedrich August von Hayek, who emphasised the corresponding advantages in his book on 'The Denationalization of Money', published in 1976.

precious metal. Thus, it was possible to turn freely issued paper money into a homogenous product, which fostered its acceptance as a means of payment. However, when banknotes have to be backed by fixed amounts of gold or silver, it becomes much harder to adjust the money supply in response to ongoing changes in the volume of economic transactions caused by seasonal or business-cycle fluctuations. It is indeed difficult to maintain the full convertibility of paper money without producing sequences of excess and scarce liquidity that can, in turn, destabilise the financial system. In the case of a free-banking system, the severity of this problem is underscored by the experiences of the United States after 1836, when the charter of the Bank of the United States was not renewed by Congress and, thus, the first attempt to establish a central bank failed. Owing to the seasonal cycles in the agricultural sector, which used to dominate the US economy, payment and loan volumes tended to be significantly higher during the planting and harvesting season. As commercial banks were unable to match the increasing demand for money, the banking system became notoriously unstable. This problem was only overcome after 1913, when the Federal Reserve System was established, with the key task of providing sufficient liquid reserves throughout the year.[10]

Despite the benefits that central banks offer the financial and payment systems, many critics had, and still have, serious reservations regarding the corresponding concentration of public power in monetary affairs. Nonetheless, the issuing of uniform banknotes and other forms of currency has ultimately prevailed worldwide. Nowadays, almost every country has a central bank.[11] Moreover, none of the few remaining countries without a central bank has a free-banking system. Rather, they either have planned economies with severely restricted monetary systems (e.g. North Korea), adopted a common currency (e.g. the euro area), or have imported the currency from another country (e.g. Ecuador, which uses the US dollar).

2.3   Era of the Classical Gold Standard

Money emerged when ancient societies began to exchange a broad range of goods. Early circulating media were typically based on coins made of precious metals such as gold, silver, or copper. Until the advent of paper money, it

---

[10] See, for example, Miron, Jeffrey A., 1986: Financial Panics, the Seasonality of the Nominal Interest Rate, and the Founding of the Fed, The American Economic Review 76, 12–140.

[11] A list compiled by the Bank for International Settlements (BIS) currently contains around 200 central banks around the world.

was, at least in Europe, customary to settle large transactions with gold coins, whereas silver or copper coins were the preferred means of payment for smaller, everyday purchases. Bimetallic systems, in which a currency is based on two precious metals, survived for a relatively long time. A well-known nineteenth-century example of such a system is the Latin Monetary Union between France, Belgium, Italy, Switzerland, and Greece. In these countries, two five-franc coins containing, in total, 45 g of silver were equivalent to a ten-franc coin containing 2.9 g of gold. In other words, the price ratio between silver and gold was officially fixed at 15.5 to 1.[12]

Fixing a price ratio between, for example, gold and silver turned out to be a weakness of bimetallic systems, because a shift in the supply or non-monetary demand of the involved precious metals created a powerful incentive to hoard the relatively more valuable form of money, whereas the nominally overvalued form would flood into circulation. This principle of 'bad money' driving out 'good money' is also known as 'Gresham's Law', named after Thomas Gresham (1519–1579), an English financier and merchant during the reign of the Tudors. In the long-term, most bimetallic standards struggled to survive in the face of a sufficiently large wedge between the market and the official prices of the involved monetary metals.

Unlike bimetallism, the gold standard refers to the monometallic currency system that dominated in the decades around 1900. The triumphant advancement of currencies based on gold owed much to the role of Great Britain as the world's leading economic and political power. Accordingly, the pound sterling, which had de facto been backed by gold since the eighteenth century, had obtained the status of international currency par excellence. Hoping to replicate the economic progress associated with the British monetary system, countries such as France, Germany, Japan, and the United States, subsequently abandoned their mixed currency systems in favour of monometallic standards. In particular, the years between 1880 and the outbreak of World War I in 1914 are often referred to as the era of the 'classical gold standard', during which major currencies were officially valued in terms of gold at the so-called 'mint-par'. For example, one pound sterling and one French franc were officially worth 7.322 and 0.2903 g of gold, respectively.[13] The overriding goal of central banks was to enforce the mint-par by standing ready to exchange

---

[12]This ratio is obtained by dividing 45 g of silver by 2.9 g of gold, that is $45/2.9 \approx 15.5$.

[13]The definitions of the actual mint regulations were complicated. Different currencies were defined in terms of gold of various fineness levels and according to different weights. For example, whereas the British mint regulation stipulated that '480 ounces troy of gold, 11/12th fine, shall be coined into 1869 Sovereigns', the French mint regulation said that '1000 g of gold, 11/12th fine, shall be coined into 155 Napoleons (of 20 francs each)'. The mint-pars mentioned above use the conversion that a troy ounce

banknotes, on demand, at the official gold price. As long as this exchange was possible, a currency was said to be convertible. From an economic point of view, the move towards a monometallic standard gave rise to an international monetary system with fixed exchange rates. For example, in the case of the above-mentioned mint-pars, the official exchange rate between Britain and France equalled 7.322 g per £/0.2903 g per Fcs. or 25.22 £/Fcs. Substantial deviations from the fixed parity were untenable, because they would create international differences in gold prices and, in turn, opportunities for making easy profits by shifting gold and financial capital between countries with low and high gold prices. Using the same example of Britain and France, if the market exchange rate climbed to 25.30 Fcs./£, it would be possible to convert one pound sterling to 25.30 French francs and, subsequently, exchange these for $25.30 \times 0.2903 = 7.34$ g of gold. However, transferring this amount back to Britain would yield an arbitrage profit of $7.34/7.32 \approx 1.003$ or 0.3%. In the end, the increasing demand for French francs from such transactions would push the market exchange rate towards a rate concurring with the mint-pars.

Until now, the burden and hazards of gold transactions have been ignored. The practical implication of the cost and risks of shipping bullion between countries was that the market exchange rates of metal-based currencies could depart to some degree from the mint-pars without triggering international gold flows. For example, Fig. 2.2 depicts weekly data for the aforementioned franc-to-pound-sterling exchange rate from 1880 to 1914. Compared with what is observed in modern foreign-exchange markets (see Sect. 2.6), the corresponding fluctuations were small and confined to a narrow band whose width depended on the cost of international gold transactions.

To be on the gold standard, a country had to hold a sufficiently large stock of bullion reserves. Otherwise, the convertibility of banknotes at the mint-par would have been an empty promise. Importantly, central banking is not a precondition for a convertible currency, since private banks can, in principle, also adopt the responsibilities of note issuing. However, as mentioned above, metal-based monetary systems often restrained free-banking systems from providing an elastic (i.e. sufficiently flexible) money supply. Thus, it is, perhaps, not surprising that several central banks were founded around the turn of the twentieth century to, among other things, better handle the domestic and foreign obligations resulting from the international gold standard. Reflecting the overarching importance attached to storing and

---

equals 31.1035 g (see Clare, George, 1902: *A Money-Market Primer and Key to the Exchanges*, Effingham Wilson, p. 74).

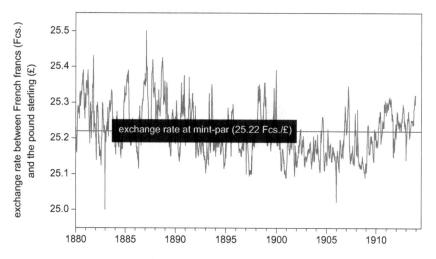

Fig. 2.2 An exchange rate during the gold standard. Source: Herger, Nils, 2018: Interest-parity conditions during the era of the classical gold standard (1880–1914)—evidence from the investment demand for bills of exchange in Europe, Swiss Journal of Economics and Statistics 154

managing the national reserve, some central banks, such as that of the United States, which were founded during the heyday of the gold standard, are called 'reserve banks'.

In any case, entrenched trade imbalances can undermine an international monetary system, within which countries compete for a fixed amount of gold. To understand why, consider the scenario of an export surplus, which implies that the claims on other countries, through selling goods and services abroad, exceed the corresponding liabilities from imports. The associated export of capital can, of course, be funded via foreign loans. Providing short-term trade finance, especially by means of so-called 'bills of exchange', was indeed a common practice during the gold standard. Nevertheless, within the framework of the gold standard, bullion shipments provided the ultimate means for counterbalancing entrenched trade deficits or surpluses. During the nineteenth century, mainly Britain, but also other industrially advanced nations such as Germany or France, exported comparably large amounts of goods and capital. Because of the resulting net gold inflows, it was quite easy for these countries to maintain freely convertible currencies. However, it is impossible to design an international trading system without some countries running import surpluses. During the era of the classical gold standard, mainly the colonies in Asia and Africa, as well as parts of Latin America, attracted large amounts of foreign goods and capital to develop their economies. Although import surpluses are not harmful per se, under a fixed exchange-rate regime, they tend to empty a country's international reserves and, at the time, they gave rise to gold outflows, which eventually made it difficult to maintain a fixed mint-par. Therefore, the gold standard was not applied across the globe, but rather in a select number of nations, including Britain, France, and Germany. Many currencies were only partly convertible. Countries such as Austria-Hungary and Russia even issued largely inconvertible paper money.

Although it seems contradictory, even during the heyday of the gold standard, most international payments were *not* carried out with gold.[14] Furthermore, despite the inherent monetary constraints of monometallic currency systems, around 1900, both cross-border trade as well as foreign investment grew to levels that were, by many measures, only surpassed when the economic globalisation driven by modern information technology took off during the 1990s.[15] This growth raises the question of how the leading central banks preserved the mint-par for decades, despite having to deal with massively greater volumes of trade and capital flows during the wave of globalisation before World War I. As already indicated above, balance-of-payments deficits ultimately entailed a loss, or 'drainage', of bullion reserves. Thus, a sufficiently large upsurge in imports and the associated capital outflow could eventually empty a country's reserves, put the convertibility of its currency at risk, and ultimately destabilise the international monetary system. However, the so-called 'discount policy' turned out to be a potent tool against drainage. In particular, if capital outflows became unsustainable, the central bank could raise the domestic level of interest rates to discourage drainage, attract foreign investment, and, hence, protect the domestic bullion reserve. In practice, the manipulation of interest rates occurred primarily via discounting bills of exchange, which used to be the dominant instrument for financing trade and short-term capital flows. By allowing commercial banks to pledge certain classes of bills as collateral against liquid reserves, and, thus, charge interest at the official discount rate, central banks gradually became aware that they can regulate the level of interest rates across the economy. Figure 2.3 shows that the Bank of England began to pursue a more active discount policy from the middle of the nineteenth century onwards. As will be discussed in detail in Sect. 4.2, the manipulation of an official discount rate to affect the economic

---

[14] See Eichengreen, Barry, 2000: *Globalizing Capital—A History of the International Monetary System*, Princeton University Press, pp. 24ff.
[15] See Obstfeld, Maurice, and Allen M. Taylor, 2004: *Global Capital Markets*, Cambridge University Press, Chap. 2.

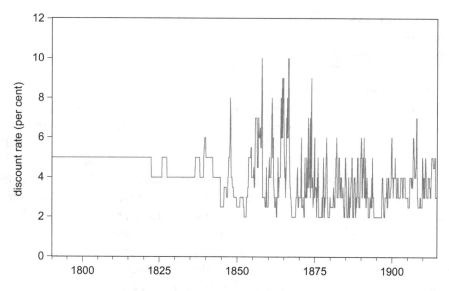

Fig. 2.3 Discount rate of the Bank of England until 1914. Data source: Bank of England

environment reflects an early version of the most important tool in the box of modern monetary policy.

To this day, gold currencies are surrounded by widely held nostalgic feelings. Colloquially, the term 'gold standard' can even refer to a 'best practice' in nonmonetary contexts. Indeed, regardless whether money circulates in the form of gold coins, or that of bullion-backed banknotes, metal-based currency systems hinder an excessive increase in the money supply. More specifically, as long as central banks were committed to keeping their currencies convertible, they were unable to print massive amounts of paper money to inflate away the national debt. As shown in Fig. 2.4, which depicts the long-term development of the price level and inflation in the United States and Britain, the average increases in the price level were indeed markedly lower during the period of the classical gold standard, than in the twentieth century. In that sense, the dogma of giving the central bank the overriding task of preserving the purchasing power of the currency is rightly associated with the monetary architecture of the decades before 1914.

However, the gold standard suffered also from several drawbacks that eventually led to its demise and replacement by an international currency system structured around fiat money and floating exchange rates. More specifically, aside from the above-mentioned problems with providing an elastic money supply, the overriding goal of enforcing the mint-par and protecting the

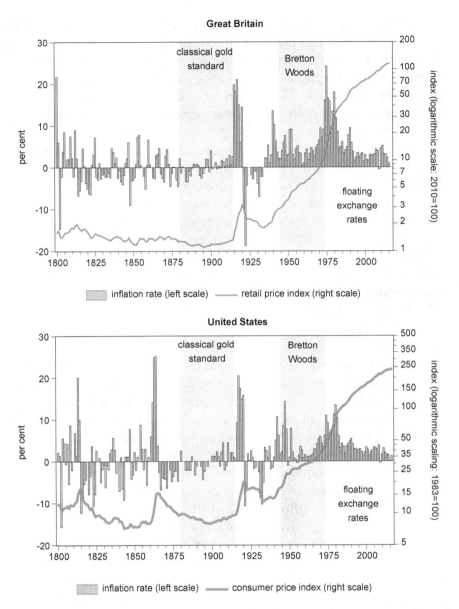

Fig. 2.4 Price developments across two centuries (1800–2016). Data source: https://www.MeasuringWorth.com

bullion reserve are a weakness of any proper metallic standard. In particular, to keep their currencies convertible, central banks had to adhere to the 'rules of the game', according to which discount rates had to be increased to stem large gold outflows regardless the levels of unemployment or inflation. The consequences of a monetary policies preoccupied with preserving the mint-par are clearly evident in the inflation data in Fig. 2.4. In particular, during the quarter of a century before World War I, inflation was too low. Due to chronic gold shortages, the price level even followed a negative trend. Entrenched deflation was, to some extent, an inherent feature of metallic currency standards and arose when the extraction of gold could not keep pace with a growing economy and population. A more or less constant supply of metal-based currency, combined with a growth-induced increase in the number of monetary transactions, implied that only average price-level decreases could boost the purchasing power of the circulating medium. More generally, changes in the volume of newly mined gold or silver, rather than the decisions of the central bank, determine the monetary policy stance in a metal-based currency regime. Strange as it might seem, during the gold standard, the money supply depended partly on new discoveries and technological progress made in the mining sector, both of which have clearly nothing to do with optimal monetary policy.

Deflations can create or prolong economic downturns by redistributing wealth from lenders to borrowers or inducing households to postpone consumption in anticipation of falling prices. It is therefore not surprising that deflationary trends gave rise to fierce political debate regarding the merits of the gold standard. A case in point is the 'free silver' debate in the United States, which featured prominently in the 1896 presidential election. In particular, the demonetisation of the silver coin in the United States during the 1870s was believed to have caused the entrenched deflation of the following decade. Falling prices were of great concern to the indebted farming communities in the American West and South, whereas the Northeast, where the financial and manufacturing sectors were concentrated, partially benefited from cheaper agricultural products. Reflecting this political conflict, William Jennings Bryan, the Democratic Party candidate, essentially represented the interests of the West and South by openly supporting the free-silver movement, which called for a remonetisation of silver to boost the money supply. Conversely, the Republican candidate, William McKinley, came out as a proponent of the gold standard. McKinley won the election owing to the votes of the Northeast. Nevertheless, the long-lasting deflationary trend was reversed at the turn of the twentieth century. Due to the mechanisms described at the end of the previous paragraph, major gold discoveries in Canada, Australia, and South Africa around 1900 pushed the average price-level changes back into positive territory (see Fig. 2.4).

Erratic shifts between inflationary and deflationary periods are another drawback of a monetary system that is not primarily concerned with maintaining price stability. At the time of the gold standard, rapid year-to-year shifts between increasing and decreasing price levels were quite common. The corresponding uncertainty imperilled mainly the working class, whose income consisted of modest, and essentially nominally fixed salaries. Thus, ordinary workers were quite exposed to the loss of purchasing power, when inflation turned out to be unexpectedly high (as shown in Fig. 2.4, inflation could easily shoot up to 5 or even 10% even in peacetime).

Finally, the stabilising features of a gold-backed currency clearly only apply as long as a central bank sticks to the rules. However, during wars or other national emergencies, gold convertibility was routinely suspended. For example, the currency school had blamed the instability of the price level, with inflation rates in Britain reaching 30%, on the suspension of the convertibility of the pound sterling in 1797 (compare Sect. 2.2).

2.4   World War I and the Great Depression

When World War I broke out in 1914, the central banks of the belligerent countries quickly suspended the gold standard to contribute to the war effort by issuing large amounts of inconvertible banknotes. Unsurprisingly, this monetary expansion gave rise to a marked upsurge in inflation. In particular, average prices in the United States and Britain doubled between 1914 and 1920, whereas Germany witnessed even higher levels of inflation (see Fig. 2.5). As mentioned above, war-induced inflation was nothing new. However, when hostilities ended with the armistice agreement of 1918, the old European powers in particular had amassed unprecedented amounts of debt, which consisted partly of inconvertible paper money. All the nations involved in the war, regardless of whether they were victorious or defeated, had to find ways to reduce this financial burden.

One way to deal with the debt overhang was to simply inflate it away. Germany essentially pursued this path, which led to one of the most notorious hyperinflations in monetary history. Having already suffered from relatively high levels of inflation during the war, and being confronted with demands for war reparations by France and Britain, Germany saw average prices increase by the unbelievable factor of around 500 billion between January 1919 and December 1923. In practice, prices repeatedly doubled within months, and, towards the inflationary climax in 1923, multiplied within days. This hyperinflation had clearly dramatic repercussions. Because all monetary assets

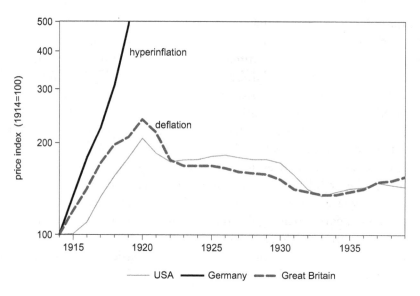

Fig. 2.5 Price level between 1913 and 1939. Hyperinflation or deflation. Data sources: MeasuringWorth (USA, Great Britain), Preisniveau fuer Ernaehrung. Statistisches Jahrbuch fuer das Deutsche Reich

suffered from an ongoing collapse of purchasing power, significant time had to be wasted converting money into goods and real assets as quickly as possible. Moreover, massive inflation tends to redistribute enormous amounts of wealth. In particular, people living on fixed incomes or savings in bank accounts suffered from the quick erosion of their financial claims, whereas, for example, real-estate owners were partly protected or could even benefit from high levels of inflation. Owing to these arbitrary financial effects, as well as the resulting tensions within society, the German hyperinflation had to eventually be stopped by means of a currency reform. In particular, to rebuild the trust in monetary affairs, a newly issued currency, the so-called 'Rentenmark', was backed by physical capital, such as real estate and land, which were assets whose values had not been eroded by inflation. This historical encounter with hyperinflation has left its mark on Germany's collective memory. Arguably, the experience of a whole generation losing large parts of their savings still resonates within German views on monetary policy.

To regain the stability of the classical gold standard, the more traditional way to deal with the debt overhang from World War I was to restore the convertibility of the currency. Of course, it was only possible to re-establish the pre-war mint-pars by reducing the amount of money in circulation to pre-1914 levels, thereby reconciling the currency with the available gold stock.

The drawback of such a policy of monetary restraint was that it required, at least temporarily, a substantial increase in interest rates, which had adverse effects on investment, employment, and gave rise to deflation. Figure 2.5 illustrates that the United States, which went back on the gold standard in 1920, essentially chose this path, as did Britain, which followed suit in 1925. Especially for Britain, the economic costs of deflation were high. During 1920, unemployment increased dramatically. Furthermore, although Britain won the war, it ceded its position as the world's leading creditor nation to the United States. Therefore, deflationary monetary policy had additional, unpleasant side-effects in terms of increasing the real debt burden.

During the second half of the 1920s, the Anglo-Saxon world, and even Germany, witnessed a short period of benign economic conditions, relatively stable financial systems, and widespread increases in prosperity. Unfortunately, these positively remembered years of the 'roaring twenties' ended abruptly with the reappearance of the fateful combination of deflation and debt when the New York stock market crashed in the autumn of 1929. The following economic downturn is called the 'Great Depression' because it was not only severe but also long-lasting, and affected virtually all parts of the global economy. In the United States, average prices, and, in turn, incomes, dropped by more than 20%. Hence, many households and firms found it impossible to service their debts, which were typically denominated in fixed, nominal terms. The result was a series of defaults and bankruptcies which propagated through the banking system. In the United States alone, thousands of banks failed. Furthermore, since the United States were the largest international lender nation at the time, they began to withdraw foreign loans, which transmitted the crisis to Europe and the rest of the world. Consequently, economic production and international trade collapsed leading to mass unemployment.

The Great Depression was caused by several, interrelated economic and political problems. However, from a monetary perspective, the vicious cycle between deflation and debt and the resulting waves of bank failures were primarily responsible for the severity, long duration, and international extent of the crisis. This 'debt-deflation mechanism' was most forcefully put forward as explanation for the sharp downturn of the 1930s by the American economist Irving Fisher (1867–1947). It is somewhat unclear why this mechanism and its most important proponent are rarely associated with the Great Depression. Conversely, by highlighting the role of economic demand and proposing fiscal stimulus as a remedy for economic downturns, John Maynard Keynes (1883–1946) became famous outside the field of economics. One reason for this difference might be an irony of history. Irving Fisher publicly declared that stock prices had 'reached what looks like a permanently high plateau' only a couple of weeks before the savings of many ordinary Americans were wiped out by the New York stock-market crash.[16] In contrast, John Maynard Keynes was perhaps just lucky to have made the equally erroneous statement that 'we will not have any more crashes in our time' in front of a smaller audience and a couple of years before the crash.[17]

If central banks had pursued an aggressive lender-of-last-resort policy during the Great Depression, they would likely have been able to break the vicious cycle between deflation, the increase in the real debt burden, and the collapse of the financial system and economic activity. Of course, to implement such a policy, a large reduction in the discount rate and a generous provision of central-bank reserves would have been warranted. It was, however, impossible to reconcile the corresponding monetary expansion with the traditional mint-pars of the gold standard. In principle, under any metal-based currency system, the amount of central-bank money can be expanded overnight by simply increasing the mint-par. Nevertheless, despite an ongoing deterioration in economic conditions during the early 1930s, the leading central banks at the time (i.e. the Bank of England, Banque de France, German Reichsbank, and Federal Reserve System) were reluctant to devalue their currencies with respect to gold and, hence, free monetary policy from the constraints of the gold standard. Instead, the capital flight and the corresponding pressure on bullion reserves eventually forced the Bank of England to suspend the convertibility of sterling in September 1931. Several member states of the Empire, as well as other countries, such as Sweden or Japan, soon followed suit. The US dollar was officially devalued in 1933. In contrast, some countries, such as France or Switzerland, increased their mint-pars only several years later. Devaluations proved to successfully combat the Great Depression. Indeed, Fig. 2.6 shows that a country's entrenched reduction in economic activity (here measured in terms of industrial production) only stopped after a devaluation of the currency had occurred.

With hindsight, it is perhaps hard to understand why some central banks hung on to the classical mint-pars until the bitter end. To understand this policy, it is important to realise that, for centuries, silver and gold coins and convertible banknotes had been the quintessential forms of money. In Europe and in other parts of the world, alternatives to metal-based currencies were deemed inferior monetary systems. Devaluations and inconvertible paper money had very bad reputations. Given this background, central banks had

---

[16] Quoted in The New York Times, October 16, 1929: Fisher sees stocks permanently high.
[17] Quoted in Somary, Felix, 1960: *The Raven of Zurich*, C. Hurst, p. 147.

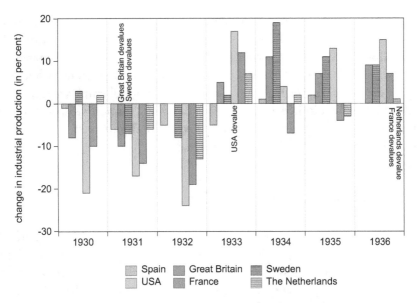

Fig. 2.6 Industrial production between 1930 and 1936. Data: Bernanke, Benjamin, and Harold James, 1990: The Gold Standard, Deflation, and Financial Crisis in the Great Depression: An International Comparison. In: Financial Markets and Financial Crises, Glenn Hubbard (Hrsg.), University of Chicago Press

the overarching task of upholding the convertibility of their currencies at a fixed mint-par. Although suspensions of convertibility and devaluations could occur, they were typically seen as exceptional emergency measures associated with large-scale instability and chaos. For the believers in the traditional monetary order, devaluing a currency represented a frivolous act which violated the property rights of banknote holders. This view is not entirely baseless. The suspension of convertibility by the Bank of England meant, for example, that within weeks, the pound sterling lost around 30% of its external value, implying that foreign investors in sterling notes suffered from a corresponding loss of purchasing power.

It is perhaps not immediately evident that the questioning of fixed gold parities represents a turning point in monetary history. In contrast to many contemporary observes, John Maynard Keynes seems to have immediately grasped that a profound reorientation of monetary policy took place during the Great Depression. At least, his assessment that the sterling devaluation 'will open a new chapter in the world's monetary history' seems to suggest this idea.[18] In any case, after the economic fiasco of the Great Depression, the view that central banks should be used to stabilise economic activity rather than following a rigid convertibility rule gained widespread acceptance. Of course, by broadening the mandate of monetary-policy to include public goals, such as managing the average price level or fostering full employment, central banks eventually adopted more prominent political roles. Correspondingly, subsequent to the experiences of the 1930s, the desire to exert public control over the monetary authority also increased.

2.5   The Bretton Woods System

The demonetisation of gold occurred in several steps. In this regard, the Bretton Woods System, which is named after the location in the United States where the post World War II monetary order was negotiated, represents an intermediate stage between ancient metal-based and modern fiat-money systems. By and large, the Bretton Woods conference, which took place in 1944, attempted to increase flexibility and international coordination in monetary affairs to avoid the disastrous deflation and financial instability during the interwar period, but retain the disciplining elements of gold-backed currencies. The result was a hybrid setup that can best be described as a 'gold-exchange standard'. In particular, the United States maintained the tradition of fixing the gold price (at $35 per ounce), whereas the remaining currencies were pegged at officially declared, but, in principle, adjustable par-values against the dollar. Notably, the gold-exchange concept was not entirely new. As mentioned above, even during the period of the classical gold standard, only the most advanced nations held their international reserves primarily in gold, and large parts of the world had inconvertible paper or silver-backed money. Furthermore, during the decades before 1914 as well as during the interwar period, it was quite common to hold international reserves in the form of foreign exchange (in particular in sterling). However, the Bretton Woods System was different insofar as gold no longer circulated as a means of payment (in the form of coins or convertible banknotes) and, as illustrated by Fig. 2.7, the international monetary architecture was centred around one, officially designated reserve currency: the dollar.[19] For the following discussion,

---

[18] Quoted in Liaquat, Ahamed, 2009: *Lords of Finance*, Penguin Books, p. 432.

[19] Of course, the Bretton Woods System only covered the Western Hemisphere. Although the Soviet Union did send a delegation to the international monetary conference in 1944, the communist countries installed a financial system, within which the state took full control over the distribution of money and

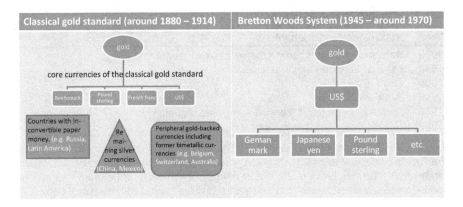

Fig. 2.7 Gold standard and Bretton Woods System

it is important to realise that after World War II, the United States adopted a special position within the Western financial system, by being the main provider of international reserves and the only country free from the obligation to intervene in the foreign-exchange market. Due to this 'exorbitant privilege', the Bretton Woods System eventually fell apart.

During the first two decades of the Bretton Woods System, the combination of rigid elements, such as backing the dollar with gold and imposing capital controls, and flexible elements, such as allowing countries to adjust their exchange-rate parities in the event of a fundamental economic disequilibrium, proved to be remarkably successful. To maintain the stability of the financial system, the International Monetary Fund (IMF) was founded to advise countries, guide them through possible adjustments of their parities, and provide emergency lending assistance during a currency crisis. In sharp contrast to the financial chaos following World War I, the 1950s and the beginning of the 1960s were characterised by an increase in prosperity and low inflation. Nonetheless, from the beginning, the Bretton Woods System suffered from several design faults. Above all, despite an unprecedented degree of cooperation between central banks as well as numerous rules for international monetary affairs, the Bretton Woods System could not achieve its ambitious goal of both providing the same level of stability as the gold standard did, and avoiding the deflationary pressure of a metal-based monetary system. Reflecting the rigidities of a monetary system organised around a more or less fixed stock of international gold reserves, it was only possible to satisfy the increasing global

the allocation of credit and foreign exchange. For the countries under the influence of communism, this choice meant that the entire financial and banking system was essentially socialised.

Table 2.2 The nationalisation of central banks

Year	Nationalised central bank
1936	Danmarks Nationalbank; Reserve Bank of New Zealand
1938	Bank of Canada
1945	Banque de France
1946	Bank of England
1948	Nederlandsche Bank; Banque Nationale de Belgique
1949	Norges Bank; Reserve Bank of India

Source: Capie, Forrest, Charles Goodhart, Stanley Fisher, and Norbert Schnadt, 1994: *The Future of Central Banking—The Tercentenary Symposium of the Bank of England*, Cambridge University Press, p. 23. Notes: Aside from the case of Belgium, nationalisation refers to a state ownership of 100% of the share capital of the central bank

demand for money, which resulted from the post World War II boom, when the United States kept creating additional dollars. However, in the long-term, this monetary expansion undermined the confidence that the United States central bank, the Federal Reserve System, would be able to convert gold at $35 per ounce. The American economist Robert Triffin (1911–1993) had identified this problem as early as 1960. Triffin's dilemma was further exacerbated by the loose monetary and fiscal policy pursued by the United States amid the Vietnam War and the 'Great Society' spending programs on education, health care, and social welfare.[20] In general, subordinating monetary policy to other areas of public policy, to the point that many central banks were nationalised (see Table 2.2), reflected the spirit of the time that governments have the wisdom to achieve a good mix between high employment and low inflation.

However, to stimulate economic activity, money growth was kept too high and nominal interest rates too low to maintain a stable price level in the long-term. Towards the end of the 1960s, the combination of expansionary fiscal and monetary policies began to result in a marked upsurge in inflation. Furthermore, as predicted by Triffin's dilemma, issuing ever more dollar reserves based on a more or less fixed amount of gold undermined the stability of the international monetary system. In particular, investors eventually began to doubt that the dollar was 'as good as gold'. Increasing gold purchases by private speculators trying to pre-empt a looming dollar devaluation provided the unmistakable sign of a crisis within the Bretton Woods System. Indeed, in 1968, central banks were no longer able to contain this type of speculation and restricted the convertibility of gold to transactions among themselves. Conversely, private transactions henceforth occurred at flexible prices on the

---

[20] See Triffin, Robert, 1960: *Gold and the Dollar Crisis*, Yale University Press.

free gold market. The segmentation of the gold market into private and public parts pushed the monetary system a step further away from its metal-based origins and, inconspicuously, removed the most important safeguard against excessive money supply within the Bretton Woods System.

The Bretton Woods System gave the participating countries only scant room to maneuver to handle inflation. In particular, as soon as the Federal Reserve System began to pursue a relatively loose monetary policy, the other central banks were forced to undertake large interventions in the foreign-exchange market. However, the corresponding dollar purchases, which were necessary to support the internationally agreed parities, resulted in a global increase in the money supply. The members of the Bretton Woods System had to import the US monetary policy including the corresponding level of inflation, whether they liked it or not. The only officially accepted remedies against an upsurge in the price level were to adjust either the parity of the dollar against gold, or that of another national currency against the dollar. Such readjustments were indeed undertaken, with the dollar being devalued to $38 per ounce in 1971, whereas the German mark, for example, had been revalued several times during the 1960s. Nevertheless, these measures had only temporary effects and did not address the fundamental problem of the Bretton Woods System that, according to the legendary words of US Secretary of the Treasury, John Connally, the dollar is 'our currency, but it is your problem'. However, this exact type of asymmetry can undermine fixed-exchange-rate systems, when the participant's views regarding the tolerable level of inflation differ too much (see Sect. 8.6). In particular, after the traumatic experiences of the 1920s, Germany was eventually no longer willing to accept a further increase in inflation to fulfil the external obligations of the Bretton Woods System. Hence, in 1973, the extraordinary decision was made to float the German mark against the other major currencies around the world.

2.6 Floating Exchange Rates and Autonomous Monetary Policy

In 1973, dramatic oil-price increases caused by the conflict in the Middle East sent shock waves across the global economy. In many countries, the result was stagflation (i.e. a combination of high inflation and economic stagnation) that damaged the Bretton Woods System beyond repair. In practice, the breakdown of the international monetary framework established after World War II implied that the leading central banks no longer fixed the external values of their currencies at predefined parities. Rather, private demand and supply on the foreign-exchange market determined the relative price of currencies such as the US dollar, the German mark, the Japanese yen, and the British pound. Such a 'non-system' with floating exchange rates was historically unprecedented. As mentioned above, although examples of inconvertible paper money or instable exchange rates had existed previously, these episodes were always seen as temporary anomalies; essentially, they were monetary symptoms of unhealthy economic or political situations. Under sufficiently stable conditions, countries had typically strived to anchor their currencies to mint-pars or other officially defined parities. Hence, although floating exchange rates are widely taken for granted today, they have only been the norm for a relatively short period of international monetary history.

In several regards, the establishment of a monetary system that was no longer organised around fixed parities was a turning point. In particular, as shown in the upper panel of Fig. 2.8, floating exchange rates have provided the impetus for an enormous growth in foreign-exchange trading. Owing to the deregulation of financial markets as well as to the progress in information technology, this growth has continued over the last few decades. With a staggering turnover of hundreds of billions per day (!), foreign-exchange trading is among the most active segments of the current financial system. At present, exchange rates react instantaneously to any kind of financially relevant news. The resulting fluctuations, which are illustrated in the bottom panel of Fig. 2.8 by means of the dollar-pound exchange rate, have clearly exacerbated the currency risks for any firm engaging in international trade or foreign investment.

Many countries were willing to face aggravated levels of currency risk to benefit from the advantages of floating exchange rates. Specifically, because central banks were no longer forced to fix the external values of their currencies, they found themselves poised to refocus monetary policy towards internal (or domestic) goals. For countries such as Germany and, later, other parts of the Western world, this newly found autonomy was used to address the increasing level of inflation, which had taken hold during the 1970s (see Fig. 2.9). In particular, inflation expectations had become entrenched and were, therefore, routinely priced into nominal wages and the cost of production and, thus, led to ongoing increases in product prices. This vicious cycle, termed the 'wage-price spiral', could only be interrupted during a period of tight monetary policy (see Sect. 7.3). In this regard, the second oil-price shock of 1979, which pushed inflation rates in many countries into double digits, turned out to be the point, after which central banks implemented the temporary interest-rate increases required to reverse the trend towards faster growth of the average price level.

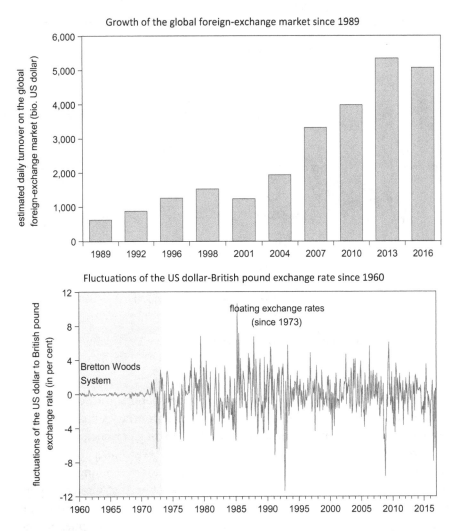

Fig. 2.8 Growth of the foreign-exchange market and volatility of the exchange rate. Data: BIS Triennial Central Bank Survey and Swiss National Bank (SNB) data portal

In the United States, the disinflation that took place during the early 1980s is closely associated with Paul Volker (*1927), under whose chairmanship the Federal Reserve System decided to tighten monetary policy. At the expense of severe but typically short-lived recessions, most central banks managed to defeat the 'Great Inflation'. The decades following the notorious combination of high unemployment and inflation during the 1970s were characterised by a so-called 'Great Moderation', during which average prices were quite stable and economic growth was only interrupted by comparatively mild

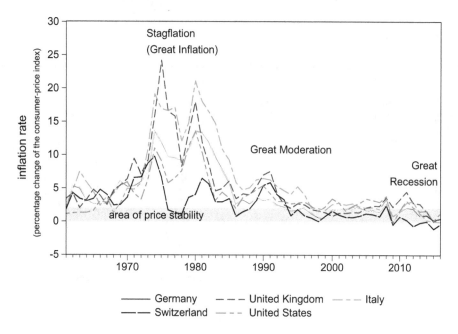

Fig. 2.9 From stagflation to the Great Moderation. Data: Swiss National Bank (SNB) data portal

downturns. This experience proved that extended periods with economically benign conditions do not require an international monetary system with fixed exchange rates, but can also occur under freely floating currencies.

Arguably, the successful disinflation after 1980 owes much to the insight that monetary policy is not a panacea against all kinds of economic problems. The experiences of the 1960s and 1970s clearly showed that monetary policy can lose its ability to reduce unemployment. Even worse, with outcomes like the wage-price spiral, inflation had turned into a self-reinforcing phenomenon whereby the public no longer believed that the purchasing power of the currency will be stable. As explained in much more detail in Chap. 7, it is perhaps in the nature of politics to seek immediate gains, such as lowering unemployment, at the expense of keeping average prices stable in the long-term. However, as shown by the Great Moderation, the political trade-off between short-term gain and long-term pain in monetary policy can be avoided. The solution is, arguably, institutional reforms fostering the independence of central banks and, in particular, their autonomy from the incentives to finance government deficits by printing money or to stimulate economic activity during an election year. Furthermore, following the pioneering role of the Reserve Bank of New Zealand during the late 1980s, many central banks adopted so-called 'inflation targets' to commit themselves to keeping average price increases within a pre-specified range, or 'band'. Specifically, inflation rates should typically be between 0% and 2%.[21] The long-term price developments depicted in Fig. 2.4 can help to clarify how an autonomous monetary policy dedicated to low inflation differs from the kind of stability produced by older metal-based currency systems. Although the gold standard was quite good at preventing rampant inflation, it was unsuccessful at limiting average-price fluctuations. Conversely, successful inflation-targeting regimes manifest themselves in both, low *and* stable inflation.

2.7 European Monetary Integration

Even though the most recent era of international monetary history has been characterised by floating exchange rates and the pursuit of monetary-policy autonomy, the modern world is far from dominated by this regime. Rather, fixed exchange rates have remained popular with small countries whose economic development depends heavily on the export of commodities such as oil, gas, or mineral resources. Because these goods are typically traded in an internationally important currency, such as the US dollar, the domestic economy can be protected from the potentially destabilising effects of exchange-rate shocks by means of a fixed exchange-rate regime. Regional monetary integrations have provided another countermovement against the global dominance of floating exchange rates. Above all, since the 1970s, Europe has embarked on an ambitious project to coordinate monetary policy. Many European countries have even ended up with the euro as a common currency.

The current European monetary architecture reflects the outcome of a decades-long process towards monetary integration that was not followed by all countries and was interrupted by setbacks. Initially, to create a zone of exchange-rate stability after the Bretton Woods System had collapsed, an

---

[21]The reason that slightly positive levels of inflation are tolerated is that commonly used price indices tend to overestimate the actual changes in purchasing power. For example, a consumer-price index measures inflation through the average price of a fixed consumer basket and, hence, ignores possible quality improvements (which would partly justify higher prices), or that consumers can switch from expensive to cheaper products. Arguably, the resulting overestimation of inflation amounts to around one percentage point (Shapiro, Matthew, and David Wilcox, 1996: Mismeasurement in the Consumer Price Index: An Evaluation, *NBER Macroeconomics Annual*). In simple words, it can also be said that price stability is achieved when 'ordinary people stop talking and worrying about inflation' (this definition is attributed to Alan Blinder, who was a Vice Chairman of the Board of Governors of the Federal Reserve System).

arrangement known as the 'European Currency Snake' was created. In particular, from the middle of the 1970s onwards, the members of the European Communities—the name under which the European project appeared at the time—tried to align their exchange rates by declaring target zones among themselves, in which the participating currencies were expected to move no more than 2.25% away from the official parities.

After the creation of the European Monetary System (EMS) in 1979, the next important step towards a European monetary union was undertaken. More specifically, the 'snake' was replaced, but the target band of 2.25% was kept. Moreover, the European Currency Unit, or 'ECU', was introduced to serve as an accounting unit among the participating European central banks. Mimicking the setup of the Bretton Woods System, the official exchange-rate parities of the EMS were adjustable. For example, during the 1980s, the Italian lire was regularly the subject of such 'realignments'. In sum, the EMS was a success story across many years, leading to the accession of countries such as Spain or the United Kingdom. However, severe problems did arise after German reunification in 1990. Due to the large demand for investment in the formerly communist East of the country, German interest rates increased together with the inflow of foreign capital. The EMS was unable to withstand this shock, leading to the widening of the target band for the Italian lire and, even more dramatically, the expulsion of the British pound in 1992.

Despite the currency crisis at the beginning of the 1990s, most members of the European project (Austria, Belgium, Finland, France, Germany, Greece, Ireland, Italy, Luxembourg, the Netherlands, Portugal, and Spain) decided to go ahead with the third, and by far the most ambitious, step in terms of centralising monetary-policy decisions by creating the European Monetary Union with the euro (which replaced the ECU) as a common currency, and the European Central Bank (ECB) as a common monetary authority. The monetary union was officially launched in 1999 and became a visible fact 3 years later with the issuing of euro-denominated banknotes and coins. Until the outbreak of the Global Financial Crisis in 2008, the euro area had witnessed a benign decade with low inflation, robust economic growth, and the accession of new members (Slovenia, Cyprus, Malta, and Slovakia; after 2008, Estonia, Latvia, and Lithuania also joined). The stability of the euro was supposed to be upheld by so-called 'convergence criteria' (also known as 'Maastricht criteria'), which obliged the member states to, among other rules, keep their government budget deficit below 3%, and their public-debt levels below 60% of GDP.[22] However, the loose enforcement, and, in some cases, the blatant violation of these rules became painfully clear after the outbreak of the Global Financial Crisis. In particular, long ignored debt overhangs in countries such as Greece, Portugal, Spain, and Ireland gave rise to destabilising effects across the entire euro area. In view of these ongoing developments, countries that adopted the euro are currently confronted with several strategic questions. Above all, the extent to which a common currency necessitates the coordination and centralisation of fiscal policy and the unification of national banking systems remains to be seen. Whether or not the member states can agree on the necessary measures to maintain the economic stability within the euro area is currently an open question.

2.8 Global Financial Crisis

The most recent challenge to central banking and monetary policy stemmed from the worldwide economic problems following the turmoil in the banking and financial system in 2008. This Global Financial Crisis originated mainly from the accumulation of bad loans in the US housing market, which eventually led to a wave of defaults by homeowners and, in turn, undermined the stability of the banks backing the corresponding mortgages. Owing to the size and interconnectedness of the US economy, the instability quickly propagated through the international financial system. In this regard, financial instruments such as mortgage-backed securities, which were originally designed to bundle credit risk, were partly responsible for the rapid transmission of instability to other parts of the financial system. These adverse events, and, in particular, the collapse of the US investment bank Lehman Brothers ended the period of the Great Moderation in North America and Europe by generating a substantial increase in unemployment, a deterioration in public finances, a worldwide decrease in international trade, and deflationary tendencies.

In 2008, the financial crisis was widely feared to mark the beginning of a new great depression (compare Sect. 2.4). Fortunately, these fears were overblown and, hence, the economic downturn is sometimes somewhat benignly called the 'Great Recession'. By arguably learning lessons from history and reacting with an aggressive expansion of monetary policy when the storm gathered pace, central banks take some credit for the fact that

---

[22]Other criteria were set regarding the convergence of inflation and money-market interest rates within the European currency area.

the economic catastrophe of the 1930s did not repeat itself. In particular, a range of measures were taken, including successive cuts of interest rates to zero, programs of quantitative easing to increase the amount of central-bank money in circulation, large interventions in foreign-exchange markets, and, most recently, the charging of negative interest rates on bank reserves. Aside from their sheer scale, and perhaps with the exception of imposing negative nominal interest rates, these policies by and large reflect the textbook monetary response to a financial crisis. Although a complete collapse of the financial and economic system has been averted, the long-term side-effects of this ultra-expansive monetary policy remain to be seen.

Although it is too early to tell, after the Great Depression and the Great Inflation, the Global Financial Crisis will probably be the next turning point in the history of central banking. Concerns as regards the stability of the financial system have e.g. already moved up the priority list of monetary authorities. In this regard, it is maybe worth remembering that the contagion of financial crises across a globally integrated economy is not an unprecedented event. Global recessions and an internationally connected financial system existed already back in the nineteenth century, and debates about the merits of lender-of-last-resort policies were already fierce at that time.

2.9   Conclusion

Although the oldest central banks can trace their roots back to the seventeenth century, they have changed tremendously across the past 300 years and, in particular, have only gradually adopted the tools and tasks associated with modern monetary policy. Although it may seem odd from today's perspective, the earliest 'central banks' were, in essence, private enterprises, which helped governments raise public funds in exchange for the privilege of issuing promissory paper (which would later become banknotes). Only much later, during the nineteenth century, did central banks begin to adopt other tasks. Early examples include lender-of-last-resort interventions in times of financial crises, services to facilitate payments between commercial banks, and the pooling of a country's international reserves. The use of monetary policy to influence overall economic conditions, including average prices and employment, established itself even later, during the twentieth century. Moreover, regarding the international, or external, dimension of guarding the currency, different historical eras were also characterised by various inter-national monetary systems. Until the second part of the twentieth century, external currency values were typically fixed via more or less close links with precious metals, such as gold or silver. It was not until the 1970s, when pure forms of fiat money, which are only convertible into themselves, became the worldwide norm.

Against this background, a blunt comparison of central-bank policies across history is prone to misinterpretations. Thus, it is important to point out that the discussion from Chap. 4 onwards reflects the current view, according to which central banks try to ameliorate macroeconomic conditions within a fiat-money system. However, before explaining the financial tools and economic relationships of modern central banking, the next chapter will review some basics about the role of money within the economy.

Further Reading

A very brief overview of the history of central banking from a US perspective can be found in Bordo, Michael D., 2007: *A Brief History of Central Banks*, Federal Reserve Bank of Cleveland.

A text dealing with central-bank history is Goodhart, Charles, Forrest Capie, and Norbert Schnadt, 1994: The development of central banking. In: Capie, Forrest, Charles Goodhart, Stanley Fischer, and Norbert Schnadt, *The Future of Central Banking—The Tercentenary Symposium of the Bank of England*, Cambridge University Press.

Many aspects of central banking are intertwined with financial history. A well-known text on this idea is Kindleberger, Charles, 2006: *A Financial History of Western Europe*, Routledge.

An excellent and concise discussion on the history of the international monetary system and, in particular, the classical gold standard is Eichengreen, Barry, 2008: *Globalizing Capital*, Princeton University Press.

For an overview of the free banking system, see Smith, Vera, 1990: *The Rationale of Central Banking and the Free Banking Alternative*, Liberty Press.

The history of the Federal Reserve System is told in Meltzer, Allan, 1989: *A History of the Federal Reserve*, University of Chicago Press.

For an early history of the Bank of England see Clapham, John, 1944: *The Bank of England*, Cambridge University Press.

A classical discussion on the monetary background of the Great Depression can be found in Friedman, Milton, and Anna J. Schwartz, 1963: *A Monetary History of the United States 1868–1960*, Princeton University Press.

An entertaining review of the Great Depression from the perspective of the major central banks at the time is Liaquat, Ahmed, 2009: *Lords of Finance*, Penguin Books.

The story of the Bretton Woods conference is told in Steil, Benn, 2013: *The Battle of Bretton Woods: John Maynard Keynes, Harry Dexter White, and the Making of a New World Order*, Princeton University Press.

3

Money: Lubricant of the Economy

Money, when acting as a medium of exchange, circulates backwards and forwards near the same spot, and may sometimes return to the same hands again and again. It subdivides and distributes property, and lubricates the action of exchange. William Stanley Jevons (British economist, 1835–1882)[1]

3.1 What Is Money?

Although the analogy of money facilitating economic transactions to oil lubricating a machine is widely popular, the words of William Stanley Jevons do not clarify what money actually is. However, it is quite difficult to come up with a satisfactory answer to this question. The following dialogue between 'Dombey and son', which has been taken from Charles Dickens' novel of the same title, illustrates precisely this problem:

'Papa! what's money?' The abrupt question had such immediate reference to the subject of Mr. Dombey's thoughts, that Mr. Dombey was quite disconcerted. 'What is money, Paul?' he answered. 'Money?' 'Yes,' said the child, laying his hands upon the elbows of his little chair, and turning the old face up towards Mr. Dombey's; 'what is money?' Mr. Dombey was in a difficulty. He would have liked to give him some explanation involving the terms circulating-medium, currency, depreciation of currency, paper, bullion, rates of exchange, value of precious metals in the market, and so forth; but looking down at the little chair,

---

[1]Jevons, William Stanley, 1875: *Money and the Mechanism of Exchange*, D. Appleton and Co., p. 15.

© Springer Nature Switzerland AG 2019
N. Herger, *Understanding Central Banks*, https://doi.org/10.1007/978-3-030-05162-4_3

and seeing what a long way down it was, he answered: 'Gold, and silver, and copper. Guineas, shillings, half-pence. You know what they are?' 'Oh yes, I know what they are,' said Paul. 'I don't mean that, Papa. I mean, what's money after all'. (Dickens, Charles, 1848: *Dombey and Son*, Bradbury & Evans, Ch. 8.)

This dialogue suggests that a description of money based on its physical nature is doomed to failure. As explained in Chap. 2, currency systems defining the value of money on the basis of gold, silver, and copper no longer exist. Today, an inconvertible banknote is nothing more than an artfully printed, but intrinsically useless, piece of paper. By only executing electronic exchanges of information between bank accounts, payments by credit or debit card are not even visible or tangible. Modern forms of money are apparently more mysterious than those that existed when Dickens wrote his novels. However, the key insight is that the material or immaterial composition of money says nothing about its economic functions.

Money should be defined not by what it is but by what it does. From this angle, money refers to all assets that are generally used and accepted means of payment for goods and services. Note that this economic definition of money is much narrower than the colloquial use of the term as often synonymous with income ('to earn lots of money') or wealth ('to have money'). The purest example of a broadly accepted circulating medium—to introduce yet another popular expression highlighting the key role of money—is cash. Today, coins and banknotes issued under the auspices of the central bank serve as legal tender; in other words, they have to be accepted by law to settle payments. As shown in Fig. 2.1 of Chap. 2, a clause saying 'this note is legal tender for all debts, public and private' is even directly imprinted on dollar bills. Of course, assets, such as checkable accounts or any other bank deposits withdrawable on demand, are also popular means for buying goods and services. In sum, the distinctive feature of money is that it serves as the commonly accepted medium of exchange. The ease with which an asset can be used to make payments, or quickly converted into a broadly accepted medium of exchange, is referred to as 'liquidity'. Cash is clearly highly liquid, because it circulates easily within the economy. In contrast, real estate is a good example of an illiquid asset. Owing to the large unit values, immobility, huge differences in quality, and considerable transaction costs required to find a buyer, it is indeed impractical to rely on home-ownership claims as principal means of payment.

Beyond functioning as medium of exchange, money typically also serves as a unit of account, or yardstick, to measure the value of economic transactions. In practice, product prices, debts, and assets are typically defined in terms of national currency units. To understand this function of money, it may be appropriate to first dismantle the myth that monetary prices reflect absolute

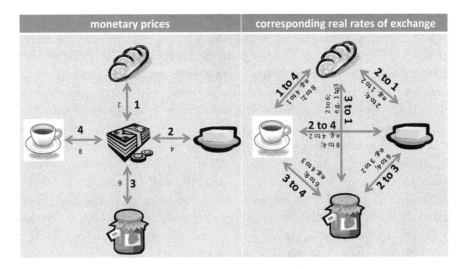

Fig. 3.1 Expressing prices with and without money

values. For this purpose, consider the stylised economy depicted in the left panel of Fig. 3.1, which comprises only a small number of goods, say bread, butter, jam, and coffee. The bold numbers reflect the assumption that the prices of bread, butter, jam, and coffee are one, two, three, and four currency units, respectively. Implicitly, this assumption gives rise to the real rates of exchange of two to one between bread and butter (that is two loafs of bread can be exchanged for one piece of butter), three to one between bread and jam, one to four between coffee and bread, two to three between jam and butter, two to four (or one to two) between coffee and butter, and, finally, three to four between coffee and jam (see right panel of Fig. 3.1). Pecuniary values are relative insofar as a hypothetical doubling of prices to two for bread, four for butter, six for jam, and eight for coffee does *not* alter these real rates of exchange, as can be seen by flipping Fig. 3.1 and consulting the corresponding numbers. Why does money still serve as a unit of account, even though pecuniary prices are themselves uninformative about real economic values? The answer is that a uniform expression of prices in terms of currency units greatly simplifies the comparison of economic value. As shown by the right panel of Fig. 3.1, without money, there are six price-pairs between the four goods in the stylised economy. However, when expressing the same relationships through a common yardstick called money, only four prices are needed (see left panel of Fig. 3.1). With more goods, this simplification becomes even more striking. For example, without money, there are 499,550 price relations among 1000 goods. As soon as one of these goods measures value, the number of prices falls dramatically to 999.[2] For the expression of prices, it is, in principle, irrelevant which good is chosen as the common yardstick. Nevertheless, it is convenient when the broadly used means of payment, which is involved in most transactions anyway, also performs the function of the unit of account. Indeed, almost everywhere, the national currency denominates payments and expresses prices. However, in a small number of cases, different terms are used for these two functions. For example, in England, 'sterling' refers to the currency, whereas 'pound' (sterling) refers to the unit of account. Similarly, 'renminbi' refers to China's currency, whereas prices are expressed in 'yuan'. Nevertheless, the unit-of-account function is so closely intertwined with money's role as means of exchange that money and the price level are closely connected. In particular, although an increase in the general price level does not alter the relative rates of exchange between goods per se, inflation does reduce the value, or purchasing power, of money. Deflation, or a decrease in the average price level, gives rise to the opposite effect.

As long as the various forms of money are not spent right away, they inevitably store value. However, this function is not a distinctive feature of money. Other assets, including interest-bearing bonds and dividend-yielding stocks, typically provide higher returns and, hence, a better way to store wealth and income for future consumption. In fact, by undermining the purchasing power of interest-free assets, inflation-induced price increases lead to negative returns on pure forms of money. Nevertheless, people are still willing to hold considerable amounts of cash owing to its liquidity, or its ability to settle payments efficiently. Still, inflation reduces the incentive to hold money. Under normal circumstances, these considerations hardly matter, and a banknote typically remains in a wallet for maybe a few days or even weeks on average. However, pervasive levels of inflation can lead to a situation, where consumers want to spend money as quickly as possible. To understand this desire to avoid painful losses of purchasing power, real-world examples of hyperinflations provide strange and illustrative stories of the outcomes of rapid price growth to exorbitant levels (see Fig. 3.2). Suddenly, daily purchases require literal heaps of banknotes, which often hold little value above that of ordinary pieces of paper. Taken together, this discussion illustrates that any form of money must retain a minimal degree of stability to fulfil the functions of a broadly accepted means of payment and a unit of account.

---

[2]In the general case with n goods and without money, the number of relative prices equals $n(n-1)/2$. If one good serves as the unit of account, only $(n-1)$ prices are needed.

Hyperinflation in Germany 1923

Banknotes that have otherwise become worthless are used as toys or wallpaper.

Images: Wikipedia Commons.

Hyperinflation in Zimbabwe 2008

Likewise, after a hyperinflation, the Zimbabwe Dollar (Zim Dollar) is used for nonmonetary purposes.

Origin of the images unknown.

Fig. 3.2 Historical impressions of hyperinflation

Of course, governments can support a national currency by granting it the status of legal tender, and firms and households have often tolerated fairly high levels of inflation. Nevertheless, when prices raise too fast, the trust in a given currency will eventually collapse and the search for an alternative means of payment—be it foreign currency or some commodity that can be exchanged in economic transactions—will begin. Hyperinflations represent extreme, and, fortunately rare, cases of a complete collapse of the currency system.[3] However,

---

[3]During the twentieth century, hyperinflation occurred, for example, in Russia (1921–1924), Germany (1922–1923), Hungary (1945–1946), Argentina (1989–1990), Brazil (1989–1990), Ukraine (1991–1994), Zimbabwe (2006–2009), and Venezuela (2018). Episodes of very high levels of inflation also occurred before 1900, such as, for example, during the French Revolution (1789) and the American Civil War (1861–1865).

they underscore that grossly unstable price levels can infringe on the social connections on which the functions of money rest. This is one reason that maintaining a low and stable level of inflation is an important goal of monetary policy.

3.2   From Commodity Money to Fiat Money

The history of money dates back thousands of years. Leaving the numerous details aside, it is remarkable that all ancient civilisations—including the early city states of Mesopotamia, the first imperial dynasties in China, the Greeks or Romans in Europe, and the Aztec empires in America—developed some version of a broadly accepted means of payment to facilitate the local exchange of goods and foster trade over longer distances. This observation is a powerful testimony to the disadvantages of the tested alternatives to a monetarised economy. For example, economic barter, that is, the direct exchange of goods, requires a so-called 'double coincidence of wants'. This notion refers to the unlikely event that a party both has the good the counterparty wants, and wants the good that the counterparty can offer. This idea may sound a bit complicated because it is complicated. Indeed, barter economies are hampered by the constant search for a suitable trading partner. In a tribal society, with only a few locally produced goods, it may be easy to identify double coincidences of wants. Conversely, when many types of goods are available and trade occurs over longer distances, it becomes almost impossible to barter. The introduction of money, which serves as a generally accepted means of payment, solves this problem and, hence, enables transactions that are in the mutual interest of the trading partners. Relevant to the quote at the beginning of this chapter, in this sense, money 'lubricates the economy' and, hence, increases welfare.

More recently, economic planning has been tested as an alternative to a monetised economy and has failed. Unsurprisingly, Karl Marx, who like nobody before or after him developed an ideological underpinning for an economic system based on government planning, was highly suspicious of the role of money and reportedly even said 'I do not like money, money is the reason we fight'. To finance a relatively lavish lifestyle, however, Marx was not loath to accept substantial amounts of money bequeathed to him by his parents or donated to him by like-minded friends.[4] Driving the point home, even during the heyday of Soviet communism in the second part of the twentieth century, cash was typically not abolished. However, it never provided a comparable level of purchasing power to that in market (or capitalist) economies, nor did it play a key role as an indicator of economic value. The people living under communism typically did not suffer from a lack of money, but rather from a lack of opportunities for spending money, because the production of goods obeyed an economic plan rather than responding to consumer needs. Furthermore, because administered prices were kept artificially low, economic scarcity was manifested in other ways, such as long queues for ordinary purchases and high prices for products sold on black markets. In planned economies, access to some degree of material welfare was often more dependent on good connections rather than money. In more general terms, despite enormous administrative efforts, planned economies have never been able to cope with the vast and detailed amount of information required to figure out the constantly changing consumer needs, nor have they been able to identify promising investment opportunities or set the right incentives throughout the production process.[5] These are some of the reasons that the planned economies of the twentieth century eventually broke down, and these factors continue to challenge the few remaining socialist countries. In contrast, when economic production and allocation are organised around free markets, in which money adopts the key role as the means of payment and the unit of account, the various consumer needs are translated into constantly evolving price signals to which large numbers of existing and potential entrepreneurs react. Even though Adam Smith's (1723–1790) celebrated 'invisible hand' metaphor has long been used to describe this process, it remains fascinating that, as history has shown, economies based on the freedom of enterprise and decentralised and seemingly chaotic production processes generate much better outcomes than even the most elaborate and seemingly ingenious plan do.

Early forms of money were almost always intimately linked with the intrinsic value of some commodity. Although different societies developed different commodity monies, the physical good, material, or substance used

---

[4] For a critical view on how Marx's personal lifestyle had little in common with that of the ordinary worker, see North, Gary, 1993: The Marx Nobody Knows. In: Maltsev, Yuri N. *Requiem for Marx*, The Ludwig Mises Institute.

[5] For a classical warning about the fallacies of economic planning that highlight, for example, the lack of suitable price signals, see Von Mises, Ludwig, 1951: *Socialism: An Economic and Sociological Analysis*, Yale University Press.

as medium of exchange had to be easy to divide into smaller units to allow for the payment of various amounts, durable so that it could store value, and easy to transport to allow for payments in distant places. Furthermore, the commodity had to have a homogeneous quality such that prices could be expressed in terms of a fixed, standardised unit of account. Finally, to avoid counterfeiting, commodity money needed to be difficult to replicate and made from a material that was not abundantly available. A number of commodities fulfil these requirements. Examples include rice, salt, pepper, shells, and precious stones. However, in most ancient civilisations, precious metals, such as gold, silver, and copper, which could be stamped into coins, turned out to be the preferred monetary material.

Clearly, the days when the value of coins depended on their metal content are long gone. Nevertheless, commodity monies have sometimes re-emerged amid the complete collapse of modern monetary systems. Probably the most widely cited example of modern commodity money is cigarettes, which spontaneously turned into a generally accepted means of payment in prisoner-of-war camps during World War II.[6] In particular, because more or less identical rations (including cigarettes) were distributed to prisoners, but preference for various kinds of food, for example, differed, the stage was set for possible gains from trade. However, even within the small world of a prison camp, it can be hard to find a double coincidence of wants and, hence, the search for more efficient ways to trade began. Within this context, the simplest solution is using cigarettes, which fulfil virtually all the requirements of commodity money listed in the previous paragraph, as a means of payment. On a much broader scale, cigarettes were also used as money in Germany during the chaotic years right after World War II as well as in the countries affected by the collapse of the Soviet Union at the beginning of the 1990s.

Although commodity money can apparently emerge spontaneously, the organisation of monetary affairs has far-reaching implications. Above all, it is of great benefit to society when a single form of money dominates to promote the functions of medium of exchange, unit of account, and store of value. Monetary standardisation exhibits a self-reinforcing tendency insofar as, for example, the most popular version of commodity money tends to be preferred. Reflecting the powerful incentive to hold the most broadly accepted means of payment, societies have often ended up with almost completely uniform money whose characteristics are enshrined in official norms, but also reflect historical social customs. Governments have always played a key role

---

[6]See Radford, Richard A., 1945: The Economic Organization of a P.O.W Camp, *Economica*, 189–201.

in defining the monetary standard through such measures as proclaiming an official means of payment, giving the central bank a monopoly over issuing uniform banknotes, only accepting the national currency for tax payments, and granting the status of legal tender. Nevertheless, governments have never been all important and, as is perhaps best illustrated by the above-mentioned episodes of hyperinflations, individuals always retain the option to abandon the official currency in response to government-produced monetary chaos.

Problems with counterfeiting and fraud provide another reason for government intervention. Aside from criminal prosecution, public measures also encompass the more or less elaborate production of officially certified money with commonly recognisable emblems. To overcome the hazards of inspecting metal-based currencies, official mints usually had the exclusive right to stamp coins with a certified weight and purity during the early stages of monetary history. The regular pattern that can be found on the edges of most coins to this day provide a nice anecdote to illustrate some of the issues associated with counterfeit money. Before the invention of these 'milled edges' (or ridges), coin holders would regularly engage in an activity called 'clipping', that is they cut off inconspicuous amounts of silver or gold. To illustrate the remarkably large extent to which this clipping was practiced, the left panel of Fig. 3.3 depicts clipped and unclipped versions of a Roman coin. As long as the holder managed to pass on a coin at its original value, which was no longer reflected in the exact metal content, clipping was a profitable business. Eventually, milled edges were imprinted to reveal such fraudulent practices. However, clipping is not a lucrative career today. Although the legal risks involved are not as great today—punishments in the past were draconian and boiling a caught clipper in hot oil was quite common during the Middle Ages—because modern coins are merely tokens, it is no longer possible to clip one's way to effortless self-enrichment.

It is an irony of history that governments themselves became the biggest adulterers of coins. This process usually involved, first, calling back all issued coins, and re-coining them at lower metal contents, and leaving their face values unchanged. Such debasement of the currency implied that more coins could be issued using the same amount of precious metal creating a profit for the government at the expense of ordinary citizens. Because, during the Middle Ages, the privilege of issuing coins rested with the feudal lord (or, in French, the 'seigneur'), the profit from debasing coins was called 'seigniorage'; this expression is still used for the profits arising from the public monopoly to issue currency (see Sect. 4.1).

Paper money constitutes a next important step in monetary history. Banknotes appeared already in China around the eleventh century amid an

Unclipped and clipped Siliqua coin from the late period of the Roman Empire.

Oldest preserved banknote. The so-called 'Ming note' (fourteenth century).

Fig. 3.3 Clipping and early paper money. Images: The Trustees of the British Museum

enormous increase in economic activity during the prosperous era of the Song dynasty. In China, paper money remained popular for hundreds of years (see the right panel of Fig. 3.3), but it disappeared by the seventeenth century owing to several episodes of rampant inflation and monetary instability during the Yuan and Ming dynasties. Conversely, around the same time, banknotes began to emerge in Europe as a by-product of goldsmiths and other industries that routinely took gold- and silverware into custody and confirmed the receipt with a piece of paper. Covered by a specific amount of conventional commodity money (i.e. coins or precious metals), these receipts turned out to provide a convenient means for large payments by avoiding the physical transfer of precious metal. By chance rather than design, the idea of a banknote was born. However, as discussed at the beginning of Chap. 2, governments sooner or later began to control these novel forms of money by establishing central note-issuing banks during the nineteenth and twentieth centuries.

In a paper-money system, the equivalent step to debasing coins is suspending the convertibility of banknotes. In the end, severing the link to precious metal gave rise to a fiat-money system, which is essentially based on government-backed claims that are only convertible into themselves. Fiat money is the norm today. However, despite the emphasis on the element of 'fiat'—which is rooted in the Latin expression meaning 'there shall be'— it is often overlooked that the main innovation of modern money is not so much that it is created by government decree. Per the discussion above, most forms of commodity money were subject to laws and regulations, through which governments tried to influence the social conventions underpinning the designated means of payment. Moreover, when, for example, gold is chosen as commodity money, a corresponding pecuniary demand is created that artificially inflates the gold price. In principle, this process is not very different from increasing the purchasing power of an inconvertible banknote to well beyond its intrinsic paper value. Taken together, the values of fiat and commodity money are, perhaps to different degrees, artefacts of what governments decree. The far-reaching novelty of fiat money instead lies in its flexibility to accommodate the supply of an otherwise useless piece of paper or even an electronic currency unit, to constantly changing financial and economic conditions. This flexibility has advantages, allowing the money supply to adjust to seasonal fluctuations, business cycles, high levels of inflation, and financial instability. Furthermore, fiat money is much cheaper to produce; it does not require precious metal, for example, which therefore becomes available in larger quantities for industrial purposes. Conversely, after removing the direct link to a physical good, the monetary authority can also abuse its newly found freedom by overissuing money. Many of the early attempts to introduce inconvertible paper money indeed ended in a fiasco. Examples—some of which have already been mentioned—include the paper-money systems of the Ming dynasty, the Banque Royale scheme in France, the overissuing of so-called 'Assignats' after the French Revolution, and the suspension of sterling convertibility during the Napoleonic wars, which all led to upsurges in inflation or even outright monetary chaos. Historical experiences suggest that, relative to, for example, gold-backed currencies, successful fiat-money systems require relatively elaborate safeguards to limit the amount of money in circulation. It has always been crucial to maintain the public's trust in a currency; this trust can be undermined by misconduct by both officially backed and private financial institutions, which are closely associated with the monetary system. However, whereas in the past suspensions of convertibility were an unmistakable sign that something was wrong within the currency system, it is presently much more difficult to detect whether monetary rules and mandates have been broken. Therefore, under fiat-based money, maintaining trust has become more important than ever before. In particular, in modern two-tiered banking systems, the trust in money is maintained through giving central banks the legal mandate to guarantee the purchasing power of the currency, and supervising commercial banks.[7]

3.3 How Much Money Circulates Through the Economy?

As indicated in the historical discussion of the previous section, in a world where cash coexists with sophisticated electronic payment systems, money is quite different thing than what it used to be when coins were the dominant means of payment. Owing to the ongoing changes and innovations in the monetary system, it is not easy to estimate how much money circulates through the economy. Theoretically, money encompasses all assets that are commonly accepted to settle economic transactions. However, in practice, depending on the interpretation of such terms as 'commonly accepted', the quantity of money can include a range of more or less liquid assets. Moreover, the quantity of money is not constant but typically increases across time to accommodate the growing number of transactions in an expanding economy. Within a given year, seasonal effects can also give rise to noticeable fluctuations in the demand for money, because, for example, many invoices fall due at the end of a month or year. Today, central and commercial banks constantly adjust their money supplies to absorb the trends and fluctuations in monetary demand.

In narrow terms, money encompasses cash in circulation, which can, according to Fig. 3.4, be further divided into coins and banknotes. This physical, non-interest-bearing form of money is sometimes referred to as 'currency'. However, in modern economies, intangible means of payment, especially book money deposited in the accounts of financial institutions, such as banks, have become increasingly more important. It is nowadays easy to draw on the corresponding assets to make payments by means of direct transfers to other accounts. Technically, cashless payments occur via

---

[7]In a two-tiered banking system, banks occupy strategic positions in the monetary system. Recently, cryptocurrencies aspire to challenge the monetary role of banks through the use of innovative technology. In particular, a cryptocurrency, such as bitcoin, relies on a publicly available compute code, which specifies an algorithm to create new currency, determines how monetary transactions can be made, and keeps a record of current and past transactions. However, until now, cryptocurrencies represent a speculative asset rather than a commonly accepted means of payment. Furthermore, similar to the early forms of commodity money, cryptocurrencies could be vulnerable to a collapse in trust and suffer from an inflexible money supply (especially in times of financial crisis). For a monetary discussion of cryptocurrencies, see Bank for International Settlements, 2018: *Cryptocurrencies: looking beyond the hype*, BIS Annual Economic Report 2018.

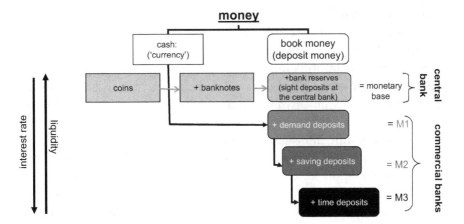

Fig. 3.4 A synoptic disposition of monetary aggregates

financial instruments, such checks or direct debits (often in electronic form). Direct financial transfers between accounts of course provide a convenient and safe way to settle regular and/or large transactions. The advent of book money is closely intertwined with the development of the banking industry. Specifically, the corresponding innovations arose mainly in response to the hazards of funding long-distance trade. The delays and risks which arose when goods were transported to far-away places introduced important caveats to cash payments. Starting in the Middle Ages, Italian bankers and, later, their colleagues in Northern Europe first developed innovations such as bills of exchange, which were written orders to pay a certain amount of money in a given place at a given date, to liberate merchants from the risk of carrying large amounts of coins. Much more recently, the substantial progress in computer and information technology has given enormous impetus to cashless payments by greatly facilitating access to deposits in bank accounts. It is therefore, perhaps, not surprising that electronic transactions of bank deposits are today the main means of payment for firms and households.

Owing to these recent monetary innovations, some believe that it is time to abolish cash. The corresponding proposals typically cut into a deep ideological debate between those who distrust government power and, hence, would like to preserve the privacy and freedom of cash payments, and those who believe in the merits of government control to combat such activities as money laundering and, hence, would like to make financial transaction as transparent as possible. Despite these possible advantages, a cashless economy is likely to suffer from several practical drawbacks, and its advocates may be as wrong than those who thought that the banknote would soon disappear when checkable accounts were introduced more than 100 years ago. The value of cash as an indispensable and safe means of payment for certain classes of transactions is likely underestimated. For example, consider purchases in remote places without access to information technology. Moreover, some groups of the population, such as the elderly, may lack the technological skills to manage electronic payments. Finally, a monetary system relying entirely on electronic payment systems would be completely exposed to breakdowns of and attacks on the corresponding information technology.

Turning to intangible means of payment, the most liquid form of book money is held as sight (or demand) deposits by financial institutions in their account at the central bank. These balances are referred to as 'bank reserves', which are a means of payment between banks and form part of the ultimate reserve of the banking system (see Fig. 3.4). For regulatory reasons, commercial banks are required to cover a fraction of their deposited assets with liquid assets at the central bank. These so-called 'minimum-reserve requirements' provide one instrument via which the central bank can influence the broad amount of money within the economic system (see Sect. 4.3). Furthermore, commercial banks can, and often do, hold excess reserves above the legal minimum. A voluntary holding of book money at the central bank is of particular importance in times of financial instability, when aggravated levels of uncertainty create ample incentives to maintain access to precautionary liquidity buffers (see Sect. 5.5). Taken together, the amount of cash in circulation and bank reserves define the monetary base, which is also referred to by a bewildering number of other names, including M0 as well as central-bank, narrow, base, and high-powered money.[8] As reflected by some of these expressions, central banks can be thought of as laying the pecuniary foundation of state-backed money based on which private economic agents build the various storeys of the monetary and financial system. Against this background, in overly simplistic terms, monetary policy is the ongoing adjustment of the monetary base to trigger further effects to the broad monetary architecture and, in turn, overall economic conditions such as the average price level.

The discussion until now may have created the false impression that the central bank is the only, or at least the most important, financial institution that supplies money. In reality, the monetary base provides one of many components. By issuing close substitutes to cash, such as demand, saving,

---

[8] To be precise, central-bank money and the monetary base are not identical concepts per se. For example, coins are issued by the government and not by the central bank in the euro area, England, and Switzerland (the central bank typically distributes the coins). In these cases, coins are not included in central-bank money. Of course, coins only account for a tiny fraction of the monetary base.

and time deposits, commercial banks play a particularly important role in the creation of the broadly defined monetary aggregates, referred to as M1, M2, and M3. In particular, M1 encompasses the public's transaction balances. Aside from cash and traveller's cheques, this category includes book money held as demand deposits in checkable accounts, negotiable order of withdrawal (NOW) accounts, and so on. The components of M1 are cash or can be converted into cash without constraints or pre-notifications (at sight) to immediately settle financial transactions. The add-on part of M1 is typically highly liquid, but also interest bearing. In addition, the monetary aggregate M2 also encompasses saving deposits, that is, bank accounts that typically pay slightly higher interest rates but that cannot be accessed in an unconstrained manner by freely withdrawing arbitrarily large amounts. Nevertheless, it is easy to turn saving deposits into a suitable means of payment. Hence, M2 is still very liquid and, therefore, also called 'quasi money'. Finally, the even broader concept of M3 adds time deposits and, hence, encompasses all potential means of payment available within the economy. The additional parts of M3 include such financial instruments as money-market funds and repurchase agreements, which are primarily held by large financial institutions rather than individuals. Although these assets characteristically mature only at a specific date in the near future, they are still sufficiently liquid that M3 can be referred to as 'near money' or 'broad money'.

Taken together, Fig. 3.4 suggests that, in practice, the concept of money can be stretched from a narrow, to a quasi, and, finally, to a broad definition and, depending on the definition, encompass assets that are more or less liquid and non-interest bearing. Quantitatively, the corresponding monetary aggregates are typically distributed like an inverted pyramid, in which the bottom corner consists of cash and the top edge includes the add-on parts of M3 (see Fig. 3.5). The increasing quantity of money when moving towards the top edge implies, of course, that modern circulating media consist primarily of intangible book money. This observation often holds for the monetary base, which encompasses not only cash but also intangible bank reserves. Hence, monetary policy expansions today occur primarily through specific transactions with commercial banks rather than through physical note printing.

The composition of the monetary aggregates can change rapidly. As a case in point, consider the effect of a financial crisis. As will become clearer from the discussion in Chap. 5, financial instability typically triggers a flight to safety implying, among other things, that banks and other financial institutions reallocate assets into more liquid forms of money. In their capacity as lenders of last resort, central banks can respond to this reallocation by expanding the monetary base. Conversely, the add-on parts of M3 shrink often dramatically,

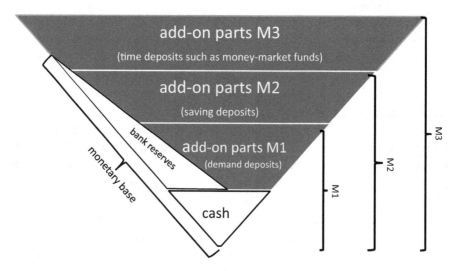

Fig. 3.5 Inverted money pyramid

reflecting a declining desire to invest in, for example, money-market funds. Hence, it is important to realise that statements about the evolution of the money supply can depend heavily on the specific definition of money being used.

3.4 Private Money Creation Inside Commercial Banks

Owing to the invention of cashless payments and, more recently, electronic payment systems, deposits in accounts offer functionally almost equivalent services to the coins and banknotes in wallets. Reflecting these developments, modern commercial banks play a major role in the creation of broadly defined monetary aggregates. In this regard, the key concept is the 'multiplier', which links official means of payment backed by credit from outside the private sector, which are therefore also called 'outside money', with those that are backed by credit created inside the private sector and, hence, are called 'inside money'.

In general, money and credit are to some degree interrelated as shown by, for example, the refinancing of commercial banks via the central bank, which often occurs in the form of short-term credit (see Sect. 4.2). Furthermore, it is also quite common to buy certain goods, such as cars, by means of consumer loans and the link between money and credit manifests itself directly in credit-card payments.[9] As a theoretical curiosity, it would, in principle, be possible to abolish money and replace it with a pure credit system, in which payments are always made on account, and balances are sporadically settled against each other.[10] In reality, however, an economy based entirely on credit has never existed, and probably will never exist. For many transactions, outright monetary payments are preferred, because firms are reluctant to give their products to complete strangers, who cannot be trusted to honour future financial obligations. To keep default risk at a tolerable level, credit is typically only granted to well-known, or creditworthy, individuals. In that sense, distrust is the root of all money.[11] Of course, the various forms of credit and loans provide a useful complement to the monetary system and are of particular importance for financing investment projects whose benefits will only materialise in the distant future. Conversely, the distinctive role of money is to providing a liquid means of payment to immediately settle economic transactions.

The interrelationships encapsulated in the money-and-credit multiplier can best be understood by looking at the connections between the stylised balance sheets of the central bank and the commercial-banking system. Figure 3.6 provides the corresponding lists of assets (left-hand side of the balance sheet) and liabilities (right-hand side of the balance sheet). For a conventional savings-and-loan bank, demand deposits are the most important liability. First, consider the scenario depicted in the left panel of Fig. 3.6, in which deposits are completely covered by reserves held at the central bank. Under this so-called 'narrow banking', or '100-per-cent reserve', system, commercial banks merely transfer central-bank money into deposits which are offered to the public. Recall that the monetary base consists of bank reserves and cash in circulation, whereas M1 includes the demand (or sight) deposits held by the public and cash in circulation. Hence, if deposits coincide with bank reserves, the monetary base and M1 are equivalent.[12] In other words, no money-and-

---

[9]Technically, credit-card payments do not immediately enter M1. Rather, they represent short-term loans from the credit-card company. The monetary side of the transaction occurs only when the invoice from the credit-card company is settled by the cardholder.

[10]This proposal was made by the Swedish economist Knut Wicksell (1851–1926) in his principal contribution *Interest and Prices* (1898, McMillan and Co.).

[11]This line of argument was developed by Nobuhiro Kiyotaki and John Moore in a paper entitled 'Evil is the Root of all Money', which was presented during the 2001 edition of the Clarendon Lectures at the University of Oxford.

[12]Perhaps, mathematical formulae can help to clarify this point. For the present scenario, we have that monetary base=cash+reserves. In case only demand deposits are considered (e.g. we contemplate M1), we

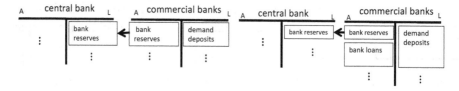

Fig. 3.6 The money multiplier

credit multiplication would take place, and commercial banks would merely serve as depots for central-bank money.

In a narrow banking system, deposits lay completely idle, meaning that they cannot be used to refinance bank loans. However, across a sufficiently large number of bank accounts, only a fraction of these deposits are typically withdrawn. Because most deposits remain untouched, it is typically unnecessary to fully cover them with liquid reserves. This insight provides a stepping stone for the fractional-reserve banking system, in which deposits are partially backed by reserves and partially lent out as bank loans (see right panel of Fig. 3.6). In this case, the term 'deposits' is, of course, somewhat of a misnomer, as bank accounts are typically more than mere money depots. Perhaps intriguingly, in the case of fractional reserves, the distinction between inside and outside money becomes important. In particular, by expanding their balance sheets, commercial banks are able to issue their own forms of broadly defined money which are backed by loans and credit created inside the private sector. The extent to which money-and-credit multiplication can occur depends crucially on the fraction of deposits covered by bank reserves. For example, if 10% of deposits are covered and 100 currency units of reserves are held at the central bank, the balance sheet of the commercial banking system can be expanded up to a total of 1000 currency units. Hence, in this example, the multiplier effect equals 1000/100=10 (e.g. by a factor of ten).[13]

---

have furthermore that *M1=cash+demand deposits*. A 100% reserve system implies that *reserves=demand deposits*. Hence, *M1=monetary base*.

[13] The exact formula of the money-and-credit multiplier can be derived from the definition of monetary aggregates. Consider the example of M1, which is defined as *M1=cash+demand deposits*. Furthermore, we have that *monetary base=cash+reserves*. Define the reserve ratio by *m=reserves/demand deposits* and the fraction of cash *c=cash/demand deposits*. Now we have that

$$\underbrace{\frac{M1}{\text{monetary base}}}_{\text{money multiplier}} = \frac{\text{cash } + \text{ demand deposits}}{\text{cash } + \text{ reserves}}$$

Despite widely held beliefs to the contrary, commercial banks cannot freely produce money from nothing.[14] Rather, banks act as intermediaries between lenders and borrowers and, hence, can only credit inside money to deposit accounts when there is a corresponding private demand for loans (see also Sect. 5.2). This demand is, in turn, limited by such things as the quality and quantity of profitable investment opportunities. Similarly, although commercial banks can create broadly defined money, they cannot create wealth with the stroke of a pen. Throughout the process of money-and-credit multiplication, any increase in the volume of demand deposits and, by extension, the amount of liquid assets circulating through the economy is by definition matched by an equivalent amount of bank loans. Because the corresponding changes in assets and liabilities exactly offset each other, the creation of inside money has no effect on overall wealth (recall that money and wealth are not the same). Finally, Fig. 3.6 only considers reserves, loans, and deposits. Under this stylised scenario, inside money and credit clearly have an intimate relationship. In contrast, real-world financial systems are more complex. Indeed, most credit and loans are nowadays backed by non-deposit liabilities and, during the last decades, the correlation between the amount of money in circulation and the volume of outstanding credit has declined to quite low levels.[15]

Money-and-credit multiplication relates to several topics discussed above. Historically, the comparison between narrow and fractional reserve banking systems reflects, partly, the emergence of the dual banking system, in which the central bank issues state-backed money but commercial banks play the main role of both providing private credit and demand deposits to households and firms (see Sect. 2.2). Moreover, the money-and-credit multiplier is also closely associated with the definition of monetary aggregates discussed in Sect. 3.3.

$$= \frac{c \times \text{demand deposits} + \text{demand deposits}}{c \times \text{demand deposits} + m \times \text{demand deposits}}$$

$$= \frac{1+c}{1+m}$$

Hence, the money-and-credit multiplier within the banking system decreases with the fraction of reserves m and cash c.

[14] For a paper demystifying this belief, see Tobin, James, 1963: Commercial Banks as Creators of 'Money', Cowles Foundation Paper, 205.

[15] See, for example, Schularick, Moritz, and Alan M. Taylor, 2012: Credit booms gone bust: monetary policy, leverage cycles and financial crises, 1870–2008, *The American Economic Review*, 201, 1029–1061.

From a graphical perspective, the inverted pyramid of Fig. 3.5 illustrates the possibility that the amount of inside money far exceeds the amount of outside money.

At a first glance, it is perhaps astonishing to hear that large amounts of money are created inside the banking system by private agents—nowadays mainly commercial banks.[16] Why should a central bank equipped with a currency monopoly tolerate this activity? In general, this question touches on the very broad debate about the appropriate role of the government within the monetary system and, thus, resonates with the above-mentioned disputes between the currency and banking schools and between the proponents and opponents of a free banking system (see Sect. 2.2). However, the arguments discussed thus far may help to explain why privately created forms of money have been an integral part of virtually any economic system. In particular, as long as firms and households can more or less freely lend and borrow economic assets, regulating and controlling every money-and-credit-related aspect within the banking system is simply a daunting task. Historical experience with, for example, the nationalisation of banknotes, which provided the impetus for the development of demand deposits, impressively demonstrate the ability of inventive commercial banks to come up with new, liquid financial products (see Sect. 2.2). To avoid similar reactions if a country wishes to establish a full-reserve banking system, the central bank would have to engage in a regulatory cat-and-mouse game with commercial banks to prevent the development of financial products that could be turned into broadly accepted means of payment. In this regard, it is maybe worth remembering that monetary conventions not only arise from government decrees but also reflect the actual payment habits of private individuals. Finally, a monetary system based entirely on officially backed money would probably also stifle innovation. It is at least doubtful that a central bank dominating all parts of the monetary system would, over the past decades, have developed such widely appreciated financial innovations as chequable accounts or, more recently, credit cards and electronic payments.

---

[16]In principle, this type of activity is not restricted to commercial banks, as anybody can create inside money as long as he or she manages to issue financial claims which are broadly accepted as a means of payment. Of course, by being close to the money and capital markets, specialising in monitoring credit, and running parts of the payment system, commercial banks are in a unique position to create inside money.

3.5   An Overview of the Money Market

To prepare the ground for the remaining discussion, it is perhaps useful to incorporate further parts of the monetary system into the just-mentioned connections between the central bank and commercial banks. Specifically, in a synoptic manner, Fig. 3.7 broadens the picture by adding, for example, the role of the private sector (households/firms), which holds claims on the commercial banking system by depositing money in bank accounts. In contrast, private individuals typically have no direct access to the book money created by the central bank.[17]

The public sector, which has a long history of monetising public expenditures, is quite different. Indeed, the direct links between fiscal and monetary authorities can be traced to the origins of central banking (see Sect. 2.1). The funding of public debt via government-bond purchases by the central bank is often referred to as 'financing public expenditure via printing money'. However, this expression is outdated. Today, interventions in government-bond markets are not settled by printing additional banknotes but rather by booking money in the form of bank reserves, which are newly created whenever the amount of government bonds on the asset-side of the central bank's balance sheet increases.

To summarise, money is often mysteriously referred to as the lubricant of the economy. This chapter should have demystified the economic role of money, which is merely a commonly accepted means of payment. Having said that, the monetary framework does have powerful economic and social effects. Against this background, the manifold connections between the central bank and the other parts of the economic system provide the basis for some of the remaining chapters of this book. In particular, Chap. 4 is devoted to monetary-policy instruments, which encompass a range of transactions via which the central bank changes interest rates and the money supply. The connections between the central bank and commercial banks are also a key element in safeguarding the stability of the financial system, as discussed in Chap. 5. Finally, the link between the central bank and the government maps into interrelationships between fiscal and monetary policy, which are important for controlling inflation. The corresponding topics are discussed in Chaps. 6 and 7.

---

[17] Of course, ordinary citizens have access to central-bank money by holding cash.

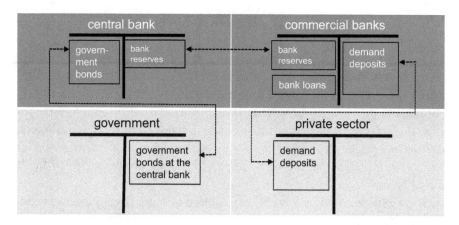

Fig. 3.7 Overview of the money market

Further Reading

For a detailed history of the various forms of money, see Kindleberger, Charles P., 1984: *A Financial History of Western Europe*, Routledge (especially Part I).

A more entertaining discussion on the history of money is Ferguson, Niall, 2009: *The Ascent of Money: A Financial History of the World*, Penguin Books.

The microeconomic aspects of money are discussed in textbooks on 'Money, Credit, and Banking'. A good example is Mishkin, Frederic S., 2013; *The Economics of Money, Banking, and Financial Markets*, Pearson.

For a more advanced discussion of recent developments in economic theory on money and credit, see Nosal, Ed, and Guillaume Rocheteau, 2017: *Money, Payments, and Liquidity*, MIT Press.

4

Monetary-Policy Instruments

It would be evident that all the evils of our currency were owing to the over-issues of the Bank, to the dangerous power with which it was entrusted of diminishing at its will, the value of every monied man's property, and by enhancing the price of provisions and every necessary of life, injuring the public annuitant and all those persons whose incomes were fixed, and who were consequently not enabled to shift any part of the burden from their own shoulders. David Ricardo (British economist and member of parliament, 1772–1823)[1]

4.1 The Central Bank's Balance Sheet

In the introductory quote, David Ricardo, who was mentioned in Sect. 2.2 as a prominent representative of the currency school, laments the upsurge in inflation after Britain suspended the convertibility of sterling in 1797. Economic history includes other examples of an inadequate money supply undermining the purchasing power of the currency. In recent centuries, the task of 'guardian of the currency' has increasingly fallen to the central bank, which, nowadays, is expected to constantly adjust the monetary base to absorb shifts in money demand, and prevent the over- or undersupply of money from causing an inflation or deflation, respectively. However, in a world with fiat money, it is perhaps no longer clear what this policy actually entails. To avoid talking about the details, interventions expanding the monetary base are

---

[1]Ricardo, David, 1809: The price of gold, Letter contributed to the Morning chronicle, p. 14.

assets origination of central-bank money	liabilities composition of central-bank money	
securities from refinancing operations (e.g. repos; formerly discount operations)	cash in circulation (banknotes and coins)	*monetary base*
securities from open-market operations	bank reserves (sight deposits of commercial banks)	
international reserves (gold and foreign-exchange reserves)	distributed profits	
	other liabilities	
other assets	net worth (equity)	

Fig. 4.1 Stylised balance sheet of a modern central bank

often presented to the public using catchy phrases, such as 'the central bank is printing money' or 'liquidity is pumped into the economy'. But how would you describe a tightening of monetary policy? It is at least noteworthy that expressions like 'the central bank is shredding money' or 'liquidity is pumped out of the economy' are unheard of.

Several classes of monetary policy instruments (or tools) are available to control the monetary base, determine the level of interest rates, and manage the corresponding direct and indirect effects on such things as the aggregate supply of money and credit. These instruments can best be explained by means of the central bank's balance sheet. To this end, Fig. 4.1 depicts a stylised case that is slightly more detailed than that depicted in Fig. 3.6. As usual, the right-hand side lists the liabilities and, thus, reflects the composition of the monetary base in terms of cash in circulation and bank reserves held as sight deposits by commercial banks. Printing banknotes and, in some cases, stamping coins as well as the logistics of cash distribution have traditionally been the responsibility of central banks. However, reflecting the declining role of cash as a means of payment (see Sect. 3.3), the days when more or fewer banknotes were put into circulation to carry out monetary-policy are long gone. Nowadays, central banks tend to merely satisfy the demand for cash, thereby matching the cyclical movements in economic transactions. In the modern world, monetary policy is instead manifested in marked changes of the aggregate-reserve position. In particular, by expanding its reserves, the central bank increases the aggregate amount of narrow money, whereas a contraction of the aggregate-reserve position takes narrow money out of circulation. Traditionally, reserves did not pay interest. However, recently, some central banks have discovered that imposing positive or negative interest rates on bank reserves provides an innovative monetary-policy instrument.

Turning to the asset-side, it is often overlooked that central banks do not issue money for free. Instead, each liability in terms of banknotes or reserves in circulation is covered by an underlying asset. A corresponding list can be found on the left-hand side of the central bank's balance sheet. Although the asset-side is often structured according to the type of financial claim (e.g. government bonds, foreign exchange, loans and advances to commercial banks, gold holdings, etc.), to disentangle the different monetary-policy instruments, it is useful to contemplate a structure that reflects the origination of the monetary base. In particular, refinancing operations with commercial banks provide a way to create central-bank money. The discount policy mentioned in Sect. 2.3, under which central-bank money was lent against bills of exchange as security, represents an early example of this class of monetary-policy instruments. In concurrence with developments in the financial industry, refinancing operations subsequently moved to so-called 'Lombard loans', which permitted commercial banks to borrow reserves, at the 'Lombard rate', against a broader basket of financial securities. Today, refinancing operations are typically arranged in the form of a 'repurchase agreement' (or repo), which combines a spot transaction issuing a short-term central-bank loan against collateral with a simultaneous forward transaction stipulating the date and conditions of the corresponding repurchase (see Fig. 4.2). Furthermore, assets can also end up with the central bank through open-market operations, that is, direct purchases or sales of securities in (open) financial markets. Similarly, central-bank money can originate from direct interventions in foreign-exchange markets. The amount of foreign-exchange assets resulting from such transactions are a country's international reserves, which are not to be confused with the reserves on the liability-side. Under metallic currencies, gold or silver holdings were the key reserves, whereas 'foreign-exchange reserves' (or in short 'forex reserves' or 'FX reserves')—e.g. banknotes, deposits, and bonds denominated in foreign currency—currently

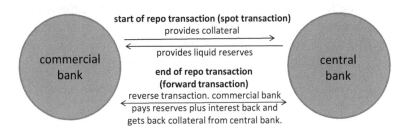

Fig. 4.2 Repo transaction

serve as the main vehicle for the international monetary system. International reserves are also a prerequisite for conducting foreign-exchange interventions.

The central bank's balance sheet shown in Fig. 4.1 contains additional items, such as profits and net-worth, which are, of course, related to the notion of seigniorage, or the pay-offs resulting from the monopoly in issuing officially recognised forms of money. Still, seigniorage revenue arises from several sources, overlaps only partially with accounting profits, and does not lend itself to straightforward measurement.[2] A first source of seigniorage income is associated with the growth in central-bank money. Additional banknotes or bank reserves, whose production costs essentially nothing, indeed encapsulate a transfer of economic claims from private households and companies to the central bank. However, even when the monetary base does not grow, the currency monopoly can still yield a profit. In particular, a comprehensive notion of seigniorage recognises that the asset-side of the balance sheet in Fig. 4.1 includes interest-bearing items, whereas the liabilities-side contains cash and reserves that carry relatively low or even no interest. In combination, an interest-rate spread arises that provides a second source of seigniorage. To explain this idea in other words, the holders of cash or bank reserves provide the central bank with cheap or even interest-free loans. On the asset-side, the corresponding funds can partly be reinvested in securities yielding financial income (e.g. interest, dividends, etc.).

For fiscal policy, the profit distributed by the central bank to the treasury matters. The corresponding transfers, which are also called 'fiscal seigniorage', originate, of course, in the above-mentioned sources of central-bank income. However, the bank can temporarily retain profits to bolster its net-worth position. Hence, the concepts of seigniorage and central-bank profit do not perfectly overlap. Furthermore, the accounting profit of central banks can react markedly to erratic price fluctuations on financial markets. Above all, the accounting value of international reserves reacts to exchange-rate changes. In particular, a depreciation of the domestic currency manifests as an accounting profit, because the nominal value of assets denominated in foreign currency increases when the foreign currency buys more domestic currency units. By the same logic, an appreciation of the domestic currency gives rise to an accounting loss on the international-reserves position of the central bank.

---

[2]A thorough discussion of the different forms of seigniorage can be found in Baltensperger, Ernst, and Thomas Jordan, 1997: Principles of Seigniorage, *Swiss Journal of Economics and Statistics*. A textbook discussion on seigniorage can be found in Walsh, Carl E., 2017: *Monetary Theory and Policy*, MIT Press, Ch. 4.

Although governments typically welcome regular transfers of central-bank profits, they are by no means an adequate indicator of the quality of monetary policy. Rather, historical experience suggests that it is dangerous to tie monetary policy too closely to fiscal considerations. Although massive growth in central-bank money might initially provide an easy means to eliminate public debt, the associated expansion in the central bank's balance sheet will eventually create money in excess of demand and, in turn, boost inflation. In the introductory quote, David Ricardo draws attention to the negative consequences of such a policy on the value of property as well as detrimental effects when fixed incomes are undermined by the collapsing purchasing power of money. Seen from this angle, seigniorage represents an 'inflation tax' (for more details, see Sect. 7.2). Against this background, it should be clear that under a modern approach to monetary policy, the pursuit of price stability rather than profit maximisation is the primary goal of central banks. This goal stands in sharp contrast to that of commercial banking, for which a sustainable, high profit is probably a good indicator for success.

The balance sheets published in the annual reports of central banks are much more detailed than that shown in Fig. 4.1 and typically contain additional items, such as tangible assets or banknote stocks on the asset-side. Furthermore, even though cash and bank reserves determine the monetary base, other liabilities may be included. For example, similar to the treasury issuing government bonds, some central banks have issued their own-debt certificates. In doing so, the total amount of assets and liabilities no longer maps directly into the monetary base. In principle, the monetary base can shrink, even if the balance-sheet total increases when a central bank is able to reallocate sufficiently large amounts of bank reserves into own-debt certificates.

Returning to the question of how central banks implement monetary policy, the corresponding instruments encompass a set of specific financial transactions to change the size and composition of the monetary base and, in turn, affect interest rates, the money supply, and credit conditions throughout the economy. Against this background, the remainder of this chapter reviews some of the most important classes of monetary-policy instruments.

4.2 Refinancing Operations, Discount Policy, and the Base Interest Rate

Regular refinancing operations with the banking system provide one of the most important instruments for conducting monetary policy. More specifically, by granting short-term loans to commercial banks and other financial institutions—typically via the above-mentioned repo transactions—central banks can change the amount of liquid reserves and, in turn, affect other important financial variables. The broad impact of refinancing operations rests on the fact that the interest rate, the type of collateral (usually liquid securities with high credit-ratings), and the term to maturity (usually not more than several weeks) at which commercial banks can borrow reserves from the central bank provide landmarks for the entire financial system. When, for example, a central bank raises the interest rate, or otherwise tightens the conditions for borrowing bank reserves, the refinancing costs of commercial banks increase, whereas their demand for refinancing operations is likely to decrease, as is the broadly defined amount of money (see Fig. 4.3). Hence, these measures constitute examples of a tightening of (or contractionary) monetary policy. The opposite effects arise under a loosening of (or expansionary) monetary policy.

Because of their monopoly in issuing currency, central banks wield great influence on the level of interest rates within a given currency area. In particular, owing to the virtually risk-free and liquid nature of central-bank money, the rate charged on refinancing operations typically provides the basis for interest rates on bank deposits, fixed-income securities, mortgages, and so on. The various add-on values reflect, for example, different default risks (the lower a borrower's creditworthiness, the higher the interest rate is) or

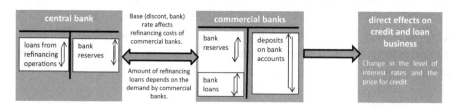

Fig. 4.3 Effects of refinancing (or discount) policy

the term to maturity (interest rates on long-term assets are usually higher).[3] Nevertheless, interest rates typically move essentially in tandem with the rate charged on refinancing operations (see the top panel of Fig. 4.4). Hence, a central bank raising its interest rate marks a tightening of monetary policy insofar as the (opportunity) cost of holding money or receiving credit increases throughout the financial and banking system and, in turn, downward pressure is placed on economic activity. Of course, the opposite effects tend to arise under a loosening of monetary policy, that is, a reduction in the central bank's interest rate.

In addition to its direct financial effects, the interest rate charged on refinancing operations provides also a clear signal of the central bank's assessment of the prevailing economic conditions. It is therefore not surprising that official announcements about the interest rate charged on refinancing operations are eagerly awaited and usually prominently discussed in the media. In practice, the corresponding decisions are typically announced in terms of a 'base (interest) rate', which is sometimes also called the 'official interest rate'. In particular, as part of ordinary or extraordinary meetings of the relevant decision-making body, central banks announce whether they have decided to raise, lower, or leave unchanged the base interest rate. The exact process and corresponding expressions differ between countries. For example, bearing witness to the historical origin of interest-rate decisions in the discounting of bills of exchange, the corresponding measures are sometimes still referred to as the 'discount policy'. Furthermore, some countries, such as Japan, communicate monetary-policy decisions through a discount rate, even though bills of exchange are an outdated financial product. In other cases, central banks can announce monetary-policy decisions directly in terms of the refinancing rate, which is referred to as the 'repo rate' by the Swedish Riksbank, the 'bank rate' by the Bank of England, and the 'main refinancing rate' by the European Central Bank, to give a few examples. Other countries, such as the United States or Switzerland, announce their base interest rate by means of a target band, within which a given money-market interest rate for short-term loans between commercial banks is allowed to fluctuate. Concretely, in the United States, the target band refers to the so-called 'federal funds rate', and

---

[3]The difference between short-term (e.g. those on money markets) and long-term (e.g. those on capital markets) interest rates is reflected in their term structure. Across various points in time, the observed term structure of interest rates can be positive (meaning that long-term rates are relatively higher), or negative. The positive slope is deemed normal in the sense that it is the most common scenario, because investors typically want to be compensated for the higher level of uncertainty when holding an asset that pays out in the distant future.

Joint movement of interest rates for the case of the United States. Changes in the base interest rate (target band of the federal-funds rate) affect the development of interbank rates (federal-funds rate embedded in target band) and (depending on the maturity and credit risk) also the interest rates charged on bank loans, government bonds, and commercial paper.

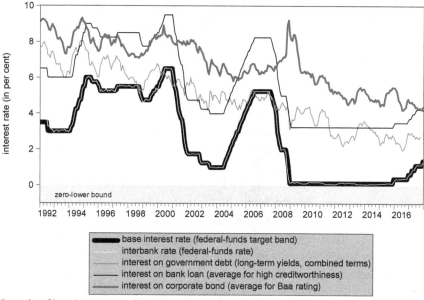

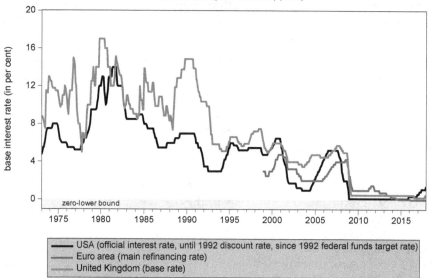

Fig. 4.4 Base interest rate and the development of market interest rates. Data: FRED database of St. Louis Federal Reserve

in Switzerland it refers to the 'Libor'.[4] Finally, the size and structure of the policymaking body setting the base interest rate depends on the organisation of the central bank. Prominent examples include the Federal Open Market Committee (FOMC) of the Federal Reserve System, the ECB-Council for the euro area, and the Monetary Policy Committee (MPC) of the Bank of England.

Base interest rates change across time in accordance with the business cycle and the level of inflation. During a recession, they are typically cut to stimulate economic activity. However, as shown in the bottom panel of Fig. 4.4 for the examples of the United States, the euro area, and Japan, the interest rates associated with refinancing operations cannot be reduced to an arbitrarily low level, but rather are subject to a minimum called the 'zero-lower-bound'. Negative refinancing rates are difficult to manage, because they essentially imply that commercial banks would be paid for holding reserves at the central bank. Such a situation would clearly create incentives to hoard unnecessarily large amounts of bank reserves, which therefore lose much of their impact on the general financial and economic environment. In economics, the strange effects that arise when interest rates approach their lowest possible level are described as the 'liquidity trap'.[5] However, even when refinancing operations are ineffective in an environment with extremely low interest rates, monetary policy as such has not necessarily become ineffective. Other instruments discussed below, such as open-market operations, are still available to further loosen monetary policy.

---

[4]The acronym 'Libor' stands for London interbank offered rate, which is an indicative (i.e. non-binding) reference rate for short-term interbank loans denominated in various currencies between the major banks in the London financial market. Owing to London's leading position in international financial affairs, the Libor provides the basis for a range of key commercial interest rates around the world. Because the Libor is a subjective assessment of the borrowing costs of large banks, it is prone to manipulations. Therefore, there are currently attempts to replace the Libor with a benchmark based on money-market interest rates on actual financial transactions. See Duffie, Darrell, and Jeremy C. Stein, 2015: Reforming LIBOR and Other Financial Market Benchmarks, *Journal of Economic Perspectives* 29, 191–212.

[5]This expression was coined by John Maynard Keynes to explain why monetary policy was, arguably, ineffective during the Great Depression of the 1930s. In principle, a liquidity trap can arise whenever banks, firms, or households hoard central-bank money. However, the incentives to do so are particularly large when the opportunity costs of holding money are low, that is, when nominal interest rates are close to zero.

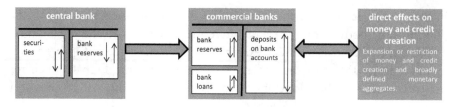

Fig. 4.5 The direct effects of reserve requirements

4.3   Reserve Requirements

Compared with refinancing operations, requirements regarding the amount of reserves to be held at the central bank constitute a cruder instrument to affect the conditions within the commercial banking system. To understand how monetary-policy implementation via reserve requirements works, recall from the discussion on the money-and-credit multiplier in Sect. 3.4 that the reserves-to-deposit rate restricts the aggregate amount of loans, which commercial banks can issue based on a certain amount of deposits. More specifically, an increase (decrease) in required reserves represents a tightening (loosening) of monetary policy, as fewer (more) bank loans and deposits can be created with the same monetary base. Figure 4.5 depicts the corresponding connections in a schematic manner.

Central banks typically stipulate and regularly check that commercial banks hold a bare minimum of reserves. Various channels are available to fulfil this requirement. The above-mentioned refinancing operations provide just one of several options. However, in contrast to the setting of the base interest rate, central banks are typically reluctant to consider regular changes of the minimum-reserve requirements.[6] The main reason that reserve requirements are no longer a popular monetary-policy instrument is that they are only levied on designated deposits and, hence, affect modern banking and financial systems in a highly selective manner. Conversely, by impacting a broad range of interest rates, a change of the base interest rate is felt by any financial firm, regardless of whether it is refinanced via non-deposits, or is mainly active in segments other than the credit and loan business. Taken together, in financially

---

[6]A prominent exception is the People's Bank of China, which routinely changes the reserve requirements of commercial banks. However, the Chinese financial system still differs markedly from those of Europe and North America, as it encompasses only a small number of state-controlled banks. Arguably, this distinction facilitates the implementation of monetary policy via reserve requirements.

advanced countries, a policy built around reserve requirements would fail to broadly affect money and credit conditions.

More often than not, policy discussions about reserve requirements arise amid much broader debates regarding the relative merits and risks of a fractional-reserve banking system. Because bank reserves link the monetary base with the amount of bank credit, it is probably not surprising that these issues receive significant attention when a credit boom results in severe financial turmoil. In particular, during the aftermaths of the Great Depression and, more recently, the Global Financial Crisis, proposals to adopt a full-reserve banking system entered the political debate. Parts of this debate were already highlighted in Sects. 3.4 and 5.4 revisits these issues from a financial-stability perspective.

Reserves provide other angles for monetary-policy implementation besides stipulating a minimum level. Traditionally, central banks did not pay interest, whereas commercial banks had strong incentives to keep their reserve holdings as low as possible. However, to better control the liability-sides of their balance sheets, some central banks (notably the Federal Reserve System in 2008) began to pay interest on reserves. However, in times of financial instability, the main problem is that commercial banks begin to hoard large amounts of central-bank money. To undermine this behaviour, some central banks have recently moved in the opposite direction by charging a 'fee' on bank reserves, which is often referred to as a 'negative interest rate'. Examples of such policies can be found in Denmark, the euro area, Japan, and Switzerland. It is important to realise that these sub-zero rates are not applied to refinancing operations and, hence, do not directly contradict concepts such as the lower bound or the liquidity trap, which were discussed above. This distinction is immediately manifested in the fact that refinancing loans appear on the asset-side of a central bank's balance sheet, whereas bank reserves represent a liability. Nevertheless, it is possible to push the nominal values of some commercial interest rates into negative territory by charging commercial banks for their reserve holdings. Still, as long as central banks also issue banknotes and coins, nominal interest rates must be subject to some lower bound, because sufficiently negative rates (e.g. sufficiently high 'fees') will drive commercial banks to eventually return to their historic habit of holding reserves in terms of (interest-free) banknotes in their vaults (see Sect. 2.2). Against this background, the potential role of negative interest rates is connected with the discussion of the future role of cash within the economy (see Sect. 3.3). In particular, some advocates and critics of abandoning cash base their views on

Fig. 4.6 Direct effects of open-market operations

the alleged advantages and risks, respectively, of removing the lower bound on nominal interest rates.[7]

4.4   Open-Market Operations

In contrast to the various forms of refinancing operations, a second class of monetary-policy instruments draws on direct interventions in the financial system. A prominent example is purchases and sales by the central bank on the bond or money markets, in which other banks as well as private firms and individuals trade a broad range of financial assets. In other words, these financial markets are open to the public, and the corresponding monetary-policy interventions are called 'open-market operations'. Similar to other monetary-policy instruments, direct interventions in financial markets have additional effects on the aggregate amount of bank reserves circulating through the economy. As depicted in Fig. 4.6, central-bank purchases of securities from commercial banks, or other financial corporations, are settled by crediting reserves and, hence, represent a loosening of monetary policy. The opposite scenario of monetary-policy tightening begins with an open-market sale of securities by the central bank. The buyer pays these securities with money form his account with the central bank, which extracts liquid reserves from the financial system.

Technically, an open-market intervention can look very similar to a refinancing operation in the sense that it may involve the same banks and even the same securities. However, a hallmark of any direct intervention into the financial system is that the initiative conventionally lies entirely with the central bank, which determines the type, point of time, and amount of securities to be bought or sold. In contrast, refinancing loans are issued

---

[7]See, for example, Deutsche Bundesbank, 2017: *War on Cash: Is there a Future for Cash?*, International Cash Conference 2017.

on the demand of commercial banks and, hence, depend on their desire to borrow reserves from the central bank. Furthermore, open-market operations often involve financial institutions in addition to commercial banks, such as insurance companies or pension funds. Thus, it is possible to directly affect the financial conditions outside the banking system. Finally, open-market operations not only change the aggregate amount of bank reserves but also shift the demand or supply of the underlying securities. Therefore, a sufficiently large intervention affects their price, or quotation, and at least temporarily gives rise to wealth-effects. For example, substantial central-bank purchases of a given financial asset will entail corresponding price increases.

Pursuing an open-market policy may have various motives. The desire to inject additional central-bank money during a severe financial crisis, even though the base interest rate has already hit its lower bound, has already been mentioned. Recent example of such a policy include the various programmes of 'quantitative easing' that were launched by several central banks during the Global Financial Crisis, and that essentially encompassed purchases of securities with long terms to maturity to reduce long-term interest rates. However, open-market operations are also used under normal circumstances. For example, central banks can intervene in important money markets (and also foreign-exchange markets) to iron out erratic price fluctuations. However, such fine-tuning operations are intended to stabilise the financial-market environment rather than bringing about a fundamental change in monetary policy.

Open-market operations are a potent tool in countries where large and highly developed financial markets provide ample amounts of securities denominated in domestic currency. Central banks usually prefer to hold liquid securities that are, if necessary, easy to buy and sell. Ideally, the issuer of a corresponding security should also have a high credit-rating to ensure that the default risk on the asset portfolio of the central bank is negligible. Reflecting these conditions, open-market operations typically involve domestic sovereign bonds, which represent relatively standardised debt instruments, as they are backed by the government.[8] Owing to the differences in creditworthiness and partly to the lack of deep financial markets, corporate bonds and shares (stocks) do not lend themselves to an open-market policy, because the purchase

---

[8] In this regard, a special situation has occurred in the euro area, where no government bonds (so-called 'euro bonds') are currently issued by the central government (i.e. the European Union). Therefore, the ECB conducts its open-market operations partly with government bonds of the member states. Doing so gives rise to the risk of creating distributional effects when, for economic or political reasons, the bonds of certain member states are preferred over others.

of private debt could be the gateway to inconspicuously supporting certain firms or industries, which could be at odds with monetary policy that is supposed to be in the broad public interest. To avoid such distortional effects, most central banks are reluctant to actively trade large amounts of private securities.[9]

Many countries around the world lack the necessary degree of financial development to use open-market operations as their primary monetary-policy instrument. Moreover, in small countries, regular central-bank interventions could be hampered by the small size and liquidity of local bond markets. Conversely, in countries such as the United States, which has the largest government-bond market in the world, open-market operations are widely used instruments to implement monetary policy.

4.5   Foreign-Exchange Interventions

Direct interventions in the foreign-exchange market can be interpreted as a particular type of open-market policy whereby the central bank purchases or sells various foreign assets that are typically summarised by the term 'foreign exchange'. In practice, the corresponding interventions often involve a commercial bank which is willing to trade money or financial securities denominated in a given foreign currency against central-bank reserves denominated in the domestic currency (see Fig. 4.7). Similar to open-market operations, foreign-exchange purchases create additional reserves, expand the monetary base, and, hence, reflect the loosening of monetary policy. The converse effects arise when the central bank sells financial assets denominated in foreign currencies.

In most cases, the desire to manage or even fix the exchange rate provides the principle motive for foreign-exchange interventions. In particular, any sale of foreign exchange by the central bank is associated with an increasing relative demand for domestic forms of money and, hence, tends to appreciate the international purchasing power of a given currency. The opposite effects arise from a purchase of foreign exchange. A country may wish to manage its exchange rate for reasons related to rather broad, international macroeconomic

---

[9]A recent example of private asset purchases involved so-called 'mortgage-backed securities' (MBS). These securities were at the centre of the Global Financial Crisis as they provided the vehicle which transmitted the losses from decreasing real-estate prices in the United States to other parts of the banking and financial system. To prevent a destabilising cascade of potential bank failures, in 2008, the Federal Reserve System introduced rescue programmes including, among other things, the purchase of substantial amounts of MBS.

Fig. 4.7 Foreign-exchange interventions and their direct effects

considerations. Above all, the international value of a currency impinges on the relative prices between domestic and foreign assets as well as those of imported and exported goods and services (see Chap. 8). Although the various exchange-rate regimes have many advantages and disadvantages, in the present context, it is sufficient to understand that under a fixed exchange-rate regime, foreign-exchange interventions become the dominant monetary-policy instrument, because the central bank must be ready to trade its currency at the predefined external value to stabilise the exchange rate. To that end, it is imperative to hold a sufficient stock of international reserves. Otherwise, a central bank would not be in the position to prevent depreciation by selling foreign exchange and, hence, support the value of the domestic currency.

Aside from foreign-currency transactions by the central bank, capital controls represent a much cruder instrument for intervention in foreign-exchange markets. The corresponding taxes, limits, and outright prohibitions on cross-border financial transactions were an integral part of, for example, the Bretton Woods System (see Sect. 2.5). However, with the financial liberalisation of the last decades, most restrictions and regulations on the international financial system have been dropped. In the developed world, capital controls are nowadays only deployed as emergency measures to stem capital flight during a severe currency crisis (see Sect. 8.6 for more details). Conversely, in many developing countries and emerging markets, capital controls are still relatively widely used to manage the amount and composition of cross-border financial transactions.[10]

---

[10]For a state-of-the-art discussion on capital controls, see International Monetary Fund, 2011: Recent Experiences in Managing Capital Inflows—Cross-Cutting Themes and Possible Policy Framework.

4.6   Overview of Monetary-Policy Instruments

Recall that central banks conduct monetary policy to achieve economic objectives, such as maintaining the purchasing power of a currency, fostering high employment, or stabilising the financial system. To do so, central banks must be able to influence the prevailing conditions within the monetary and financial system. Against this background, this chapter has reviewed the most commonly used monetary-policy instruments (or tools).

To this point, the discussion has focused on the isolated effects of each monetary-policy instrument. Refinancing operations at the base interest rate were thought to affect other interest rates in the economy, open-market operations to impact the prices of the involved securities, and foreign-exchange interventions to move the exchange rate in a given direction. However, modern financial systems are highly integrated, and any monetary-policy intervention will immediately lead to adjustments in all relevant money and capital markets. Figure 4.8 endeavours to illustrate the joint effects of the various monetary-policy instruments on the monetary and credit conditions as well as on asset prices and exchange rates. Consider, for example, the well-known interaction between interest and exchange rates. More specifically, a monetary-policy induced increase in the level of interest rates increases, of course, the nominal

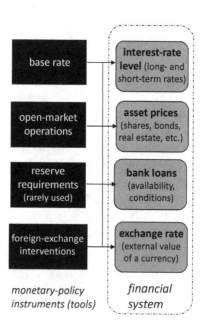

Fig. 4.8   Monetary-policy instruments

yield on domestic assets. To the extent that foreign investors would like to participate in these developments, capital inflows also increase. However, on the foreign-exchange market, the additional demand for domestic securities triggers the appreciation of the domestic currency. Furthermore, when the central bank decides to raise or lower its base interest rate, the values of financial assets are also affected. For example, a changing interest-rate environment alters the present values of fixed-income assets such as bonds. Finally, because the stock market provides an alternative, or substitute, for fixed-income investments, a monetary-policy induced reduction in the interest-rate level can boost stock prices as the corresponding investments have become relatively more attractive. Similar joint effects can be observed for open-market operations or foreign-exchange interventions. However, it would be too cumbersome to discuss all of these possible contingencies.

Figure 4.8 shows only the most commonly used monetary-policy instruments. Additionally, central banks have in the past imposed rather rigid rules and regulations on, for example, the legal level of interest rates or the allocation of credit. A good example of these policies is the interest-rate ceilings on various types of deposits stipulated by the so-called 'Regulation Q' in the United States during the decades after 1933. Following the deregulation of financial markets starting in the 1970s, direct price controls of commercial interest rates are no longer broadly applied. Moreover, in addition to actual monetary-policy interventions, central banks can also affect monetary conditions in more subtle ways. Above all, by publicly assessing the current financial and economic situations, providing forward guidance about future monetary policy, reserving the right to make monetary-policy interventions under certain circumstances, and applying moral suasion on financial matters, it is to some degree possible for a central bank to talk interest or exchange rates in a certain direction. Of course, the effect of public statements that are not immediately backed up by actual monetary interventions depends crucially on the standing of a central bank as moral authority on monetary and financial matters.

Depending on monetary traditions, the prevailing economic conditions, and the current exchange-rate regime, central banks have employed vastly different instruments to implement monetary policy across different countries and time periods. In many cases, refinancing operations with commercial banks and changes in the base interest rate serve currently as the standard monetary-policy instrument. However, in countries with large and highly developed financial markets, open-market operations can play an important role. The same can be said for foreign-exchange interventions in small, open economies, whose economic conditions are largely a reflection of developments in international trade and finance. Furthermore, the various monetary-policy instruments do not always affect financial systems in the same way, but their effectiveness depends on the development, international openness, and the stability of the financial system, among other factors. Hence, appropriate choices of monetary-policy instruments differ not only between countries, but also across time. A case in point is the outbreak of a financial crisis, during which refinancing operations tend to lose their effectiveness when interest rates approach their lower bound, or the increased level of uncertainty make banks reluctant to issue new loans regardless of the available amount of liquid central-bank reserves. Hence, in times of crisis, central banks typically attach more weight to open-market operations or foreign-exchange interventions, as was the case during the most recent Global Financial Crisis, during which 'unconventional' measures such as 'quantitative easing' were introduced. Although some words of warning are appropriate regarding the novelty of some of these policies—as mentioned above, quantitative easing is essentially a specific form of traditional open-market operations—it is certainly true that an unstable financial environment poses a challenge to setting monetary policy. The next chapter addresses this issue.

Further Reading

Brief overviews of monetary-policy instruments can be found in most macroeconomic textbooks. A good example is Abel, Andrew B. and Ben. S. Bernanke, 2001: *Macroeconomics*, Addison-Wesley, Ch. 14.

A macroeconomic textbook discussion on monetary policy instruments from a European perspective is Miles, David, Andrew Scott and Francis Breedon, 2014: *Macroeconomics - Understanding the Global Economy*, Wiley, Ch. 13.

A more detailed textbook discussion on monetary policy tools from an American perspective can be found in Mishkin, Frederic, 2018: *The Economics of Money, Banking, and Financial Markets*, Pearson, Part 4.

5

Money, Credit, and Banking

I felt that the Fed had always been the agency that picked up the pieces when there was a financial crisis, and it was invented to do exactly that. Janet Yellen (American Economist and Chair of the Federal Reserve System from 2014 to 2018, *1946)[1]

5.1 The Financial System and Financial Stability

This chapter shifts the focus to the interrelationships between the central bank, the financial system, and commercial banking. Thus far, the discussion has shown that the central bank adopts a key position within the financial system in the sense that monetary-policy decisions, which affect the level of interest rates and other monetary variables, have effects on commercial banks as well as on financial markets. For this and other reasons, any form of financial instability, or fully-blown crisis, quickly turns into an urgent monetary-policy issue as soon as problems, such as widespread bank failures, arise. Therefore, the supervision of the financial system, and, specifically, the way in which commercial banks allocate money and credit are of great concern for setting monetary policy.

The financial system encompasses a set of interrelated markets and institutions which are involved in the transfer of assets between households, companies, and other units with current surpluses of funds (usually called lenders,

---

[1]Time Magazine, 20 January 2014.

© Springer Nature Switzerland AG 2019
N. Herger, *Understanding Central Banks*, https://doi.org/10.1007/978-3-030-05162-4_5

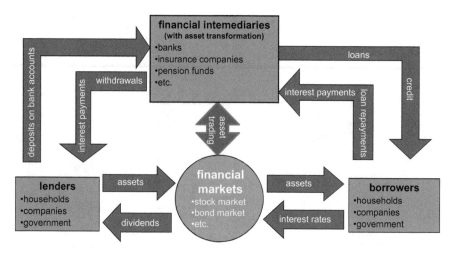

Fig. 5.1 Direct and indirect methods of finance

creditors, or savers), to those with corresponding deficits (borrowers, investors, or spenders). Hence, the characteristic feature of financial transactions is that they give rise to intertemporal exchanges between lenders and borrowers in terms of a stream of current and future payments. Concrete examples include the provision and repayment of loans and credit, the payment of interest, and the distribution of dividends. Financial transfers can occur via two broadly defined methods. As is synoptically illustrated by Fig. 5.1, financial markets provide a forum for direct methods of finance between borrowers and lenders, as in the case of a company raising equity by issuing shares and, hence, selling a claim on future profits, or by issuing debt-instruments, such as bonds, with contractually fixed payment-streams. Furthermore, the financial system also offers indirect methods of finance involving financial intermediaries, that is, companies that specialise in matching lenders and borrowers. Above all, financial intermediaries arrange transfers of funds by collecting savings from the public and bundling them into various forms of credits, loans, and other financial products. Commercial banks are the prime example of this type of activity. However, in a similar manner, mutual funds, hedge funds, pension funds, and insurance companies also adopt intermediary positions within the financial system.

In the modern economy, financial markets and banks have become indispensable for managing assets, collecting savings, providing credit, keeping track of payments, and handling financial risks (which is the 'raison d'être' of the insurance business). The importance of these activities becomes clear when a crisis prevents the financial system from functioning properly. Adverse events, such as stock market crashes, banking failures, and currency crises, imply that savings are no longer safe, that the allocation of credit stagnates, that financial trading or the payment system malfunction, or that covering certain financial risks is suddenly very difficult. The corresponding economic consequences can be dramatic. More often than not, fully fledged financial crises have, indeed, been followed by deep recessions with substantial increases in unemployment and falling average incomes. Therefore, promoting financial stability is widely seen as an important policy goal.[2]

Why is the financial system especially prone to crises? Several explanations will be discussed in detail during this chapter, but, for the moment, it is sufficient to realise that any financial transaction encapsulates an assessment of future developments whose outcomes are inherently uncertain or subject to risk and probabilities. For example, because a credit contract is essentially an agreement regarding future payments, it will only be offered when the lender believes that the borrower will be able and willing to fulfil his financial obligations. Of course, if the borrower defaults on the interest payments or on the repayment of the borrowed amount, this belief turns out to be false. In general, because the success or failure of financial transactions are only clear with hindsight, they rely on a correct assessment of future events. However, misjudgements can occur. Furthermore, perhaps more so than any other economic activity, the financial sector lends itself to outright misbehaviour, such as fraud, embezzlement, and other forms of immoral self-enrichment. To avoid costly mistakes, both access to reliable information about future financial developments and detailed knowledge about the type of person you are dealing with are of utmost importance for successful financial transactions. However, financially relevant information is typically only partially available, is asymmetrically distributed between the involved parties and, hence, subject to manipulation. Some of these issues manifest themselves directly in the language used in finance. For example, when providing a credit, the lender has to *believe* (in Latin 'credere') to some degree that the borrower will not default. Of course, the borrower will always be in a better position to assess his default risk and to known his own intensions. Moreover, especially when the default risk is high, or when a borrower plans to commit outright fraud or embezzlement, every effort will be made to conceal this intention while negotiating for credit. Taken together, these issues imply that financial transactions are, to some degree, based on mutual trust. It immediately follows

---

[2]Of note, financial stability matters not only for economic reasons. Financial crises can also destabilise the political system. Indeed, in many cases, financial crises have led to social unrest caused by widespread frustration over the loss of savings, high inflation, mass unemployment, and so on.

that any upsurge in distrust within the financial system can have devastating consequences and lead to widespread instability.[3]

5.2   The Role of Commercial Banks

In the modern world, commercial banks are probably the most important financial player. The term 'commercial bank' refers to any financial intermediary whose main business consists of collecting deposits from the public, or refinancing itself on financial markets or via other financial intermediaries, and simultaneously transferring large parts of the corresponding funds into various forms of loans and other credit-type financial instruments. In doing so, a characteristic feature of the standard banking business[4] is that the financial features of deposits in bank accounts differ fundamentally from the features of bank loans. Recall that bank deposits, which account for a large fraction of book money, provide the vehicle for cashless payments. To serve as an alternative to banknotes and coins, deposits must be withdrawable on demand; in other words, account holders should always be able to access the corresponding funds by writing a cheque, making a withdrawal, or performing an electronic transfer to other accounts. Conversely, bank loans are inherently illiquid in that they mature at a specific future date and are earmarked for a designated project or investment. This transition from short-term and liquid demand deposits to long-term and illiquid bank loans is an example of what economists call an 'asset transformation' (sometimes also 'maturity transformation').

Because key aspects of banking and finance link the creation of book money with the issuing of various forms of loans and credit, the branch of economics devoted to these issues appears under the same title as this chapter—money, credit, and banking. This 'trilogy' is clearly connected to the discussion of money in Chap. 3. In particular, it is important to recall the pros and cons of money and credit multiplication (see Sect. 3.4): Although the flexible creation of book money by private banks represents an important achievement of modern finance, it also provides a latent source for financial instability.

---

[3] For a thoughtful academic essay on the good and bad effects of the financial sector on society, see Zingales, Luigi, 2015: Does Finance Benefit Society?, *Journal of Finance* 70, pp. 1327–1363.

[4] Other parts of the banking business, not discussed in detail here, include the exchange of money and wealth management. Furthermore, a whole range of financial services, including the raising of large amounts of capital for companies and governments, the arrangement of mergers and acquisitions, and the emission and trading of various securities, such as bonds and shares, on financial markets are summarised under the term 'investment banking'.

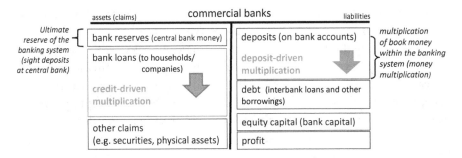

Fig. 5.2 Stylised balance sheet of the banking sector

To appreciate the connections between money, credit, and banking, it is helpful to consider the stylised balance sheet of a commercial bank in Fig. 5.2.[5] Further to the discussion above, claims on the asset-side encompass, for example, bank reserves and outstanding bank loans, which are granted as mortgages to households or as corporate credit to firms. Commercial banks can hold further claims by purchasing income-earning securities, such as government bonds and commercial paper. The liability-side of the balance sheet includes, above all, deposits in bank accounts. Furthermore, commercial banks adopt other liabilities by accepting interbank loans or raising funds from the financial system in some other way. Finally, equity (or bank) capital and profits represent liabilities towards the owners (or shareholders) of the bank.

The extent to which the deposits in Fig. 5.2 exceed the amount of central-bank reserves reflects the multiplication of book money within the banking system (see Sect. 3.4). In the absence of binding minimum-reserve requirements, commercial banks can indeed expand their balance sheets by, for example, issuing new bank loans and simply crediting the corresponding amounts to the account of the borrowing household or company. The alternative to such credit-driven multiplication is deposit-driven multiplication, by which a commercial bank manages to attract additional savings and employs these funds to provide additional loans. Owing to the inherently simultaneous nature of money and credit creation, it is difficult in practice to tell whether concrete expansions or shrinkages of a bank's balance sheet were driven by developments on the asset or liability-side. Either way, it is probably more

---

[5]In reality, the banking sector consists of a variety of depository institutions, savings institutions, investment banks, and various other financial intermediaries often appearing under slightly different names in different countries. The balance sheet of Fig. 5.2 is highly stylised and reflects the situation of a typical deposit bank.

important to realise that money multiplication is typically linked to the provision of bank credit and fractional-reserve holding.

At first, the methods which modern commercial banks use to create money and credit may seem concerning. As will soon become clear, financial-stability issues are indeed associated with fractional-reserve banking. At the same time, it should not be overlooked that fractional-reserve banking provides a way to reconcile the opposing financial needs of savers, who deposit money into bank accounts, and investors, who require bank loans. On the one hand, commercial banks provide financial services, such as processing cashless payments, safeguarding wealth, and providing liquidity, that are crucial for carrying out economic transactions. To fulfil this task, deposits must of course be liquid. On the other hand, for ordinary people as well as for most small and medium-sized enterprises, bank loans are typically the only external means to fund expensive investment projects. Of course, a loan with similar characteristics to those of a deposit in terms of being withdrawable on demand would be useless from the point of view of the borrower.

5.3   The Anatomy of Banking Crises

The fragility of commercial banks is a direct consequence of simultaneously accepting deposits that are withdrawable on demand, and issuing loans that will mature in the future. Banking crises are indeed almost as old as the banking business itself. Although it is difficult to compare the extent of the problem across time due the lack of comprehensive data, Fig. 5.3 nevertheless shows that many countries have recurrently suffered from widespread failures within the banking industry since 1800. Furthermore, systemic banking crises have often coincided with currency crises, high inflation, sovereign defaults, and stock market crashes. Given this background, it is perhaps not surprising that the word 'bankrupt', which today is used to refer to any type of commercial failure, originates in the banking sector. In particular, the term 'bank' refers to the benches (the Italian 'banca'), on which medieval money changers in Italian city-states displayed their coins. The term 'rupt' comes from the Italian word 'rotta' for the 'broken' benches of failed money changers.

Why is banking such a perilous business? First, commercial banks are subject to insolvency risk. In general, insolvency refers to a situation, in which a borrower is no longer able to honour his financial obligations. In other words, he is overindebted. In particular, commercial banks can become insolvent due to defaults on bank loans. A correct assessment of credit risk— the risk that bank customers cannot make the promised interest payments,

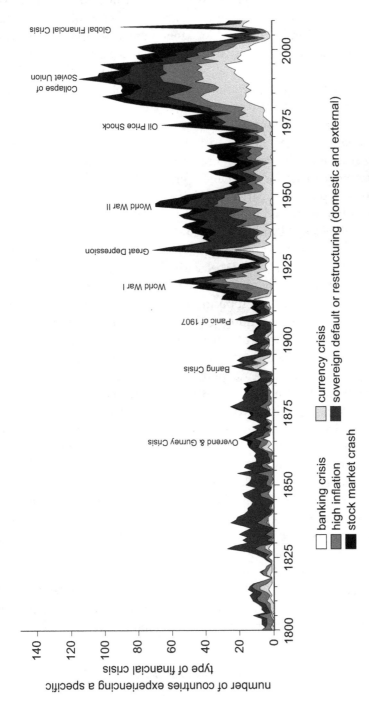

Fig. 5.3 Financial Crises (1800–2010). Data source: Reinhard, Carmen M., and Kenneth S. Rogoff, 2009: This Time is Different – Eight Centuries of Financial Folly, Princeton University Press

instalments, and so on—is indeed a key ingredient of a successful banking business. However, to avoid costly mistakes, or detect cases of outright fraud or embezzlement, detailed information about the economic and personal circumstances and the behaviour of the borrowing party is warranted. In this regard, commercial banks may well benefit from specialising in the scanning and monitoring of a large number of loan applications. Furthermore, bank staff can partly rely on past experiences and can gain knowledge from established customer relationships. Nevertheless, because the arrangement of any credit is by definition subject to future uncertainty, it is impossible to completely avoid misjudgements. Sporadic defaults are inevitable and, in principle, are unproblematic for the stability of a commercial bank. Conversely, if catastrophic economic events cause a massive upsurge in default rates or past mistakes lead to the accumulation of bad loans, commercial banks can eventually be threatened by insolvency amid increasing losses from bank-loan defaults. Similarly, insolvency can also be caused by collapsing asset prices, as when a commercial bank is hit by speculative losses to its securities portfolio. Although banks ruined by speculation tend to receive more attention, it should not be overlooked that the credit business including, in many cases, even the comparatively unspectacular mortgage business has often been the primary cause for instability within the banking industry.[6]

Second, commercial banks suffer from peculiar liquidity risks which generally refer to the risk that an individual or a company does not have access to sufficient amounts of money to settle imminent financial obligations. In other words, there is an inability to pay. Compared with other industries, the traditional banking business is subject to highly idiosyncratic liquidity risks which are inherently intertwined with the asset transformation and the fractional-reserve holding associated with the balance sheet of Fig. 5.2. Although liquidity issues should not arise under normal circumstances, as when depositors make only sporadic withdrawals, a commercial bank is, in principle, always at risk when large numbers of depositors decide, for whatever reason, to make massive withdrawals, which could exhaust the liquidity buffer consisting of, among other things, bank reserves. The fundamental discrepancy between liquid deposits and illiquid bank loans lies at the heart of such banking panics, which are driven by depositors' loss of confidence that the balances on their bank accounts are safe. This fear can, in turn, initiate a vicious cycle, in which liquid bank reserves decrease rapidly due to indiscriminate

---

[6]See Admati, Anat, and Martin Hellwig, 2013: *The Bankers' New Clothes*, Princeton University Press, pp. 93ff. See also Saunders, Anthony, and Marcia Millon Cornett, 2008: *Financial Institutions Management - A Risk Management Approach*, McGraw Hill, Ch. 10.

withdrawals, which in turn aggravates illiquidity risks and, in an extreme case, leads to a run on and subsequent collapse of a commercial bank. The top-right circle in Fig. 5.4 illustrates the corresponding mechanism. In principle, a bank-run can result from irrational fears that suddenly turn into hysterical withdrawals. In practice, however, bank-runs rarely occur out of the blue but rather arise when the public becomes aware that a bank is struggling with considerable amounts of bad loans or sufferings from other problems.

Until well into the twentieth century, the banking system regularly witnessed cases of nervous depositors literally running to their local bank branches to withdraw their money as quickly as possible for fear of an imminent bankruptcy. However, as a reaction to the massive number of bank failures during the Great Depression (see Sect. 2.4), deposit-insurance schemes were launched to provide financial compensation to depositors who lost money from their bank accounts. The key aspect of these schemes was that the expectation of receiving compensation would help to reinforce the trust in the banking system and, hence, short-circuit the vicious cycle of the top-right circle shown in Fig. 5.4, as depositors would no longer have an incentive to make indiscriminate withdrawals. Indeed, since the introduction of deposit-insurances schemes, classical bank-runs have become relatively rare.[7] Currently, bank deposits are seen as a rather safe way to refinance commercial banks. Nevertheless, the banking system has remained fragile, because a critical loss of confidence can also beset the non-deposit parts of a commercial bank's balance sheet. In particular, unstable commercial banks may be forced to sell-off assets in a distressed manner. Inasmuch as such 'fire-sales' result in a temporary oversupply of securities on financial markets, another round of falling prices may immediately follow, which could further undermine the trust in the solvency of a commercial bank (see the bottom circle in Fig. 5.4). In a similar vein, vicious cycles can also occur with respect to external funding through such channels as interbank loans. In this regard, news or even rumours about liquidity risks increase the short-term interest rate at which a given commercial bank can raise loans on the interbank market. Then again, such an adverse development may set-off a self-reinforcing crisis and, potentially, trigger an actual collapse of the bank (see the top-left circle in Fig. 5.4). Notably, the recent Global Financial Crisis was indeed associated

---

[7] For a review of the economic effects of deposit-insurance schemes, see Demirgüç-Kunt, Asli, and Enrica Detragiache, 2004: Does deposit insurance increase banking system stability? An empirical investigation, *Journal of Monetary Economics* 49, pp. 1373–1406. There is a lively debate as to whether deposit-insurance schemes have indeed stabilised the banking system. One drawback of issuing guarantees on deposits is that doing so can give commercial banks a false sense of security and induce them to take higher risks when, for example, issuing bank loans. On this issue, see also Sect. 5.8.

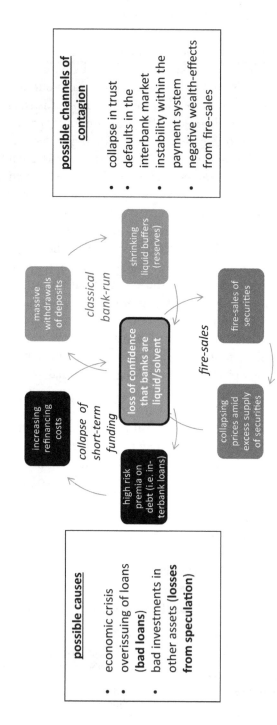

Fig. 5.4 Banking panics and banking crises

with fire-sales and freezes of the interbank market, rather than classical bank-runs. Taken together, loss-of-confidence-induced liquidity crises seem to be an inherent part of any banking system which is supposed to facilitate the access to money and credit.

Figure 5.3 shows that bank failures have often been correlated across several countries. The most notorious systemic crises, such as the Great Depression and the Global Financial Crisis, have even affected most parts of the financial and economic systems. Borrowing medical terminology, the corresponding propagation effects are typically referred to as the 'contagion of a banking crisis', which can, so to speak, spread in an epidemic manner. Another image that is often invoked is the 'domino effect', in which the failure of one commercial bank is thought to initiate a 'chain reaction'. Thus, the magnitude of the initial impulse may well depend on the size and interconnectedness of the collapsing bank. In an extreme case, the devastating effects caused by the failure of a systemically relevant bank can even tear entire financial systems down. It is easy to understand how an individual failure can escalate into a systemic crisis when considering that the vicious cycles shown in Fig. 5.4 can, in principle, propagate through the entire banking and financial system. In particular, a run on a given bank can undermine the trust in the entire banking system as long as there are reasons to believe that liquidity or insolvency problems also loom elsewhere. Furthermore, fire-sales by unstable commercial banks can, at least temporarily, depress financial markets and, hence, inflict losses on large parts of the banking and financial system. Finally, liquidity risks can propagate through interbank markets and payment systems connecting the various parts of the financial sector.

Fully grown banking crises can cause significant damage. Therefore, it is not surprising that, during the nineteenth century, the early note-issuing banks began to act as banks for the banking system and, above all, to provide emergency liquidity assistance to make sure that the payment system was stable, prevent credit crunches, and preserve the effectiveness of monetary policy (see Sect. 2.3). Today, a range of measures are available to maintain financial stability. First, setting minimum-reserve requirements plays an, admittedly relatively modest, role. More important are interventions within the context of the lender of last resort, the setting of minimum-equity rules for commercial banks (capital requirements), and the supervision of banks, the payment system, and the financial-market infrastructure. The following sections discuss these measures in turn.

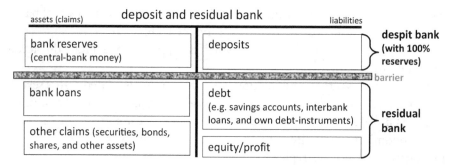

Fig. 5.5 Full-reserve banking

5.4   Bank Reserves and Full-Reserve Banking

Because the practices of money multiplication and fractional-reserve holding are important drivers of the special liquidity risks within the banking system, it is tempting to conclude that banking crises could be prevented by imposing sufficiently large liquidity buffers. Central banks could do so by simply raising the minimum-reserve requirements. However, such measures would not be a panacea against instability within the banking system. To understand why, it is insightful to consider a scenario with full (or 100%) reserves, in which banks would be forced by law to fully cover their demand deposits with liquid reserves at the central bank, meaning that money and credit multiplication would be prohibited.

Figure 5.5 illustrates that a full-reserve system would essentially split banks into deposit and residual parts. The deposit bank would merely match reserves with demand deposits and, hence, provide a depot for liquid means of payment. In contrast to a fractional-reserve system, in which deposits typically earn interest, full-reserve accounts cannot be used to fund loans and, hence, would be interest-free, or even subject to fees to cover the commercial bank's expenses for providing cashless payment services. The drawbacks of giving up interest earnings and holding large amounts of idle reserves are probably the reasons why pure deposit banks have rarely existed in practice.[8] In contrast,

---

[8] Historical examples resembling a pure deposit bank include the medieval 'exchange banks', which were established to facilitate large commercial transactions, limit the uncertainties arising from a multi-coin currency system, and serve as coin depots. Exchange banks typically held assets in the form of bullion and coins against liabilities in the form of bank deposits (book money), but they did not issue paper money (unlike the note-issuing banks described in Sect. 2.1). Early exchange banks were founded in commercial centres in Southern Europe such as Barcelona (1401), Genoa (1407), and Venice (1587). In 1609, the 'Amsterdamsche Wisselbank' (or exchange bank of Amsterdam), which is often seen as an early ancestor

residual banks would be responsible for the allocation of loans and credit, which would have to be refinanced by some non-deposit liability. Eliminating the money-and-credit-multiplication process is not problematic as long as either the residual bank has ample access to interbank loans, can issue own debt-instruments, raise equity, or the broad public is willing to invest in such products as money-market funds. However, to the extent that these conditions do not hold (e.g. if households or firms are reluctant to hold risky bank shares or prefer the safety and liquidity of demand deposits), the allocation of credit could be impaired.

By keeping demand deposits fully liquid, a full-reserve system eliminates the risk of a classical 'bank-run'. As long as money in bank accounts is matched by equivalent amounts of central-bank reserves, commercial banks are indeed positioned to deal with arbitrarily large withdrawals. Hence, no depositor would have an incentive to panic and try to empty his account as quickly as possible. Based on this observation, proposals to abandon money and credit multiplication have often been made during episodes of severe financial instability. Probably the most famous example is the so-called 'Chicago Plan', which was designed during the Great Depression by several economists at the University of Chicago. In particular, they suggested dealing with the pervasive financial instability at the beginning of the 1930s by fully covering checkable deposits with reserves held within the Federal Reserve System. However, this idea was not pursued by the government of President Franklin D. Roosevelt.[9] In any case, abolishing money and credit multiplication is unlikely to be a game-changer in the fight against financial instability. Although classical bank-runs would no longer occur, liquidity risks would still remain—and may even be aggravated—in other parts of the banking and financial system. In fact, the residual bank would have to refinance credits using liabilities with potentially incongruent maturities and, hence, would still be subject to liquidity risks, destabilising defaults, or dangerous losses on asset portfolios. Of note, during the recent Global Financial Crisis, the biggest sources of instability were

---

of modern central banks, was founded. As an internationally connected financial centre, Amsterdam was at the time awash with coins of various origins and quality. To deal with these coins, merchants were forced to make large commercial transactions through the Wisselbank, which would check the quality of the coins before depositing them and issuing a commonly recognised form of book money against them. See, for example, Kindleberger, Charles, 2006: *A Financial History of Western Europe*, Routledge, pp. 46ff.

[9] For a discussion on the layout of the Chicago Plan, see Fisher, Irving, 1935: *100% Money*, Allen and Unwin.

indeed stand-alone investment banks and money-market funds[10]—financial institutions that do not accept deposits.

Despite the fact that full-reserve requirements would be costly without eliminating some of the most important risk factors in commercial banking, the corresponding discussion draws attention to an often ignored aspect of modern forms of money. In a world with fractional-reserve banking, money held in bank accounts is not exactly the same as cash, but rather provides a very close substitute in terms of liquidity and safety. In particular, conventional deposits are exposed to idiosyncratic liquidity risks. Of course, owing to deposit-insurance schemes, this risk is usually negligible. Still, bank deposits essentially encapsulate only a claim to receive the ultimate means of payment (especially cash) on demand from a *specific* commercial bank and, hence, are imperilled in case of bankruptcy. Conversely, cash and bank reserves represent the central bank's promises to pay and, hence, lose their (nominal) values only in the extreme event of a collapse of the government's monopoly in issuing currency.[11] Taken together, this comparison underscores that only the central bank ultimately determines how much money circulates though the economy. The following sections demonstrate that this distinction matters greatly during a financial crisis.

5.5   The Lender of Last Resort

Owing to the monopoly in issuing currency, central banks are bound to provide liquidity to financial institutions suffering from, for example, panicky withdrawals by depositors. To prevent liquidity risks at an individual bank from escalating into a systemic crisis, central-note issuing banks gradually adopted the role of lender of last resort during the nineteenth century (see Sect. 2.2).[12] Monetary authorities such as the Federal Reserve System were even specifically founded to fulfil this task. A lender-of-last-resort policy

---

[10]Investment banks are discussed in footnote 4 of this chapter. A money-market fund refinances itself primarily by issuing short-term debt and reinvesting the corresponding financial means in liquid assets. Money-market funds are typically employed to manage the excess liquidity of large investors.

[11]After a political revolution, foreign invasion, or civil war, it is of course possible that the public monopoly in issuing currency collapses. More commonly, governments (as represented by the central bank) do not fully honour their promises to pay on, for example, issued banknotes by creating inflation and, hence, reducing the purchasing power of the currency.

[12]Originally, 'lender of last resort' was a jurisprudential term. In particular, in French, 'dernier ressort' referred to a court, whose judgement was final in the sense of not being open to appeal. The monetary meaning of 'lender of last resort' implies that commercial banks cannot formally protest at another authority when the central bank refuses to provide emergency liquidity assistance.

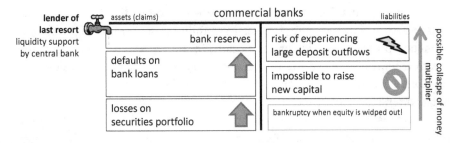

Fig. 5.6 Liquidity assistance by the lender of last resort

implied that, under certain conditions, commercial banks suffering from liquidity shocks could turn to the central note-issuing bank for emergency assistance. Aside from supporting financially distressed commercial banks, lender-of-last-resort interventions can nowadays also involve other financial firms or financial markets where catastrophic crashes are looming.[13] Concrete measures encompass the lending of reserves, the transfer of unstable parts of the balance sheet (including bad debt or junk assets) to a so-called 'bad-bank', or emergency purchases of assets that have become illiquid. Finally, the central bank can also merely act as a crisis manager by, for example, coordinating the resolution of a failing commercial bank.

Lender-of-last-resort interventions typically employ instruments, such as refinancing operations or open-market interventions, that are quite similar to those routinely used in monetary policy. However, emergency interventions are characterised by a highly selective application of these instruments in the sense that central-bank reserves are supplied at specific terms to a specific financial firm. In a schematic manner, Fig. 5.6 illustrates the mechanism of a lender-of-last-resort intervention in the classical case of a distressed commercial bank which has been hit by dangerously large losses on its bank-loans or asset portfolio. When it is difficult to counter these losses by raising new capital, or when even massive withdrawals of deposits are imminent, equity could wiped out, resulting in bankruptcy. By providing liquidity in terms of additional bank reserves, the central bank can support a failing commercial bank.

Lender-of-last-resort policies are not intended to merely rescue banks, but rather to tackle the idiosyncratic liquidity risks in commercial banking

---

[13]Central banks are not the only lenders of last resort within the financial system. For example, the International Monetary Fund (IMF) can act as the international lender of last resort for crisis-hit countries (see Sect. 8.6).

and prevent contagion effects from spreading across the financial system (see Sect. 5.3). Furthermore, financial instability poses a massive problem for monetary policy. In particular, disruptions in the process of money and credit creation tend to undermine the channels via which monetary-policy interventions affect the broad economy. In more detail, the public and commercial banks often react to an increasingly unstable financial system by hoarding cash and bank reserves. However, at the aggregate level, this bolstering of liquidity buffers can trigger a collapse of the money-and-credit-multiplication process. Finally, when the central bank does not step in as the lender of last resort, the corresponding decline in the amount of broadly defined money (M1, M2, M3) might well result in a drop in aggregate prices, that is a deflation. This chain of events more or less describes the Great Depression (see Sect. 2.4). Hence, the macroeconomic motive for a lender-of-last-resort policy is to ensure stable supplies of money and credit.

The principles of a successful lender-of-last-resort policy can be traced to Henry Thornton (1760–1815) and Walter Bagehot (1826–1877). In particular, to stabilise the banking system, they recommended that central banks be ready (1) to provide generous liquidity assistance during a crisis (or lend freely) (2) at a high interest rate (3) against good collateral priced according to its value during 'normal times'.[14] As long as these principles are observed, idiosyncratic liquidity issues within the banking and financial system will arguably disappear. Similar to a deposit-insurance scheme, a lender-of-last-resort policy is supposed to short-circuit the vicious cycles giving rise to massive withdrawals of deposits, the fire-sale of assets, or the collapse of other sources to refinance commercial banks (see Fig. 5.4). As long as it is commonly known that the central bank will react to such adverse events by lending freely as required by the first principle mentioned above, a collapse in confidence— which was identified in Fig. 5.4 as the main driver of banking crises—could indeed be averted. Furthermore, charging a high interest rate, which should be above the market interest rate in normal times prior to the crisis,[15] should prevent commercial banks from turning to the central bank for liquidity assistance when alternative sources of refinancing are still available. The lender of last resort is intended for emergency situations and should only be put

---

[14] For a thorough discussion of the lender-of-last-resort principles see Goodhart, Charles, 1999: Myths about the lender of last resort, *International Finance* 2, pp. 339–360.

[15] This practice is often wrongly referred to as charging a 'penalty rate' above the market interest rate. However, such a penalty rate does not work, when financial markets freeze amid a crisis. Concretely, such collapses typically manifest themselves in sudden, massive increases in market interest rates. Applying an even higher interest rate in a lender-of-last-resort intervention would simply indicate that the central bank is unwilling to provide emergency liquidity assistance at acceptable conditions.

into action during extraordinary circumstances. Finally, in both normal and extraordinary times, central banks should only lend out reserves against good collateral, which typically refers to securities with a high credit-rating. Doing so is supposed to prevent the central bank from rescuing holders of bad debt or junk assets by essentially providing a government bailout.

Because the purpose of the lender of last resort is to safeguard the provision of liquid forms of money, a corresponding policy can, of course, only have stabilising effects when the financial system is actually suffering from liquidity problems. Above all, these cases include that of a commercial bank experiencing a temporary shortfall of cash and reserves and, hence, having difficulties fulfilling its imminent financial obligations. When a bank is insolvent, the situation is completely different, as financial obligations can never be honoured. In this scenario, a lender-of-last-resort intervention would not prevent but would merely postpone bankruptcy. In concrete terms, liquidity assistance to an insolvent financial firm essentially implies that current and future losses are partly transferred to the central bank.

Owing to their selective application, lender-of-last-resort interventions are among the most delicate activities of a central bank. Furthermore, in many cases, making the crucial distinction between illiquidity and insolvency has proven to be difficult. At the end of the day, the actual losses on, for example, bank loans and other assets will determine whether or not a distressed commercial bank will eventually be able to honour its obligations towards its depositors, debtors, and shareholders. Of course, any statement about the future is subject to uncertainty. Furthermore, it is exactly during a crisis when the difficulty to accurately assess default risks increases. Hence, when deciding whether to make a lender-of-last-resort intervention, a central bank can never be fully certain that liquidity support has been granted to a financial firm that turned out to be broke. A more cynical version than a simple misjudgement occurs when it is quite clear that a commercial bank is insolvent, but the bank is nevertheless rescued to conceal the corresponding problems for political reasons. In these cases, emergency liquidity assistance does not solve the problem, but rather provides a way to 'kick the can down the road'. In any case, because misguided lender-of-last-resort interventions can give rise to financial losses which could be passed along to taxpayers, the rescue of commercial banks is subject to a considerable degree of political risk. Hence, the corresponding decisions are rarely made by central banks in isolation, but more commonly in cooperation with government authorities, such the ministry of finance.

Aside from creating political problems, a lender-of-last-resort policy could also be counterproductive in terms of inducing commercial banks to behave irresponsibly. In particular, a central bank that stands ready to correct all mistakes in liquidity management could lead to excessive risk taking when issuing loans, investing in securities, choosing refinancing sources, or undertaking any other banking activity. Should these risks pay off, the main beneficiaries are the bank managers and owners, who receive higher salaries and profits, respectively. Conversely, if these risks backfire and give rise to dangerously large losses, then, per the discussion above, these losses could be passed on to the central bank and, in the end, the taxpayer. Of course, such asymmetry in dealing with profits and losses violates key principles of a free enterprise system, and could incentivise perverse behaviour in the sense that a too extensive interpretation of the lender of last resort could create exactly the liquidity and insolvency risks which should have been avoided.[16]

Owing to adverse-incentive effects on policy makers and bank managers, the lender of last resort is not a panacea against financial crises. To prevent banks and other financial institutions from getting a false sense of security, central banks typically emphasise that receiving emergency liquidity assistance is a privilege, not a right. Nevertheless, the experiences of past banking and financial crises suggest that neither the central bank, nor the government can afford to remain inactive in the face of catastrophic financial shocks.

Despite the potential losses for the taxpayer and the concern that mistakes are no longer fully borne by financiers and banks, modern financial systems probably require a lender of last resort in some form. However, the resulting dilemmas could become pervasive when commercial banks become systemically relevant, meaning their collapse would threaten the stability of the entire financial system. In this scenario, the adverse effects of a lender-of-last-resort policy are endemic. The enormous shocks and catastrophic economic consequences following the failure of a systemically relevant bank make it practically impossible to avoid some form of public rescue. Of course, this situation virtually eliminates the prospect of bankruptcy and, hence, the most important disciplinary element of a competitive market economy. Therefore, the corresponding issues are referred to as 'too-big-to-fail problem'. With systemically relevant banks and other financial firms that are highly interconnected with the financial system, the conflicts between the stability enhancing and adverse effects of a lender-of-last-resort policy can only be

---

[16]In economics, the adverse-incentive effects arising from regulatory interventions are described using the somewhat cumbersome expression 'moral-hazard effect'. Moral hazard is not restricted to rescuing banks. These problems are endemic in, for example, the insurance business, where generous coverage can undermine the incentive to take adequate care of the insured object. Many other examples can be found in other areas of economics and politics.

avoided through additional regulatory measures, such as banking supervision or capital regulation.

5.6 Banking Supervision and Capital Requirements

Thus far, the discussion has shown that an unstable financial system can hamper the implementation of monetary policy and, more generally, cause massive economic damage. Therefore, it is desirable to avoid systemic financial crises arising in the first place rather than trying to deal with the resulting problems by, for example, providing emergency liquidity assistance or bailing out fragile banks. Of course, a financial system that is supposed to provide funds for risky investments and deal with all kinds of economic uncertainties, but is completely resilient to a crisis, will probably never exist. Nevertheless, more modest goals could be to design regulatory measures fostering prudent behaviour in banking and finance to at least reduce the probability of a financial crisis or make sure that individual failures do not tear down the entire financial system.

Perhaps contrary to widely held beliefs, finance and banking belong to the most heavily regulated sectors of the economy. In particular, most countries around the world impose a range of prudential rules and measures that are meant to prevent financial crises. Section 4.3 discussed the example of minimum-reserve requirements, which are typically not imposed on industries other than banking (non-banking firms are not forced to have accounts at the central bank). Other sector-specific regulations include compulsory insurance policies for deposits (deposit insurance), capital requirements for commercial banks, the regulation of entry in the sense that commercial banks and other financial firms often need a government licence to operate (chartering/licencing), on-site and off-site examination of commercial banks, specific accounting and disclosure requirements for financial data, and government supervision of most parts of the payment system. Owing to constant changes in the political and economic environment, the composition and design of these measures has hitherto been regularly revised and adjusted in a constant process of de-regulation and re-regulation.

Overall, the requirements to hold a minimal amount of (equity) capital is probably the most important instrument of prudential banking regulation. To illustrate these so-called 'capital (adequacy) requirements', Fig. 5.7 returns to the stylised balance sheet of a commercial bank. Capital requirements refer to

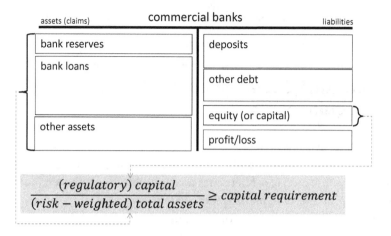

Fig. 5.7 Capital-adequacy requirements

the liability-side and, more specifically, determine the adequate composition of debt and equity to refinance a bank. In particular, the minimum requirements are typically defined in terms of a ratio of equity to total assets. The simplest case uses unweighted values as directly reported on the balance sheet. A corresponding ratio of, say, 5% of pure equity—which is not uncommon in practice—also indicates how much a bank is leveraged, because various forms of debt, such as deposits and interbank loans, inevitably account for the remaining liabilities in the balance-sheet total. The caveat against building a regulatory framework based on balance-sheet values is that they ignore differences in risk-taking. For example, providing venture capital to start-up companies may require the same amount of minimum capital than holding a highly diversified portfolio of securities with a high credit-rating. To account for such differences and, thus, force banks to set more capital aside for risky investments, it has become common practice during the last couple of decades to weight the asset-side according to the probability of default. Hence, banks holding risky assets should hold more capital. The corresponding international standards have been developed by the so-called 'Basel Committee' at the Bank for International Settlements (BIS).[17] Although it is in theory adequate

---

[17]The Bank for International Settlements (BIS) was founded in the 1930s to settle German reparations resulting from World War I more efficiently (see Sect. 2.4). Aside from some remaining tasks regarding international payments, the BIS today serves mainly as a forum for the exchange of ideas on monetary and financial issues. Membership in the BIS is restricted to the most important central banks around the world. Since the 1980s, another key task of the BIS has been to develop international minimum standards for capital requirements. Referring to the Swiss city where the BIS is headquartered, the corresponding

to employ risk weights to determine minimum capital requirements, in practice, the calculation of the corresponding ratios is quite complicated. In particular, vagaries arise regarding the separation of debt and equity,[18] the valuation of assets that are not traded on financial markets and, last but not least, the calculation of sound risk-weights in an uncertain, constantly changing environment.[19] Especially for large banks, these factors have led to the establishment of entire departments that deal with both implementing and finding loopholes in the 'Basel rules'.

Capital requirements can foster financial stability, because capital represents the loss-absorbing component of a balance sheet. Hence, a bank holding more capital is more resilient to adverse events, such as an upsurge in defaults on loans, collapsing asset prices, and unexpectedly large deposit withdrawals. Under a free enterprise system, private companies should of course define themselves how much capital they would like to hold, thereby determining their capacity to absorb losses. However, the widespread contagion effects from failures within the financial system, as well as the too-big-to-fail dilemma mentioned above, motivate restricting commercial banks in this regard.

Capital-adequacy requirements are a preferred instrument in banking regulation, because they provide a basis for imposing potential losses on bank owners rather than letting the public, as represented by the central bank or the government, bear the consequences of bad management. In other words, unlike other regulatory measures, capital regulation does not inconspicuously reward imprudent behaviour to stabilise the financial system. Furthermore, rules about the adequate composition of debt and equity do not per se restrict a bank's ability to issue loans and, hence, do not create adverse effects in

---

measures are called the 'Basel rules' or 'Basel accords'. In the aftermath of the Global Financial Crisis, these rules have been substantially revised and extended resulting in the so-called 'Basel III' requirements.

[18] For example, the Basel III rules define the tier 1 ratio, which should be at least 4.5% and refers to the nominal capital or share capital for stock-traded companies as well as retained earnings. The total (tier 1 and 2) capital ratio, which should be at least 8%, includes common equity and retained earnings, as well as supplementary capital such as undisclosed reserves, revaluation reserves, or hybrid instruments sharing characteristics of debt and equity. Furthermore, counter-cyclical capital buffers, which should be increased in boom times and may be lowered during a crisis, surcharges for large banks, and additional liquidity requirements, have been introduced.

[19] These issues reflect some of the problems that were partly responsible for the 2008 financial crisis. In particular, valuing assets based on market prices (so-called 'mark-to-market') can aggravate a banking crisis when the collapse of security prices inflicts immediate losses on commercial banks, which, in turn, further undermines the confidence in the stability of the banking system. This is an example of the vicious fire-sales mechanism discussed in Sect. 5.3. Furthermore, in determining the risk-weights, assets, such as mortgage-backed securities, were seen as safe and, hence, had to be backed by relatively little capital. However, during the crisis, it turned out that these securities were much riskier than originally thought and, due to the collapse of the US real-estate market, were subject to large losses that essentially initiated the Global Financial Crisis (see also footnote 9 of Chap. 4).

terms of blocking funds that would otherwise have been available for economic investments.

Commercial banks must typically hold a government licence, or charter, which can be withdrawn when, upon examination, prudential regulations are violated. In countries such as the United Kingdom (and currently also for large banks in the United States and the euro area), the central bank is responsible for licensing (chartering) and, hence, supervising and checking the capital adequacy of commercial banks. The main advantage of placing banking supervision under the auspices of the central bank is to provide the monetary authority with direct access to a wealth of information about the banking sector as well as a large degree of control over the financial system. However, in many countries (and in some parts of the banking system in the United States and in the euro area), the banking and financial system is supervised by separate authorities. The advantage of having designated banking and financial supervisors is avoiding conflicts of interest should the goals of maintaining price stability and financial stability contradict each other as well as a concentration of power within the central bank.

It has recently become customary to split the issues in banking regulation into micro- and macroeconomic aspects. The so-called 'microprudential regulation' deals with the stability of individual financial firms. Because modern monetary policy is mainly concerned with broad economic developments, macroprudential issues, which refer to the stability of the financial system as such, are typically more relevant to the central bank. The experiences from the Global Financial Crisis suggest that this distinction is not merely semantic. Despite its global scale, the crisis originated in a relatively small segment of risky mortgages, the so-called 'subprime mortgages', in the American real-estate market. The bundling of these bank loans into tradable securities, called mortgage-backed securities (MBS), provided the channel through which defaults due to the collapse of US house prices after 2007 spread through the financial system. The uncertainty about which commercial banks held MBS on their balance sheet, the size of these holdings, and hence the losses suffered, destroyed the confidence in the stability of the banking and financial system. Owing to the size of the American financial sector, this development had worldwide repercussions. These events underscore that financial instability cannot always be traced back to individual banks, but can also result from their interconnectedness via derivative financial instruments or the interbank market. As with other systems, in the complex world of finance, the whole is often more than the sum of its parts. Seen from a macroprudential angle, a financial crisis is an episode during which destabilising feedback effects propagate through the system, implying that a seemingly small event, such as the collapse of an individual bank, can suddenly have far-reaching consequences, such as panicky withdrawals, a massive reluctance to provide credit, or crashing asset prices.

5.7 Overseeing the Payment System and Financial-Market Infrastructure

The public is probably not sufficiently aware of the importance of an efficient and stable payment system and financial-market infrastructure. Similarly, the infrastructure that is sometimes loosely referred to as the 'plumbing of the economy' receives rarely attention in economic-policy debates. However, it should be straightforward that the framework ensuring that the various forms of money and other assets can safely, cheaply, and quickly be traded is of utmost importance. Issuing, trading, settling, clearing, registering, and confirming financial claims and liabilities may seem unspectacular. However, within the financial system, their role is comparable to the road and rail network for moving goods. Like the transportation infrastructure, the payment and financial-market infrastructure can, in principle, be provided by the government or by private companies. In practice, it is indeed the case that central and commercial banks simultaneously manage various parts of the infrastructure underpinning modern financial transactions. In any case, during the last decades, far-reaching innovations regarding the electronic processing of information and computer technology have revolutionised the ways in which payments are made and assets are traded. At the same time, the development of electronic payment systems has also increased the interconnectedness within banking and finance. Hence, the propagation of individual financial failures, which can undermine the stability of the entire financial system, can swiftly arise from contagion effects across the payment system and the financial-market infrastructure (see Sect. 5.3).

Among other factors, the stability of the financial infrastructure depends on the ways in which assets are traded and transactions are settled. Large parts of financial trading, such as trades on derivatives and foreign-exchange markets, are simply conducted on a bilateral basis between commercial banks and other financial firms. Such trades are referred to as direct, or 'over-the-counter' (OTC), transactions. By arranging trades bilaterally, the costs of maintaining a trading platform can be avoided, and financial products can be customised more flexibly. Conversely, the corresponding trades and payments are more obscure and, hence, more difficult to supervise. As shown in Fig. 5.8,

counterparty 1
(usually a commercial
bank or a financial firm)

counterparty 2
(usually a commercial
bank or a financial firm)

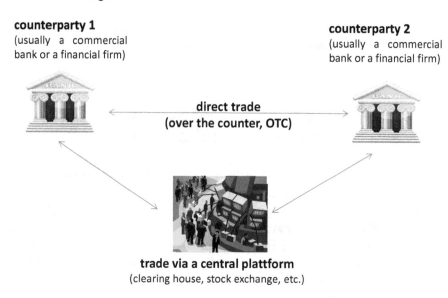

direct trade
(over the counter, OTC)

trade via a central plattform
(clearing house, stock exchange, etc.)

Fig. 5.8 Possible arrangements of financial trades and payments

trading platforms acting as clearing houses or central counterparties provide alternative ways for organising trades and payments. A prime example of such a platform is the stock exchange. However, a large fraction of oil trading, but also trades of certain standardised contracts for foreign currencies and bonds, also occur on dedicated platforms. The corresponding advantage is that information regarding prices and trading volumes is summarised on the trading platform, which facilitates the supervision and regulation of financial markets. The disadvantage is that central clearing requires the traded products to be standardised. For assets, such as oil, or identical securities, such as common stocks, this disadvantage is perhaps not serious. Conversely, it is difficult or even impossible to standardise certain agricultural products or insurance policies for specific individuals or objects.

Broadly speaking, there are two ways to settle payments. First, under a real-time-gross-settlement system, each transaction is settled individually more or less instantaneously. To deal with the millions of transactions arising at commercial banks or on certain financial markets, a system dealing with every individual debit and credit entry requires, of course, relatively large liquidity buffers. Conversely, by only sporadically balancing the net amounts that accrue during certain intervals, a net-settlement system can operate with substantially lower amounts of liquidity, as long as the incoming and outgoing payments on each account partly cancel each other out. In other words, the liquid amounts required to net-settle payments depend merely on the average balances rather than their accumulated value during a certain period. Furthermore, compared with gross settlement, fewer actual transactions take place under a net-settlement system. This gain in efficiency comes, however, at the expense of safety, as it is not immediately clear whether a counterparty has enough money to ultimately make the pledged payment. In sum, the choice between a gross and net-settlement system encapsulates a trade-off between efficiency and safety.

Taken together, some oversight and coordination are probably warranted to guarantee a smooth and stable processing of financial transactions. By directly managing some parts of the payment system (in particular regarding payments of reserves between commercial banks) and adopting a supervisory and regulatory role for other parts of the payment and financial-market infrastructure, central banks have traditionally fulfilled this task. During the Global Financial Crisis, it was indeed the case that those parts of the payment system that were under some form of oversight by the central bank, or other authorities, such as the securities or stock-exchange supervisor, worked quite smoothly. Conversely, instability did occur in the shadow-banking system. In particular, certain forms of over-the-counter trading (e.g. with MBS) have arguably led to opacity and, hence, amplified the downturn amid the financial-instability-induced upsurge of uncertainty about the default risks within the banking system.

5.8   What Are the Limitations of Financial Regulation?

Major financial crises almost inevitably lead to debates on regulatory reform. Until now, the corresponding outcome has almost always been an expansion of banking and financial-market regulation. It is therefore not surprising that the cornerstones of the current framework can be traced back to specific historical events. The lender of last resort, which resulted from the frequent banking crises during the nineteenth century (and, in particular, the failure of Overend and Gurney in 1866 described in Sect. 2.2); deposit-insurance schemes, which were invented during the Great Depression of the 1930s; and international minimum standards regarding capital-adequacy requirements, which are a legacy of the globalisation of the financial system during the 1980s and the Global Financial Crisis after 2008, all bear witness to this relationship.

Most financial crises have arisen after households, firms, or banks have been 'inexcusably imprudent in keeping [...] cash [...], but relying on credit [...] which would enable them to borrow whenever they pleased'. Over-borrowing can indeed cause widespread financial instability as soon as the inevitable upsurge in credit defaults occurs and/or liquidity starts to evaporate. Typically, such adverse developments trigger interventions by the central bank, which is then called to lend 'by every possible means and in modes [...] never adopted before'. When reading these quotes, it is probably tempting to assume that they refer to some financial turbulence in the recent past. In fact, the first quote talks about the situation at the Pole and Thornton Bank, which caused financial instability in England in 1825. The second quote is attributed to the governor of the Bank of England at that time, Jeremiah Harman, who was about to experiment with an early form of a lender-of-last-resort intervention.[20] However, when contemplating the history of financial crises as summarised in Fig. 5.3, one may wonder why banking panics, speculative excesses on financial markets, and the over-issuance of credit do not seem to occur less frequently despite the tremendous reform and expansion in banking and financial regulation.

No matter how many promises bankers and politicians will make during the next crisis that such an event will never happen again, it is probably impossible to design a well-functioning, but completely stable financial system. As mentioned at the beginning of this chapter, the main purpose of the financial system is to provide society with a forum to trade financial claims and the associated risks. To recapitulate, failures in financial transactions result from adverse future political and economic events as well as misjudgements regarding the behaviour of the involved parties. Thus, risk and uncertainty are part of the game. The associated losses can be caused by mistakes, but also, sometimes, by outright fraud and embezzlement. In this regard, commercial banks and other financial firms usually receive most of the blame. In the past, numerous scandals have indeed occurred, in which bankers have acted irresponsibly and engaged in excessive risk-taking or have blatantly abused their positions at the expense of their clients.[21] However, because any financial transaction involves at least two parties, the instinctive tendency of human

---

[20]The first quote is attributed to Marianne Thornton, the sister of Henry Thornton, who was one of the founding fathers of the classical lender-of-last-resort doctrine (see Sect. 5.5).

[21]Two examples are cited in footnotes 3 and 8 of Chap. 2. Another notorious scandal arose from the bank of Charles Ponzi, who at the beginning of the 1920s promised depositors in Boston (USA) an annual interest rate of up to 45%. However, these interest rates could only be sustained via a pyramid scheme, in which newly deposited money was immediately used to pay other depositors. Until today, this type of fraud is still referred to as a 'Ponzi scheme'. To date, the largest financial scandal occurred around

beings to blame others for their own mistakes is important in this context. It would indeed be too simple to blame only commercial banks for problems within the financial system, or to believe in conspiracy theories which typically do not account for the complex causes of financial crises. One example is non-fraudulent credit defaults, which reveal that a bank has apparently poorly screened bank-loan applications, but at the same time also represent a failure of the credit-taker to assess his financial capabilities. Similarly, sovereign defaults are often blamed on reckless speculators, especially by politicians presiding over a period of fiscal profligacy, or by citizens who ask for comprehensive public services and low taxes, but believe that an increasing public-debt level will never have concrete consequences. In very broad terms, major problems in money and finance tend to arise when the financial system has been the subject of unrealistic expectations.

For similar reasons, regulatory interventions are never a panacea against crises within the banking and financial system. For example, it would be completely naive to believe that central banks, or other supervisory authorities, cannot make bad judgments or behave irresponsibly. Moreover, there are good reasons to believe that comprehensive regulatory interventions can themselves become a source of instability. The potentially counter-productive effects of an indiscriminate lender-of-last-resort policy have already been mentioned. Another prominent example of the ambiguous effects of monetary policy on financial stability is the setting of interest rates during financial crises. Since they are typically associated with recessions, central banks tend to lower their base interest rates in times of widespread financial instability. However, doing so could inconspicuously give rise to speculative price increases in the stock or real-estate markets, which provide alternative investment opportunities to interest-bearing securities. In general, it is challenging to pursue a low-interest-rate monetary policy without increasing the risk of financial-market bubbles. Thus, central banks have had difficulty to dealing with speculative bubbles. In this regard, a widely cited dictum attributed to the former governor of the Federal Reserve System William McChesney Martin (1906–1998) says that it is the task of the central bank 'to collect the punchbowls as soon as the party really gets going'. However, in practice, it is often unclear when the party has gotten out of hand, or, in other words, when financial market prices no longer reflect fundamental developments. The track record of central banks and other pundits to forecast crises is indeed at best mixed—although, of

---

the financier Bernard Madoff in 2008, who for decades had operated an investment fund based on the principles of a 'Ponzi scheme'. The eventual collapse resulted in losses amounting to billions of US dollars.

course, some experts are quite good at 'backcasting' a crisis or continuing to forecast a crisis until it eventually happens. This should not be surprising. In the case of an unmistakable speculative bubble, financiers have every incentive to sell their overpriced assets to avoid the forthcoming losses. However, this behaviour tends to dampen financial market prices and, hence, pre-empt a financial bubble from occurring in the first place. Thus, policies trying to prevent financial crises rest on the controversial belief that central bankers and financial regulators are better at identifying financial excesses than are financiers and bankers, whose profits and jobs directly depend on correctly anticipating adverse developments.

The discussion in this chapter should not obscure the fact that modern central banks pursue goals regarding the broad development of the economy, rather than only that of the financial sector. It would indeed be misleading to evaluate the success of a given monetary policy according to, say, the reaction of the stock market. The next chapter turns to the effects and trade-offs inherent in monetary policy and discusses, in particular, the extent to which macroeconomic goals, such as price-level stability and high employment, can be achieved.

Further Reading

Probably the most widely used textbook on money, credit, and banking is currently Mishkin, Frederic S., 2018: *The Economics of Money, Banking, and Financial Markets*, Pearson.

At a more advanced level, the economics of banking and the financial system is presented in Freixas, Xavier, and Jean-Charles Rochet, 2008: *Microeconomics of Banking*, MIT-Press.

For a textbook discussion on the various risks affecting financial intermediaries see: Saunders, Anthony, and Marcia Millon Cornett, 2017: *Financial Institutions Management—A Risk Management Approach*, McGraw Hill.

A comprehensive historical account of financial crises can be found in Reinhard, Carmen M., and Kenneth S. Rogoff, 2009: *This Time is Different - Eight Centuries of Financial Folly*, Princeton University Press.

Another historical view on financial fragility organised around the experiences of different countries is Calomiris, Charles and Stephen H. Haber, 2014: *Fragile by Design*, Princeton University Press.

A book explaining the role of capital requirements is Admati, Anat, and Martin Hellwig, 2013: *The Bankers' New Clothes*, Princeton University Press.

It is still difficult to find a book on the Global Financial Crisis that presents a critical review of all the involved parties in a well-balanced manner. In this regard, a good choice is Rajan, Raghuram G., 2010: *Fault Line—How Hidden Fractures Still Threaten the World Economy*, Princeton University Press.

A number of personal accounts and books tell stories of recent spectacular cases of financial failure, including Lowenstein, Roger, 2001: *When Genius Failed* (Harper Collins) on the collapse of the Long-Term Capital Management Fund in 1998; Arvedlund, Erin, 2009: *Madoff - The Man who Stole $65 Billion* (Penguin Books); and McDonald, Larry, 2009: *A Colossal Failure of Common Sense* (Ebury Press) on the collapse of Lehman Brothers in 2008.

6

The Initial and Final Effects of Monetary Policy on Inflation, Output, and (Un)employment

Inflation is always and everywhere a monetary phenomenon. Milton Friedman (American Economist, 1912–2006)[1]

6.1 Monetary Macroeconomics

This chapter endeavours to provide a non-technical review of broadly accepted findings in monetary macroeconomics, that is, the discipline studying the effects of monetary variables, such as the money supply or nominal interest rates, on macroeconomic outcomes, such as the aggregate movement of prices, consumption, investment, and employment (and its counterpart, unemployment). In addition to Monetarism, as represented in the opening quote by its most famous proponent Milton Friedman, the discussion also visits other schools of economic thought including Keynesianism, and introduces ideas associated with economists who never managed to turn themselves into household names. Often, terms such as 'Monetarism' or 'Keynesianism' are used in a deeply ideological sense to indicate whether someone supports the free-enterprise system or believes in welfare improvement through government intervention. Unfortunately, this interpretation is far removed from these terms' original economic meaning. Pushing ideology aside, the scientific debates and historical experiences of the last 200 years or so have given rise

---

[1]Friedman, Milton, 1970: The Counter-Revolution in Monetary Theory, IEA Occasional Paper no. 33, p. 11.

© Springer Nature Switzerland AG 2019
N. Herger, *Understanding Central Banks*, https://doi.org/10.1007/978-3-030-05162-4_6

to a set of broadly established views, or theories, about the economic effects of money. In particular, when put in the appropriate context, many of the seemingly antagonistic statements in monetary economics are surprisingly uncontroversial. As explained in much more detail in this and the next chapter, when making economic statements, it is crucial to distinguish between the initial, or short-term, effects of money over a couple of quarters, and final, or long-term, effects across many years.

The following analysis of the macroeconomic effects of money draws on many of the aspects of central banking that have already been discussed. To recapitulate, central banks' use of monetary-policy instruments to affect the level of interest rates, the volume of credit, and the exchange rate is discussed in Chap. 4. It was previously mentioned that a well-functioning monetary system facilitates payments and fulfils other important functions, such as the provision of a standardised measure of economic value. Chapter 5 is devoted to the ways in which central banks can foster financial stability and, hence, safeguard the capacity of the financial and banking system to provide money and credit. Taken together, the discussion thus far has already provided clues to how the effects of central-bank interventions do not end at the boundaries of the monetary or financial system, but rather spread across the entire economy. Given this background, monetary policy encompasses a range of measures taken by the central bank and, typically to a minor extent, other government authorities to improve macroeconomic outcomes by regulating the amount of money and credit circulating through the economy. To achieve broadly recognised policy goals, such as price-level stability and low unemployment, a central bank should, of course, be able to manipulate interest rates, the supply of money, credit conditions, and exchange rates, whereas in the second stage, the corresponding interventions should have further effects on the aggregate environment, that is, across all sectors of the economy. Following the previous discussion of the narrower aspects of central banking, this chapter focuses on the aggregate, or macroeconomic, level of monetary policy.

6.2   Money and Inflation: The Neutrality of Money

Despite the almost supernatural powers that are often attributed to money, according to established theory backed by overwhelming empirical evidence, monetary policy has surprisingly little, or even no, effect on long-term economic welfare as represented, for example, by a country's average income level, economic growth, or severity of poverty and unemployment. To understand the absence of this relationship, it helpful to introduce the distinction between real and nominal variables. Real variables reflect economic phenomena that have direct value. The textbook example is consumption, which is typically constrained by an individual's income and wealth. Of course, the true, or real, value of income or wealth depends on its power to purchase consumption goods. Thus, not only are pecuniary amounts important, but the price level and the future path of inflation matter as well.[2] Despite the outstanding role given to consumption in economic analysis, an individual's well-being can, of course, be increased in many other ways; common examples include spending time with family and friends and being in good health. However, although it is possible to put a price on enjoying free time by, for example, considering the lower income one is willing to accept for working less, or sum up the costs of curing a disease, the real benefit of having a good time or of feeling well is not directly reflected by a specific amount of money. Recognising that money enters the equation only indirectly, as a means of payment or unit of account, leads to the trivial insight that poverty cannot be miraculously alleviated by printing banknotes. Hence, the following conclusion arises: as long as individuals do not suffer from 'money illusion'—meaning they are not interested in money per se—monetary policy is unlikely to create the vast differences in economic welfare observed around the world.

The relationship of nominal variables (i.e. those measured in dollars, euros, pounds, etc.) with money is completely different. Reflecting money's function as a unit of account, the general price level and its fluctuations across time, that is inflation, are textbook examples of nominal variables. Moreover, the interest and exchange rates published in the financial press are also expressed in currency units and, hence, constitute nominal variables. Unsurprisingly, sustained monetary developments have pervasive nominal effects. More specifically, when a central bank issues more cash or allows commercial banks to create more deposits than necessary to lubricate commercial transactions, inflation will sooner or later readjust the purchasing power of money. That a sustained increase in the average price level cannot be caused by real variables,

---

[2]In practice, measuring general price trends is not trivial. To do so, a representative consumer basket must be defined. Then, based on this basket, a price index is calculated so that the development of purchasing power is comparable across countries and time. The corresponding calculation is usually done relative to a certain base year, in which the index is, by definition, normalised to 100 points, that is $P_0 = 100$. The percentage change in the index across time measures inflation. If the price index climbs in year t to, for example, $P_t = 103$, inflation during that period was $(103/100 - 1)=0.03$ or 3%. Using the price index, it is also possible to convert nominal values into real economic values. For example, the real values at time t and 0 can be compared by applying the factor $100/103$. In particular, when Y_t reflects the nominal value of an economic variable such as income, then $y_t = Y_t * (100/103)$ is its real value, which has been corrected by the change in the purchasing power of money.

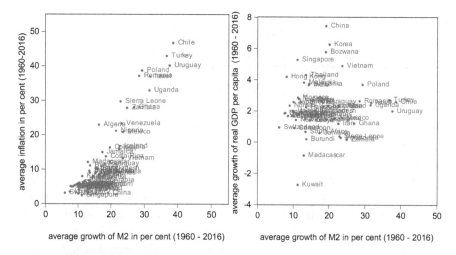

Fig. 6.1 The growth of money, prices, and economic output. Data sources: M2 growth and inflation: International Financial Statistics (IMF). Growth of real GDP per capita: World Development Indicators (The World Bank)

but rather arises when the stock of money outgrows real economic output, is a stylised fact. The long-term correlation between the growth rates of money and prices (or inflation) is indeed striking. For many countries, this relationship is illustrated in the left panel of Fig. 6.1, in which the average increase in M2 across several decades is plotted on the horizontal axis against the average inflation rate during the same period.[3] In contrast, as depicted in the right panel, an increase in M2 has no apparent relationship with real economic development as measured by the average growth rate of the real gross domestic product (GDP) per capita. Confirming the above claim, ongoing economic growth and all the comforts derived from this growth apparently do not depend on the amount of money a country has created.

More or less proportional effects also arise between other nominal variables. In particular, a close connection has widely been observed between the nominal interest rate, which the central bank can control by manipulating the base rate (see Sect. 4.2), and expected inflation. A priori, lenders have every incentive to demand higher nominal interest rates the more average prices are expected to increase. In doing so, the anticipated loss of purchasing power of future payments can be offset. Across time, pervasive levels of inflation

---

[3] Figure 6.1 ignores several countries, which reformed their currency systems due to becoming independent, joining a common currency, or suffering from hyperinflation. For these countries, structural breaks and missing data prevent the calculation of long-term averages.

are indeed associated with higher nominal interest rates. This relationship, which is depicted in the top panel of Fig. 6.2 with US data, is known as the 'Fisher effect', named after American economist Irving Fisher (1867–1947), who provided the first thorough description of this phenomenon. However, by accounting for future changes in the purchasing power of money, lenders and borrowers do not seem to care about pecuniary amounts as such. Rather, the decision to enter into a credit contract depends on the true return on saving and the true cost of investing, as reflected by the *real* interest rate, which is approximately given by the difference between the nominal interest rate and expected inflation.[4] Real interest rates have been quite stable across time and have barely reacted to the marked changes in the inflationary environment during the last few decades. Instead of monetary policy, fundamental factors including an economy's potential to grow, and hence deliver real returns on investment, or a country's demographics, as, for example, more savings are warranted to support an aging population, arguably determine the real level of interest rates.[5]

The proposition that, in the long-term, real economic activities evolve independently from developments in the monetary sector, which, in turn, are closely linked with nominal phenomena such as inflation, is called the 'neutrality of money'. This property has far-reaching implications for the strategic conduct of monetary policy. In particular, by exploiting the close connections between money and inflation, a central bank should be able to proliferate price stability by choosing an adequate level of nominal interest rates or limiting the supply of money. Conversely, a policy aiming to foster economic growth is doomed to fail because, in real terms, money ultimately only provides a convenient means of payment. A massive cash injection, or a low nominal interest rate, cannot miraculously create goods and services out of nothing, or come up with technological and organisational innovations,

---

[4]The exact formula of the real interest rate is given by

$$\text{real interest rate} = (\text{nominal interest rate} - \text{inflation rate})/(1 + \text{inflation rate}).$$

As long as inflation is relatively low, the denominator on the right-hand side is approximately equal to one and can be neglected. Hence, the value of the real interest rate is approximately given by

$$\text{real interest rate} \approx \text{nominal interest rate} - \text{inflation rate}.$$

For example, with a nominal interest rate of 5% and an inflation rate of 3%, the real interest rate is approximately 2%.

[5]For discussions on the determinants of the real interest rates see, for example, Fessenden, Helen, 2015: *Real Interest Rate*, Econ Focus, Federal Reserve Bank of Richmond. A more extensive review can be found in Obstfeld, Maurice, and Linda Tesar, 2015: *Long-term Interest Rates: A Survey*, Washington, President's Council of Economic Advisors.

Fisher effect illustrated with long-term US treasury yields. Changes in nominal interest rates reflect, in large parts, changes in expected inflation. The value of the expected (or ex-ante) real interest rate is positive and comparatively stable across time.

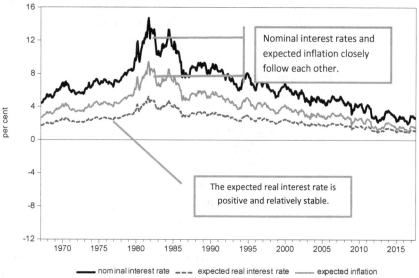

Due to price shocks, the realised (or ex-post) real interest rate can fluctuate heavily.

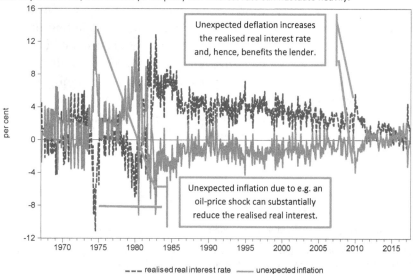

Fig. 6.2 Fisher effect. Notes: Nominal interest rates reflect long-term government bond yields. Inflation reflects the change of the consumer price index (CPI) for all items less food and energy. Inflation expectations are derived according to the method of Mishkin, Frederic, 1981: The Real Interest Rate: An Empirical Investigation, NBER Working Paper No. 622

which have historically been the driving forces of sustained increases in prosperity. The causality runs rather in the opposite direction. Central banks should constrain the amount of money in circulation to account for the fact that economic resources, such as labour, capital, land, or energy are scarce. Otherwise, an oversupply of money will sooner or later erode the purchasing power of a currency. However, to keep inflation under control, the money stock does not necessarily have to remain constant. Rather, its ongoing adjustment should absorb the seasonal fluctuations and other cyclical patterns in economic activity in the short-term, and also match the secular increase in transactions in a growing economy in the long-term. Building on earlier ideas postulated by the currency school (see Sect. 2.2), Monetarism is probably the most widely known doctrine emphasising that money matters for inflation and business-cycle fluctuations. In particular, based on a large body of historical economic analysis, the Monetarists advised central banks to adopt rigid rules according to which monetary aggregates should grow in a foreseeable manner.[6]

To avoid a common misunderstanding, it is important to realise that the neutrality property does not refer to the monetary framework as such. Adequate formal rules and informal norms underpinning an efficient payment and credit system are, of course, important for creating and spreading prosperity and, hence, provide real economic value. Many economic transactions simply will not take place without a broadly accepted circulating medium. As is evident from the historical episodes of financial crises or hyperinflations, monetary chaos can be very harmful.

In a similar vein, the neutrality property of money does not imply that inflationary outcomes are irrelevant. As a background observation, note that even seemingly small changes in the average rate of inflation lead to surprisingly large differences. As a rule of thumb, the period over which prices

---

[6]Prominent Monetarists include Milton Friedman (1912–2006), Allan Meltzer (1928–2017), and Karl Brunner (1916–1989). In its heyday during the 1970s, some ideas postulated by Monetarism were implemented in the actual conduct of monetary policy. In particular, after the collapse of the Bretton Woods System, some central banks began to announce explicit growth targets for monetary aggregates. However, reflecting changes in payment habits and financial innovations in the 1980s, the unstable behaviour of monetary aggregates proved to be a caveat against this approach. Therefore, during the 1990s, most central banks switched to a so-called 'inflation-targeting regime', in which the development of the average price level serves directly as a monetary-policy goal (see Sect. 2.6). However, the intellectual heritage of Monetarism resonates to this day in discussions about the role of monetary aggregates as economic indicators, the drawbacks of discretionary monetary policy, and the importance of central-bank mandates. An insightful overview of the key propositions of Monetarism can be found in Friedman, Milton, 1970: *The Counter-Revolution in Monetary Theory*, Institute of Economic Affairs Occasional Paper, no. 33.

double can be gauged by dividing the number seventy by the inflation rate.[7] To appreciate the leveraged effects of persistent price increases, consider the following comparison: With 1% inflation, it takes 70 years for the average price level to double. With 5% inflation, the corresponding period shrinks to only 70/5≈14 years.

For various reasons, inflation is costly. First, direct costs arise when firms are forced to constantly update their price schedules to changes in the purchasing power of money. This phenomenon is described by the catchy expression of 'menu costs', which alludes to the outlays when restaurants must reprint their menu cards with new prices. However, by infringing on the functions of money, sustained price movements cause the most damage in an indirect manner (see also Sect. 3.1). In particular, inflation tends to reduce the demand for money and, hence, undermines its role as a broadly accepted means of payment. Furthermore, by changing the yardstick of economic value, an inconstant price level modifies the monetary unit of account. In essence, this modification is as confusing and unpractical as if measures of distance or weight were redefined slightly differently each year. At least in the long-term, ongoing changes in the purchasing power of money hamper price comparisons. Most people understand these changes when contemplating the seemingly laughable prices charged for basic goods, such as food, fifty or one hundred years ago. Inflation gives rise to further distortions, because prices across a range of products do not necessarily react equally fast to monetary changes and, hence, partly lose their roles as indicators of economic scarcity. A well-known example of this is the so-called 'bracket creep', which arises, when

---

[7]This 'rule of seventy' is the result of the exponential nature of price-level growth, that is

$$P_t = P_0(1 + \pi/100)^t.$$

Here, P_0 is the initial and P_t the final price level, π is the inflation rate (in per cent), and t the period under consideration. A doubling of the average price level implies that $P_t = 2 \times P_0$. By means of natural logarithms, the doubling time t can be calculated by

$$t = \frac{\ln(2)}{\ln(1 + \pi/100)}.$$

According to the Taylor-rule, we have approximately that $\ln(1 + \pi/100) \approx \pi/100$. Furthermore, we have that $\ln(2) = 0.693... \approx 0.7$. Hence, the rule of 70 arises, since

$$t \approx \frac{0.7}{\pi/100} = \frac{70}{\pi}.$$

tax payments are defined in monetary units, but tax laws are only infrequently updated. Hence, it is possible that an individual may merely receive a nominal wage increase to absorb the effect of inflation, but nevertheless ends up paying more taxes, by moving into a higher tax bracket even though his real income has remained constant.

By reducing the capacity to reliably transfer purchasing power into the future, inconstant prices also infringe the store-of-value function of money. In this regard, unexpected surges in inflation, which can lead to massive wealth redistributions between lenders and borrowers, are most important. More specifically, the extent to which the above-mentioned Fisher effect correctly adjusts the nominal interest rate to inflationary effects depends, of course, on the correct anticipation of future price trends. When inflation turns out to be unexpectedly high and the corresponding loss in purchasing power has not been fully reflected in nominal interest rates, the *realised* real interest rate falls in hindsight. Such a scenario, of course, harms lenders and benefits borrowers, whose repayment burdens are reduced in real terms. Bearing witness to all kinds of price shocks that constantly hit the economy, including changes in energy and food prices, the development of the realised real interest rate is far from smooth and stable. Rather, as shown in the bottom panel of Fig. 6.2 with US data, unexpected inflation arising, for example, from the oil-price crises of the 1970s can even push the realised real interest into negative territory, implying that households and firms were actually rewarded for living on borrowed money (in real terms). This situation may seem positive, because borrowing becomes very attractive, which may, in turn, stimulate economic activity and lower unemployment. Why should we not live with permanently high levels of inflation? The problem is that a discrepancy between the realised and expected real interest rate cannot last long. Because human beings learn from past mistakes, lenders cannot be forever fooled into offering real interest rates at a loss. Rather, expectations are revised as soon as the inflationary environment appears to change. It is only possible to keep the realised real interest rate low by constantly raising the inflation rate. However, doing so would be associated with an unsustainable upsurge in the price level. Rampant inflation is itself a source of economic uncertainty. In particular, the faster that average prices grow, the more volatile they tend to be, which, for example, hampers the financial calculation of investment projects by increasing the difficulty of assessing the real value of future returns.

In general, sustained movements of the average price level inflict direct and indirect costs on all individuals, albeit to various degrees. Above all, low-income members of society are likely to suffer disproportionately from inconstant prices, because common ways to guard against inflation, such as investing in physical assets like real estate or holding foreign currency, are typically unavailable to the poor. Massive inflation not only causes economic harm but also leads to social instability if not violent unrest. Rapidly increasing prices (in particular those of food staples) have, indeed, played a part in some of the most notorious uprisings in history, including in the American (1776), French (1798), and Russian (1917) Revolutions.[8] Although a decay in the purchasing power of money is typically not the deeper cause of social unrest, it can tip an already fragile political situation into open revolt or revolution.

In sum, a stable monetary standard is most likely in the common interest. As long as a monopoly over issuing currency has been given to the central bank, it seems almost natural to bestow it with the mandate to maintain the purchasing power of the currency. To do so, the amount of money in circulation needs curtailing and adequate levels of nominal interest rates must be imposed. In most countries, price stability is nowadays, indeed, a key ingredient of the 'monetary constitution' and is often seen as a public task comparable to upholding a stable political and legal order, without which it would be difficult to do business, or even pursue an ordinary life.[9] Section 7.3 addresses the issue of how the complex interrelationships between inflation and the corresponding expectations are a key factor for successful monetary-policy outcomes. The following discussion, however, focuses on the initial effects of money.

6.3   Employment, Interest, and Money: The Transition Mechanisms of Monetary Policy

The previous paragraphs on the neutrality property emphasise the long-term nature of these relationships. As long as individuals have the flexibility and time to adjust their behaviour to fundamental monetary developments, the close connection between monetary and nominal phenomena, such as inflation, is intuitive. However, what about the initial effects of money? When prices and wages are not constantly updated, because, for example, they have been fixed by contracts, the short-term situation could appear quite different. In particular, when a monetary injection is not immediately compensated by higher prices, an at least temporary increase in purchasing power will

---

[8]See, for example, He, Liping, 2017, *Hyperinflation: A World History*, Routledge.

[9]To understand the role of the government in monetary affairs along these lines see Friedman, Milton, 1959: *A Program for Monetary Stability*, Fordham University Press, pp. 4–9.

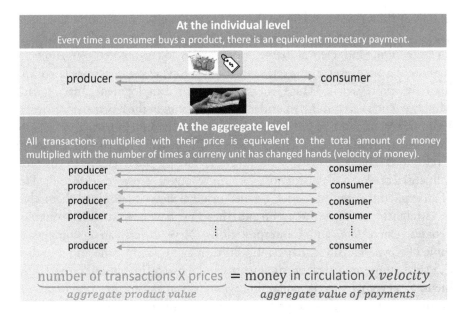

Fig. 6.3 Illustrating the quantity equation

arise in some parts of the economy. In other words, under the influence of inflexible prices, money can be non-neutral. This idea is easy to grasp by aggregating monetary expenditures for economic products in the so-called 'quantity equation', which is illustrated by Fig. 6.3. In any given period, it turns out that the aggregate product value, that is, the number of economic transactions multiplied by their prices, must coincide with aggregate monetary payments, that is, the total amount of money in circulation multiplied by the average number of times a currency unit changes hands (called the 'velocity of money'). In a non-barter economy, this relationship holds automatically, as every purchase of an economic product is counterbalanced by a monetary payment. Therefore, in the long-term, when the number of produced goods and services is fixed by technology and stable payment habits fix the velocity of money, the amount of money in circulation maps directly to the average price level. This relationship is simply the neutrality property of money encapsulated in the quantity equation. Clearly, this relationship breaks down when prices are inflexible (or even fixed) or the velocity is not constant.

The time frame over which the effects of money are neutralised may matter because 'in the long-term, we are all dead'. This sarcastic statement can be found in one of the earlier writings of John Maynard Keynes (1883–1946), entitled 'A Tract on Monetary Reform'. In this book, he follows in the footsteps of eminent British economists by studying the consequences of monetary fluctuations and he reaches rather traditional conclusions, such as an unstable value of money is costly to society, inflation is essentially a monetary phenomenon, and central banks can employ open-market operations to stabilise the price level. However, to the public, Keynes' name is associated with his views expressed in 'The General Theory on Employment, Interest, and Money', which was published under the impression of the Great Depression in 1936, and focused on explaining output fluctuations and, in particular, reasons that large-scale unemployment can persist. By bringing the short-term to the forefront of economic analysis, the 'General Theory' has been one of the most influential books in the history of economic thought. However, due to the lack of an explicit theoretical model, Keynes' original views do not lend themselves to a straightforward interpretation and, therefore, have been subject to ongoing debates, extensions, and reinterpretations. Nevertheless, an encompassing topic of Keynesianism is that erratic shifts in aggregate income and spending can create unnecessarily large downturns and massive, involuntary unemployment. A key challenge is explaining why such unsatisfactory outcomes can persist without giving rise to price, or wage adjustments. Aside from the above-mentioned price rigidities and instabilities in the velocity of money, according to the 'General Theory', psychological factors creating a crisis of confidence can also prevent a quick restoration of full employment. In particular, aside from traditional risk-and-return considerations, pervasive uncertainty about future developments is considered to be a major impediment to short-term investment decisions. Quoting Keynes' famous 'animal spirits' analogy:

> Most, probably, of our decisions to do something positive, the full consequences of which will be drawn out over many days to come, can only be taken as a result of animal spirits—of a spontaneous urge to action rather than inaction, and not as the outcome of a weighted average of quantitative benefits multiplied by quantitative probabilities. [...] It is safe to say that enterprise which depends on hopes stretching into the future benefits the community as a whole. But individual initiative will only be adequate when reasonable calculation is supplemented and supported by animal spirits, so that the thought of ultimate loss [...] is put aside as a healthy man puts aside the expectation of death. This means, unfortunately, [...] that slumps and depressions are exaggerated in degree [...]. (Keynes, John Maynard, 1936: *The General Theory on Employment, Interest, and Money*, Harcourt, Brace and Company, pp. 161–162.)

Even though aggregate income and spending decisions depend on many variables, they are arguably connected to the way in which money is used, which is of primary concern for central banks. In particular, Keynes conjectured that in a depression economy, the primary function of money shifts from a means of payment to a store of value insofar as firms and households would like to hedge against collapsing stock-market or real-estate prices by holding more liquid and safe asset such as cash. However, when money is hoarded, increasing the amount of cash in circulation or creating additional deposits may no longer lead to a boost in aggregate spending and, in turn, consumption. In a similar vein, at any level of interest rates, investment may remain permanently depressed when firms are pessimistic about the future. Low interest rates could even prevent a recovery when they are widely seen as a sign of a gloomy economic outlook and, hence, fail to revive the 'animal spirits' of entrepreneurs. In an environment, in which anxious households hoard money and firms lack confidence, Keynes believed that monetary-policy interventions would be largely ineffective. To escape this situation, in which households save too much and firms invest too little, he instead advocated for a fiscal stimulus through additional government spending.[10]

By explaining how large-scale unemployment can persist without being corrected through price and wage adjustments to counterbalance the collapse in aggregate income and spending, Keynes provided one explanation for the magnitude and length of the economic downturn of the 1930s. Although the circumstances of the Great Depression were quite special, his analysis inspired several generations of economists to elaborate on the short-term effects of inflexible prices and wages. Nevertheless, it should not be overlooked that these ideas neither were discovered during the 'Keynesian Revolution', nor are exclusively associated with 'Keynesianism'. In particular, problems with persistent involuntary underemployment were commonly attributed to sluggish wage and price adjustments in the works of prominent nineteenth-century economists, including Alfred Marshall (1842–1924), whose lectures Keynes attended when he was a student at Cambridge University.[11] Furthermore, the role of mistaken expectations, which can lead to waves of optimism sustaining speculative investment booms and stock-market bubbles, has recently become a popular topic which resonates with the psychological factors of the animal-spirits story. The following quote is just one of many examples illustrating the relationship between human deficiencies and overconfidence.

---

[10]In this regard, Keynes is in sharp disagreement with the Monetarists, who blamed the Great Depression on inadequate monetary policy, which arguably led to a collapse of the banking system and, in turn, the money supply. See, for example, Friedman, Milton, 1970: The Counter-Revolution in Monetary Theory, Institute of Economic Affairs Occasional Paper, no. 33.

[11]See Niehans, Jürg, 1990: *A history of economic theory - Classical contributions 1720–1980*, The Johns Hopkins University Press, pp. 54, 59, 103, 349. See also De Vroey, Michel, 2011: The Marshallian Roots of Keynes' Theory. In: Arnon, Arie, Jimmy Weinblatt, Warren Young (eds.), *Perspectives on Keynesian Economics*, Springer, pp. 57–75.

The over-weening conceit which the greater part of men have of their own abilities, is an ancient evil remarked by the philosophers and moralists of all ages. Their absurd presumption in their own good fortune, has been less taken notice of. It is, however, if possible, still more universal. There is no man living who, when in tolerable health and spirits, has not some share of it. The chance of gain is by every man more or less over-valued, and the chance of loss is by most men under-valued [..]. (Smith, Adam, 1776: *An Inquiry into the Nature and Causes of the Wealth of Nations*, Book I, Ch. 10, Part 1.)

However, this idea is not new. Indeed, the anachronistic language reveals that this quote is from an old book; in fact it comes from 'The Wealth of Nations', written by the leading figure in classical economics, Adam Smith (1723–1790). Finally, despite their dissenting views on the ability of governments to stabilise the economy, the main representatives of Monetarism never disputed that monetary impulses have distinct short-term effects.[12] In sum, it is broadly accepted that changes in the money supply can initially have non-neutral effects.

For a detailed understanding of the effect of central-bank interventions on real economic activity in the short-term, recall from Fig. 4.8 of Chap. 4 that monetary policy directly impacts the level of interest rates, the volume of bank loans, asset prices, and exchange rates. Figure 6.4 broadens this picture by adding the so-called 'monetary-policy transition mechanisms', that is, the channels via which money gives rise to temporary effects on real incomes and spending. Thus, expenditures can be grouped into several components including private consumption, investment, government consumption, and net exports, that is, the difference between exported and imported goods and services.[13] Because government consumption is essentially determined by public-budget considerations, the impact of this component falls into the realm of fiscal policy and is, hence, not further discussed here. In contrast, consumption and investment decisions depend, at least to some degree, on the level of interest rates, the terms and conditions of obtaining bank loans, and the returns households and companies earn on their assets, which are some

---

[12] See e.g. Friedman, Milton, 1970, The Counter-Revolution in Monetary Theory, Institute of Economic Affairs Occasional Paper, no. 33, pp. 10–11.

[13] The total expenditure across the whole economy is also called the 'aggregate demand'. Indeed, according the expenditure approach to national accounting, the Gross Domestic Product (GDP) can be calculated as

$$GDP \equiv consumption + investment + government\ consumption + \underbrace{net\ exports.}_{=export-import}$$

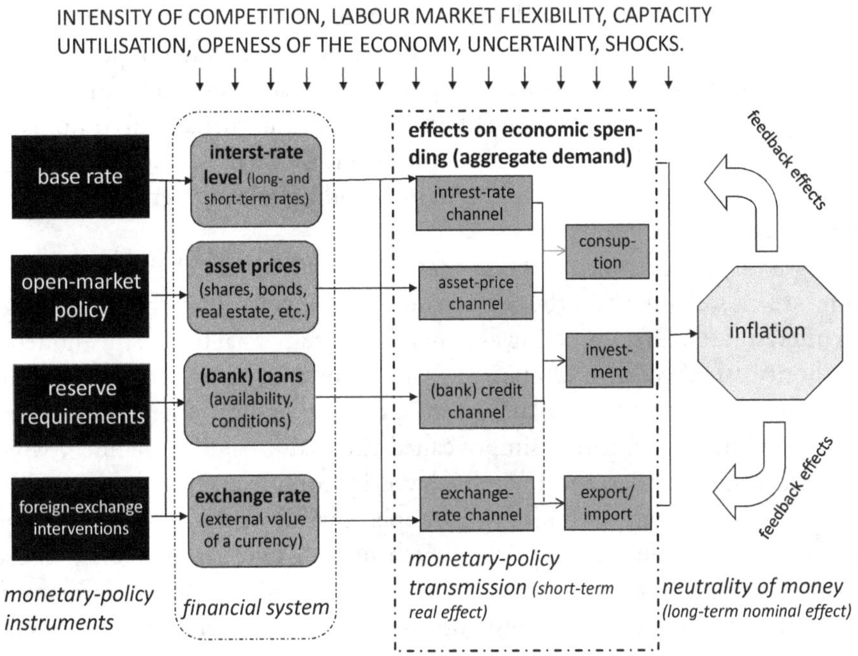

INTENSITY OF COMPETITION, LABOUR MARKET FLEXIBILITY, CAPTACITY
UNTILISATION, OPENESS OF THE ECONOMY, UNCERTAINTY, SHOCKS.

Fig. 6.4   Monetary-policy transition mechanisms

of the variables influenced by monetary policy. Moreover, the exchange rate is
clearly a key variable for the importing and exporting sectors of a country.

Probably, the interest-rate channel is the most-widely cited transmission
mechanism. Recall that the central bank's base rate wields great influence over
other nominal interest rates. Of course, savings and investment decisions by
firms and households depend on the real rate of lending and borrowing. Thus,
a central bank induced increase or decrease in the level of interest rates has real
effects, when the corresponding change occurs surprisingly and, hence, has
not already been priced into inflation expectations.[14] By changing the cost
of credit and, hence, that of investing, any shift in the real interest rate affects
real economic activity. Furthermore, the real return on bonds or bank deposits
affects savings decisions, which also reflect the amount of consumption
deferred into the future. Taken together, by reducing domestic investment
and consumption, a tightening of monetary-policy through an increase of

---

[14]In other words, inflation expectations matter for the interest-rate channel, because together with the
nominal interest rate, they determine the value of the ex-ante real interest rate (see Sect. 6.2). For example,
lower inflation expectations matched with a constant nominal interest rate increase the expected real
interest rate.

the base rate puts downward pressure on economic activity. Conversely, a corresponding loosening of monetary policy gives rise to the opposite effects and will put upward pressure on aggregate consumption and investment. Owing to its broad impact on the financial system and virtually all components of the economy, the interest-rate channel is one of the most powerful forces in modern monetary policy and plays an outstanding role in attempts to manage macroeconomic developments.

Figure 6.4 suggests that the domestic and international financial system offers further channels for the transmission of monetary policy beyond changes in interest rates. First, by acting as banker for commercial banks, the monetary authority can affect their refinancing conditions and, hence, can influence the amount of bank loans circulating through the economy. The corresponding transmission mechanism is simply called the 'bank-lending channel', which owes its importance to the key role played by commercial banks in matching savers with investors. Second, through open-market operations, central banks can directly influence asset prices, which provide another way for financial-market conditions to temporarily affect real economic demand. More specifi-cally, the asset-price channel rests on the idea that monetary policy induced changes in, for example, stock or bond prices create wealth-effects which propagate into aggregate consumption and investment. In this regard, real-estate prices are often of paramount importance, because houses or apartments constitute by far the most valuable asset held by the average person. For example, real-estate bubbles, which tend to be intertwined with burgeoning financial markets, boost homeowners' wealth, and the corresponding windfall gains have often been spent on consumption and investment binges in the past. Third, the exchange-rate channel captures the international dimension of monetary-policy transmission. It is probably commonly known that an appreciating domestic currency puts downward pressure on the export sector but is good news for importers. In particular, when the domestic currency can suddenly buy more units of foreign currency, the price of locally produced goods and services increases for foreign buyers, whereas imports become relatively cheaper. Similar effects accrue to the value of foreign assets (expressed in domestic currency). In an open financial system, the exchange-rate channel can be very crucial for explaining short-term economic fluctuations. In any case, through foreign-exchange interventions, central banks can alter the external value of their currency to affect the short-term conditions in the international sector.

Owing to their complexity, the initial effects of monetary policy can, probably, not be properly understood without the help of theoretical models. Whether you like it or not, in economics, few equations often say more than a thousand words do. The above-mentioned debates about the interpretation of Keynes' 'General Theory' are a forceful testimony to this principle. As strange as it sounds, most economists do not learn about Keynesianism by reading Keynes. In the classroom, concepts like the interest-rate channel are instead taught using a more or less elaborate version of the so-called 'IS/LM model' developed by John Hicks (1904–1989), a less-famous Cambridge economist.[15] His popular model distils the short-term interaction between employment, interest rates, and money into two equations, namely, the IS-curve, reflecting the aggregate behaviour of consumption and investment on the goods market, and the 'LM-curve', capturing the money market. In combination, these equations have proven to be a versatile framework to clarify, for example, why monetary policy can have short-term real economic effects when prices are rigid.

In the history of economic thought, the decades after the 1930s were dominated by rudimentary versions of Keynesianism, and the relationships between variables, such as money, interest rates, and employment, were analysed from a purely static and short-term perspective. Although this perspective might be understandable in view of the imminent disasters during the Great Depression, ignoring the future effects of fiscal and monetary policy also laid the intellectual foundation for overstating the benefits of cheap money and government deficit-spending. Despite the well-known shortcomings of early Keynesian analysis, it is surprising that some of the daring conclusions still receive undivided support in modern-day policy discussions. For example, a deficit-spending fiscal policy during a recession is often thought to give rise to unambiguous benefits. Based on a theory ignoring the future, more public spending and tax cuts will of course always foster economic activity and reduce unemployment. However, in reality, the situation is a bit subtler as spendthrift governments tend to pile up public debt, which encapsulates future increases in taxes and austerity budgets, implying a reduction in aggregate consumption

---

[15]The path that led to the IS/LM-model nicely illustrates many of the points made thus far. In 1933, Cecil Arthur Pigou (1877–1959), who was a fellow economist of Keynes at Cambridge University, published his 'Theory of Unemployment', which was lambasted in the 'General Theory', despite expressing quite similar views, such as that lower wages can, in principle, boost employment. However, this so-called 'Pigou effect' does not arise when wages are contractually fixed. Although their designers allegedly had personal animosities, it was indeed quickly shown that the Keynesian and Pigouvian explanations for unemployment could easily be reconciled. In particular, a year after the publication of the 'General Theory', a conference of the Econometric Society started the business of analysing what Keynes really meant. Although it tried to uncover the deviations from established economic thought, John Hicks' paper entitled 'Mr. Keynes and the 'Classics'; A Suggested Interpretation', which became famous for its IS/LM-model, essentially ended up finding considerable overlaps. For a historical overview of the IS-LM model, see De Vroey, Michel, and Kevin D. Hoover (eds.), 2005: *The IS-LM Model: Its Rise, Fall, and Strange Persistence*, Duke University Press.

and investment. Public debt ultimately must be paid by someone. Similarly, a policy of cheap money with irresponsibly low interest rates can lead to rampant inflation. Focusing on monetary policy, the final part of this chapter turns to these dynamic issues.

6.4   Bridging the Short and Long-Term

Today, the idea that monetary-policy-transition mechanisms provide, in principle, ways to manage economic fluctuations and avoid cyclical unemployment is broadly accepted. However, after a monetary-policy impulse has affected consumption, investment, or exports, how are the corresponding effects related to the long-term neutrality property of money?

A state of non-neutrality cannot persist forever. In particular, prices and wages are likely only inflexible for several quarters. In a stylised manner, the upper part of Fig. 6.5 illustrates the slow and gradual reaction of the price level to a loosening of monetary policy. Although prices are initially fixed, after some time, an increase in the money supply results in a proportional increase in the average price level to restore the neutrality property.

The price-adjustment process also determines the aggregate reactions of real income and spending to a monetary-policy intervention. As indicated by the right side of Fig. 6.4, inflation feeds back into monetary-policy transmission. This process can be understood by first contemplating the interest-rate channel, which rests on the co-movement between real and nominal interest rates and, hence, evaporates as soon as price increases are reflected in higher inflation expectations. In other words, the above-mentioned Fisher effect,

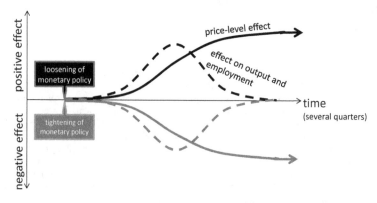

Fig. 6.5 Dynamic effects of monetary-policy interventions (stylised)

which brings real interest rates back to their sustainable levels, sooner or later reverses the monetary-policy impulse. Similar feedback effects also arise regarding the other transition mechanisms, as a looming upsurge in inflation hampers the issuing of bank loans and reduces asset prices expressed in real terms. Similarly, to offset the loss of international purchasing power, currencies tend to depreciate in the face of high levels of inflation.[16] Taken together, as shown by the upper part of Fig. 6.5, the real-economic effect of a monetary-policy intervention typically exhibits a wave-like, or hump-shaped, pattern. The peak indicating the maximum stimulus is usually reached after several quarters. In the lower part of Fig. 6.5, the mirror image of a monetary-policy tightening is depicted, which might be warranted to root out high inflation. However, this disinflation may impose a cost in the form of a temporary reduction in economic output, which is typically accompanied by an upsurge in unemployment. Section 7.3 returns to the implications of such a stabilisation crisis in more detail.

Prices do not always adjust in the same manner everywhere. For example, as alluded to by the upper edge of Fig. 6.4, widespread price collusion is likely to slow the reaction of inflation to a monetary impulse. Similar effects arise with wages, which constitute a major cost component in most economic sectors. The degree of wage inflexibility depends on the organisation of the labour market—meaning, for example, the extent to which wage-bargaining occurs in a centralised manner, the quality and quantity of labour-market regulations, and the role trade unions play in the wage-setting process. Moreover, reflecting how closely an economy operates to full capacity, the sluggishness of prices might also change across the business cycle. Above all, when firms run out

---

[16]The exact mechanism through which depreciation maps into inflation can be illustrated by the purchasing-power-parity theory. This theory is a generalisation of the so-called 'law of one price', according to which the local prices of freely tradable goods should be identical after the foreign price has been converted into domestic currency. Otherwise, arbitrage opportunities, that is, the exploitation of international price differences to make easy profits, would arise. The absolute version of the purchasing-power-parity theory expresses the same idea in terms of aggregate prices. In other words, exchange rates offset, in the long-term (when prices are flexible), international price-level differences, that is

$$\text{exchange rate} = \text{foreign price level}/\text{domestic price level}$$

The relative version of purchasing power parity, given by

$$\text{change in exchange rate} = \text{foreign inflation rate} - \text{domestic inflation rate},$$

re-expresses this relationship in terms of changes across time. Hence, exchange-rate changes reflect differences in inflation with a relatively high level of domestic inflation tending to depreciate the currency (here, a reduction of the exchange rate). This result is perhaps intuitive. When rampant inflation affects a currency, its external purchasing power can only be preserved by an increase in the cost of foreign currency in terms of domestic currency units. In other words, depreciation is an international reflection of the internal loss of purchasing power.

of spare capacity, they must resort to price increases rather than increasing production to manage any further increase in demand. Finally, inflation also arises via imported goods and services, whose prices tend to go up (down) when the domestic currency depreciates (appreciates).[17] Such exchange-rate induced price changes, which are also referred to as 'imported inflation', clearly matter more when international trade accounts for a large part of economic activity.

From the discussion thus far, it may be tempting to conclude that monetary policy provides a tool to fine-tune economic activity. A comparison with an engineering task, such as ensuring the smooth operation of a machine through controlled interventions, may come to mind. However, owing to the behavioural underpinning of economic relationships, it would be misleading to view central banking as a form of 'monetary engineering'. In contrast to technical relationships, the connection between variables such as money, inflation, and unemployment is much subtler. Similar to the money-and-credit-multiplication process discussed in Sects. 3.4 and 5.2, the aggregate relationship between variables such as money, inflation, and unemployment is not stable or mechanical. Thus, although the neutrality property encapsulates a longstanding statement about the relationship between money and other nominal variables, there is far less consensus regarding the magnitude of the initial effects of money. The relative importance of the various monetary-policy transmission mechanisms can change dramatically through time, as interest and exchange rates are usually the key factors under ordinary economic circumstances, whereas bank lending and asset prices move to the forefront in times of crisis. More specifically, marked economic booms are typically accompanied by waves of optimism and massive expansions of credit (credit boom), which are often followed by even more spectacular downturns during which banks are reluctant to issue, or even renew, loans. However, when many banks decide to adopt a wait-and-see policy, the bank-lending channel collapses, and a credit crunch can emerge. In a similar vein, bursting asset bubbles do not just imperil the stability of the financial and banking system. Rather, via the asset-price channel, they also dampen economic activity by suddenly leaving homeowners and firms overindebted, which will temporarily curtail their consumption and investment. By exacerbating the effects of a financial crisis, frictions in bank lending and crashing asset prices have in many cases been the main causes of severe economic turmoil (see Sect. 5.3). Crises

---

[17] In economics, the relationship between exchange rates and import prices is called the 'exchange-rate pass through', which is typically incomplete. Exchange-rate changes are often only partly reflected in import prices because they are rigid in the short-term, and competition between domestic and foreign companies is imperfect.

of confidence can radically change the impact of monetary policy on broad economic conditions.

In sum, economic circumstances and the time horizon matter greatly for the conduct of monetary policy. Across several quarters, and in a situation without pervasive uncertainty, it is relatively easy to influence economic activity and employment conditions. Conversely, across several years or even decades, the neutrality property of money prevails. In any case, due to the time-lag in the reaction of prices and economic activity, good monetary policy depends crucially on a central bank's ability to correctly anticipate future economic developments. At the same time, this dependence also implies that monetary-policy decisions are always prone to mistakes, because economic forecasting is, by its very nature, an uncertain business. Furthermore, unexpected changes can always redirect the future path of the economy. Well-known, but by far not the only, examples of such 'shocks' are financial crises, as well as abrupt changes in energy prices (e.g. oil-price shocks) and the eruption of political conflicts at home or abroad. The main challenge of monetary policy dedicated to controlling inflation is that the central bank must react before the destabilising price trends get out of control. Owing to the slow and gradual effects of monetary-policy interventions, it would be inadequate to merely react to current deviations from price stability. An often-quoted analogy says that central banking should be compared to the steering of a supertanker, rather than that of a car, in the sense that turning the rudder has initially only small effects. In monetary policy, as in shipping, it seems sensible to pursue a steady course, identify potential obstacles as early as possible and, hence, try to avoid a collision course with anything that could disrupt the journey to the planned destination.

Further Reading

The macroeconomic relationships between money, the average price level, and economic activity are discussed in every textbook on macroeconomics. A popular example is Mankiw, N. Gregory, 2015: *Macroeconomics*, Macmillan learning.

At the advanced level, the standard textbook on monetary theory and policy is currently Walsh, Carl, 2017: *Monetary Theory and Policy*, MIT Press.

Background information on the lives and theoretical contributions of eminent economists such as John Maynard Keynes and Milton Friedman can be found in Niehans, Jürg, 1990: *A history of economic theory - Classical contributions 1720–1980*, The Johns Hopkins University Press.

A nuanced overview of the evolution of macroeconomic ideas since the 1930s, including Keynesianism and Monetarism, can be found in De Vroey, Michel, 2016: *A History of Macroeconomics from Keynes to Lucas and Beyond*, Cambridge University Press.

An introductory overview of a modern version of Keynesianism emphasising the role of confidence crises in macroeconomic developments can be found in Farmer, Roger, 2010: *How the economy works*, Oxford University Press.

A direct account of the conduct of monetary policy during the past twenty years by a former central-bank governor can be found in King, Mervyn, 2016: *The End of Alchemy - Money, Banking and the Future of the Global Economy*, Little Brown.

7

Central-Bank Independence

Inflation is always and everywhere a fiscal phenomenon. Thomas Sargent (American economist, *1943)[1]

7.1 Why Should the Central Bank Be Independent?

Economic history suggests that monetary policy can both support and distort our daily activities. Thus, to achieve good outcomes, countries typically enshrine their monetary setup in the constitution and in various laws. In particular, the central bank's mandate—or a country's 'monetary constitution'— can stipulate more or less broadly defined monetary-policy goals (or objectives), define how they should be achieved, and prescribe procedures when they are missed. When there are several policy goals, for example, in the case of the dual mandate instructing the Federal Reserve System to achieve maximum employment and price stability, their relationship needs clarifying. These strategic issues are intertwined with the question of how independent the central bank should be from outside political interference and, above all, whether a government authority can influence, or even overrule, a given decision of the guardians of the currency. Although these questions may seem innocuous, the definition of the central bank's mandate can have far-reaching

---

[1]Sargent, Thomas, 2013: *Rational Expectations and Inflation*, Princeton University Press, p. 238.

© Springer Nature Switzerland AG 2019
N. Herger, *Understanding Central Banks*, https://doi.org/10.1007/978-3-030-05162-4_7

consequences. Hence, it is a grave mistake to treat the arrangement of the monetary constitution as an unimportant political detail.

Despite the great potential for monetary controversies, which are inherent in the entrenched trade-offs between price, financial, and economic stability, independence is nowadays a widely acknowledged ingredient for successful central banking. Astonishingly, most citizens of established democracies are ready to delegate far-reaching decisions regarding interest-rate levels or the adoption of lender-of-last-resort interventions to a body of unelected technocrats. In contrast, it is almost unthinkable that similar fiscal-policy tasks, which can also be used for economic management, would be taken away from direct government control. Although central banks do not define their mandates, their independence, or autonomy, is concretely manifested in the degree with which they (1) can conduct monetary policy free from government instruction (functional independence), (2) are free to choose the instruments to implement monetary policy (instrument independence), (3) can finance themselves and autonomously determine when to disburse profits (financial independence), and (4) form a separate legal entity (institutional independence). Furthermore, appointing the central-bank governor according to professional criteria and for a relatively long and contractually fixed term of office are also signs of independence. Of course, these criteria are typically neither fully nor simultaneously fulfilled. Rather, various degrees of independence can be observed across different central banks and time periods.

Central banks should be independent for a strikingly simple reason: independence seems to produce good results. More specifically, within a fiat-money system, autonomous monetary authorities have proven to be quite successful in delivering price stability. Arguably, the years between the establishment of the Bretton Woods System in the late 1940s and the 1980s are particularly well suited for illustrating this result. During this period, even across the industrialised world, in which countries had similar financial and political conditions, the degree of central bank independence differed substantially. For example, hoping to better manage their economies by combining the forces of monetary and fiscal policy, New Zealand, France, and the United Kingdom nationalised their central banks (see Table 2.2). However, as shown in Fig. 7.1, the level of inflation turned out to be lower in countries such as Germany, Switzerland, and the United States, where central-bank independence was largely preserved. Conversely, these countries did not suffer from lower economic growth or less stable economic activity.

As a result of the neutrality property of money (see Sect. 6.2), it is intuitive that monetary policy can deliver long-term price stability. Indeed, whereas a policy of cheap money will at most temporarily boost real spending or

Central-bank independence and inflation

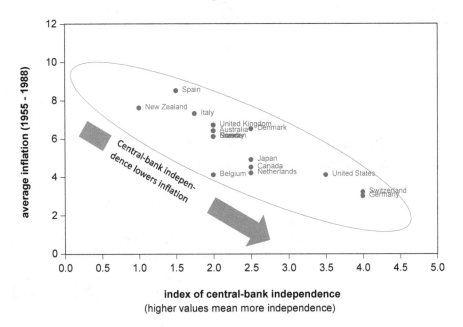

index of central-bank independence
(higher values mean more independence)

Central-bank independence and economic growth

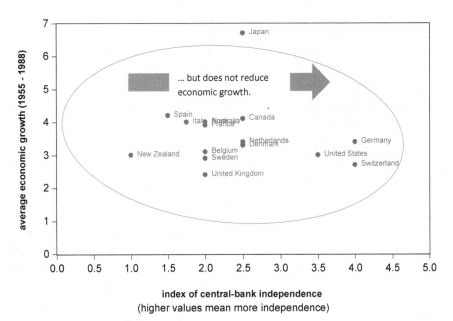

index of central-bank independence
(higher values mean more independence)

Fig. 7.1 Central-bank independence: a success story. Data: Alesina, A., and L. Summers, 1993: Central Bank Independence and Macroeconomic Performance: Some Comparative Evidence, Journal of Money, Credit, and Banking, 25, 151–162

foster production, restricting the amount of cash and deposits in circulation is a precondition for maintaining low and stable levels of inflation. However, the neutrality property does not explain why independent central banks are apparently better at resisting the short-term temptation to pursue over-expansionary monetary policy at the expense of undermining the long-term purchasing power of the currency. The next sections provide two widely cited explanations.

7.2   Independence Separates Monetary from Fiscal-Policy Considerations...

It is obviously not ideal for a currency to experience an ongoing decline in purchasing power. Hence, one may wonder why so many countries have suffered from rampant inflation, even though a central bank can restore price stability by pursuing a sufficiently tight monetary policy. A straightforward reason may be that many governments pursue other goals besides safeguarding the purchasing power of the currency. Indeed, the potential of publicly managed currencies to generate profits for the government has already been highlighted (see Sects. 3.2 and 4.1). Furthermore, recall that the primary motive for establishing the oldest note-issuing banks lay precisely in raising public funds, essentially by selling the privilege to issue banknotes (see Sect. 2.1). Thus, as long as the government controls certain parts of the monetary system, it is tempting to employ monetary policy for fiscal goals. Indeed, without central-bank transfers to the treasury, sooner or later, taxes must increase or public spending must decrease.

However, a monetary policy designed to generate as much government revenue as possible can have dire consequences. In particular, financing public programmes by issuing large volumes of currency rather than collecting taxes is, in practice, inherently associated with ongoing purchases of government bonds by the central bank. Hence, the monetary form of deficit spending results in an increase in the amount of money in circulation. Given the neutrality property, such a development will eventually undermine the value of money (see Sect. 6.2). Taken together, this chain of events inconspicuously connects public expenditures, the funding of government debt with seigniorage, and increasing average prices. Thus, from a fiscal perspective, inflation can be interpreted as a specific form of taxation. At first glance, this notion may sound odd. After all, in contrast to, say, income or corporate taxes, invoices do not exist to order the payment of an inflation tax to a government account. However, the distinctive feature of the inflation tax is that the monetary authority contributes to public finances in a rather clandestine manner. To appreciate the fiscal side of inflation, it is perhaps helpful to look back on basic forms of money and recall that, for example, a banknote simply represents a debt certificate granting the bearer the right to receive, on demand, a certain amount of fiat money from the central bank.[2] Thus, any individual with cash in his pockets holds a claim on the central bank and trusts that the corresponding financial obligation will be honoured. In the case of inflation, this expectation is not fulfilled in real terms. Because fiat money is only convertible into itself, an increasing price level inflicts a—generally hidden—loss of purchasing power on interest-free assets, such as banknotes. Nevertheless, financial losses typically benefit another party. In the present context, the readiness of the public to hold cash despite the ongoing reduction in purchasing power generates a profit on the central bank's balance sheet and, ultimately, a transfer to the treasury.

Usually, the inflation tax represents only a relatively small part of government revenue. In a typical country, the monetary base perhaps amounts to around 10% of gross domestic product (GDP). Even with an average inflation level of, say, 5%, the inflation tax is roughly 10% × 5% = 0.5% of GDP, which is small in comparison to the revenue typically raised through other forms of taxation.[3] Of course, depending on the circumstances, this share may change substantially. For example, many countries have witnessed periods of double-digit inflation. Furthermore, international-reserve currencies, such as the US dollar, are, by definition, held in substantial quantities abroad, which increases the share between the monetary base and domestic GDP. Thus, countries with relatively high levels inflation or whose currencies serve as popular international means of payment or currency reserves can raise larger amounts of inflation tax.

---

[2] It is perhaps helpful to review the origin of banknotes as 'promises to pay' in Fig. 2.1.

[3] The rule according to which the inflation tax is a function of inflation and the ratio of the monetary base to GDP results from the discussion in Sect. 4.1. Recall that seigniorage arises from the real growth in the monetary base ΔN, that is

$$\text{monetary seigniorage} = \frac{\Delta N}{P} = \frac{\Delta N}{N}\frac{N}{P},$$

where P denotes the price level. The expanded expression on the right-hand side suggests that seigniorage revenue depends on the product of base-money growth and the real base-money supply. Because real GDP equals Y/P, and money growth maps proportionally to inflation due to the neutrality property, we have that

$$\frac{\text{monetary seigniorage}}{\text{GDP}} = \text{inflation} \times \frac{N/P}{Y/P} = \text{inflation} \times \frac{\text{monetary base}}{\text{nominal GDP}}$$

(see Blanchard, Olivier, and David R. Johnson, 2014: *Macroeconomics*, Pearson, pp. 520ff.). In words, monetary seigniorage increases with higher rates of average price increases (e.g. the 'inflation-tax rate') as well as with a larger ratio between the monetary base and GDP (e.g. the 'inflation-tax base').

It is comparatively easy to monetise public debt, which, in practice, has often been a crucial consideration for employing this method of public finance. Compared with running a bureaucracy dealing with thorny tax declaration and evasion issues, putting a national currency into circulation by printing fiat money and granting it the status of legal tender is relatively simple. Even though considerable inflation is warranted to generate substantial amounts of public revenue from printing money, countries lacking a sophisticated or well-functioning public administration have often little choice, but to resort to the central bank to cover fiscal shortfalls. During a severe political crisis or military conflict, printing money is often the only remaining option. Of course, problems arise when a crisis-ridden government issues huge amounts of money and inflation spirals out of control as a result. Given this background, it is perhaps not surprising that virtually all historically recorded cases of hyperinflation have occurred in countries suffering from disastrous crises in the aftermath of a war, revolution, or other forms of massive upheaval (see Sects. 3.1 and 6.2).

Another scenario, in which an inflation tax is tempting arises when a spendthrift government has piled up an unsustainably large amount of debt whose real burden can be inflated away by an unexpected upsurge in the average price level and, hence, lower (ex-post) real interest rates (see Sect. 6.2). Recall that any unexpected inflation tends to redistribute wealth from lenders to borrowers, whereby the largest beneficiary may well be an over-indebted government. However, although it is possible to outmanoeuvre government-bond holders on some occasions, the trick of engineering a surprise inflation, which is not reflected in nominal interest rates, is not without costs. Rather, a policy of cheap money to inflate fiscal problems away is likely to ruin a government's creditworthiness giving rise to tangible economic repercussions when higher interest rates are demanded for newly issued public debt. In this way, private financiers can react to observing the devaluation of past financial claims through the manipulation of monetary conditions.

In sum, linking fiscal with monetary policy is problematic because persistently high levels of inflation are warranted to generate substantial revenue for the government. More often than not, endemic inflation is intertwined with fiscal problems, such as unsustainable government deficits and massively increasing amounts of public debt. In that sense, inflation is a fiscal phenomenon. At a first glance, this statement seems to contradict the monetary origin of inflation, and the corresponding quotes from the two Nobel laureates in this and the previous chapter appear to support the view that economists cannot agree on anything. However, upon closer inspection, these quotes do turn out to be consistent. In particular, the paragraph, which contains Milton Friedman's famous dictum, reads as follows:

> Inflation is always and everywhere a monetary phenomenon in the sense that it is and can be produced only by a more rapid increase in the quantity of money than in output. However, there are many different possible reasons for monetary growth, including [...] financing of government spending [...].[4]

In other words, when monetary policy is subordinated to public spending considerations, it is a semantic issue whether to interpret unstable prices as monetary or fiscal phenomena, because these policy areas have become closely intertwined.

An institutional remedy against the detrimental effects of high inflation is to grant the central bank a large degree of independence, meaning that monetary policy should remain autonomous from fiscal considerations, such as government-spending plans or the decision to increase or lower the tax burden. In particular, independence is manifested in the fact that the government and, in particular, the treasury, cannot influence, reverse, or even exert direct control over monetary-policy decisions. Thus, the temptation to turn to the 'banknote press' as a seemingly convenient source of public revenue is removed.

Finally, it is important to point out two common misunderstandings regarding central-bank independence from fiscal-policy considerations. First, even when prices are completely stable, central banks can still earn profits. As discussed in more detail in Sect. 4.1, with zero inflation, seigniorage revenue still arises owing to the cheap, or even free, credit provided by the holders of the monetary base. Therefore, the notion that no inflation implies no central-bank profit is incorrect. Second, the fact that monetary-policy interventions involve the purchase of government bonds is not per se an indication of a problematic nexus between monetary and fiscal policy. Owing to their standardisation and liquidity, almost all central banks routinely implement monetary policy by, for example, collateralising open-market operations with government bonds (see Sects. 4.2 and 4.4). The important factor in determining whether monetary and fiscal policy have been intertwined is the motivation for a central-bank intervention. More precisely, the question is whether refinancing operations or open-market interventions are necessary to guarantee financial or price stability, or are primarily undertaken to monetise public debt.

---

[4]See Friedman, Milton, 1970: The Counter-Revolution in Monetary Theory, IEA Occasional Paper no. 33, p. 11.

7.3 … and Fosters the Credibility of the Central Bank to Maintain Stable Monetary Conditions

The double-digit inflations that occurred in many industrialised countries during the 1970s suggest that even when governments have ample access to non-monetary sources of taxation, the average price level is not necessarily stable (see Fig. 2.9). In these cases, non-fiscal factors seem to matter. With the transition from commodity to fiat money, it has indeed become more difficult to tame inflation. Historical experience suggests that currencies that are supplied flexibly can suffer from sustained losses in purchasing power. As is often the case, gaining flexibility in, for example, the provision of money can also lead to misguided decisions. In particular, a policy of cheap money can benefit the economy by boosting output and employment in the short-term, but at the expense of maintaining the purchasing power of the currency when the neutrality property begins to dominate in the long-term. The potential trade-offs between inflation and unemployment are summarised by the so-called 'Phillips-curve', which provides a versatile framework for capturing the opportunities and limitations of achieving these economic-policy goals. Constituting a key building block in macroeconomic models to this day, the Phillips-curve is rooted in a countervailing relationship between inflation and unemployment, observed by New Zealand economist Bill Phillips (1914–1975).[5] Using US data for the 1960s, the upper panel of Fig. 7.2 illustrates that high levels of inflation are typically associated with low levels of unemployment (and vice versa). This observation gave rise to the—as it turned out erroneous—belief that the trade-off of the Phillips-curve offers a kind of economic-policy menu between price stability and full employment. Why should a country not try to move along the arrow depicted in Fig. 7.2 by tolerating slightly higher growth in the average price level, when doing so creates jobs? Would you not rather have 5% inflation than 5% unemployment?

The caveat against exploiting the Phillips-curve relationship is that you can end up with both, large-scale unemployment and high inflation. To understand why, recall that a policy of cheap money to reduce unemploy-

---

[5]In fact, Bill Phillips observed a negative correlation between increases in wages and unemployment. Because wages are a major determinant of prices and, hence, inflation, this relationship carries over to inflation and unemployment. This modification was proposed by American economists Paul Samuelson (1915–2009) and Robert Solow (*1924). Arguably, the Phillips-curve was already described by Irving Fisher in the 1920s (see Donner, Arthur, and James F. McCallum, 1972: The Phillips Curve: An Historical Note, *Economica*, pp. 322–323).

Although the trade-off between inflation and unemployment is temporarily negative...

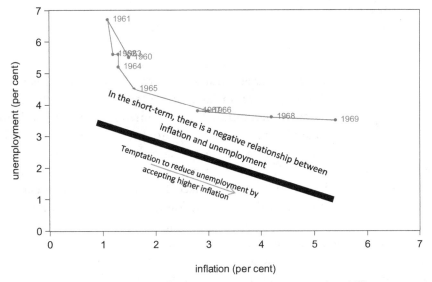

... it shifts upwards as soon as inflation expectations increase. The Phillips-curve relationship is unstable in the long-term.

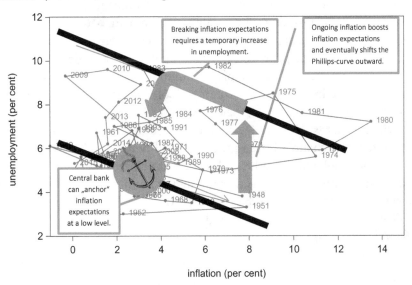

Fig. 7.2 Phillips-curve illustrated with US data. Data: FRED database of St. Louis Federal Reserve: Year-on-year CPI (for all urban consumers) change and civilian unemployment rate

ment works only temporarily. Due to the adjustment effects discussed in Sect. 6.4, the monetary stimulus to employment and output will sooner or later evaporate. Even more delicately, the corresponding process does not necessarily follow a stable pattern but can shift together with, for example, changes in inflation expectations. At this stage, it is worth further discussing the complex connections between real and nominal economic variables in general, and reconsidering the role of expectations, or beliefs about the future, with respect to the interrelationship between interest rates and inflation in particular. A monetary stimulus works best if it happens unexpectedly. Non-neutral effects only arise when a change in the monetary stance is not yet reflected in the price and wage-setting process. Consider, for example, the interest-rate channel. Given some fixed level of inflation expectations, according to the Fisher equation, a reduction in the base interest rate takes other nominal and the corresponding real interest rates with it and, hence, fosters employment through an increase in aggregate investment spending. However, the tempting conclusion that a higher level of inflation can be permanently traded-off against lower unemployment via an expansionary monetary policy is misguided. As mentioned, a monetary stimulus to the real economy rests on the discrepancy between actual and expected monetary conditions. It is now crucial to realise that human beings are not naive and, based on past experiences, eventually recognise erroneous beliefs about economic developments. It would indeed be costly for lenders or employed labour to ignore the implications of a continuing drop in the purchasing power of money. Once human beings cannot be fooled into expecting low inflation despite an unstable price level, the corresponding expectations will eventually be revised upwards. However, as soon as expectations are aligned with reality, the interest-rate channel loses much of its ability to stimulate real economic activity and employment. When it is widely anticipated that a policy of cheap money will continue, investors demand higher nominal interest rates to offset the likely decrease in the purchasing power of future nominal payments.[6]

That unstable expectations can destroy the policy trade-off apparently offered by the Phillips-curve was proven by actual events. In particular, after

---

[6]Again, the Fisher equation given in footnote 4 of Chap. 6 clarifies these connections. Approximately, we have

$$\text{real interest rate} \approx \text{nominal interest rate} - \text{expected inflation}.$$

With constant inflation expectations, any change in the nominal interest rate maps directly into the real interest rate. In the long-term, changes in nominal interest rates tend to be reflected in inflation expectations. For example, a drop in the nominal interest rates tends to increase the money supply and, eventually, inflation and, in turn, inflation expectations. According to the neutrality of money, the corresponding effects tend to offset each other in the long-term.

prolonged expansionary monetary policy, the industrialised world entered an upward spiral of inflation towards the end of the 1960s. During the 1970s, inflation was accompanied by high levels of unemployment marking the end of the belief in the stable relationship postulated by the original version of the Phillips-curve. Aside from idiosyncratic events giving rise to oil-price shocks and increasing energy prices, changes in expectations also, arguably, caused the awkward combination of economic stagnation and high inflation (or what become known as 'stagflation'). In particular, it turned out that inflation expectations can become entrenched when households get accustomed to upward price trends and, in response, demand higher nominal wages. Insofar as companies react to nominal increases in labour costs by raising product prices, the inflation that was initially expected is produced. The resulting vicious cycle, which is capable of sustaining permanently high levels of inflation, is also known as the 'wage-price spiral'. The combined forces of nominal wage increases, a raising price level, and increasing inflation expectations, as depicted in Fig. 7.3, can make it increasingly harder to return to a monetary policy dedicated to price stability.

In sum, monetary policy, prices, and unemployment have complex inter-relationships with beliefs about future inflation. Although this complexity has long been recognised, only after the replacement of the essentially static

Fig. 7.3 The wage-price spiral

IS/LM model (see Sect. 6.3) with dynamic macroeconomic models did the role of expectations or the implications of current decisions for future outcomes move to the forefront of economic analysis. This so-called 'Lucasian Revolution', named after the American economist Robert Lucas, who was probably the most important developer of this research programme during the 1970s, has dramatically increased the level of mathematics used in macroeconomic analysis, which has therefore become even further detached from ordinary economic-policy debates. To nevertheless convey the insights of dynamic macroeconomics to a broader audience, central bankers and monetary economists typically resort to verbal explanations or catchy comparisons. For example, to explain the self-reinforcing nature of a growing price level, a former president of the German Bundesbank once said.

> Inflation is like toothpaste. Once it's out, you can hardly get it back in again. So the best thing is not to squeeze too hard on the tube. (Pöhl, Karl Otto, *Institutional Investor*, 1/1980.)

The American economist Robert Solow asked. 'Why is our money ever less valuable?' His answer alluded to the sinister role of expectations. 'Perhaps it is simply that we have inflation because we expect inflation, and we expect inflation because we've had it.'[7] The capacity of human beings to catch up to a changing monetary environment and, hence, not be constantly fooled into expecting low levels of inflation is wonderfully illustrated by the Swedish economist Knut Wicksell with the following comparison.

> Those people who prefer a continually upward moving to a stationary price level forcibly remind one of those who purposely keep their watches a little fast so as to be more certain of catching their trains. But to achieve their purpose they must not be conscious or remain conscious of the fact that their watches are fast; otherwise they become accustomed to take the extra few minutes into account and so after all, in spite of their artfulness, arrive too late. (Wicksell, Knut, 1936: *Interest and Prices: A study in the causes regulating the value of money*, McMillan and Co., pp. 3–4.)

Against this background, it is certainly not surprising that, after the 1970s, economists have begun to pay more attention to the role of expectations. From this discussion, a new version of the Phillips-curve has emerged which accounts for potential changes in beliefs about future inflation. As illustrated by the

---

[7]Solow, Robert, 1979: *Technology Review* (December/January 1979, p. 31).

bottom part of Fig. 7.2, a policy of cheap money boosts not only inflation but, sooner or later, also the corresponding expectations, which destabilises the relationship between inflation and unemployment. More specifically, the relationship encapsulated in the Phillips-curve eventually shifts outwards, with the unpalatable result of a permanently higher level of inflation. In other words, a reckless monetary policy to foster employment can get ahead of itself, so to speak, when it ends up worsening the trade-off between inflation and unemployment. US data across several decades as shown in Fig. 7.2 indeed illustrate that the countervailing relationship postulated by the Phillips-curve holds only across certain periods and, hence, cannot be permanently exploited.

Taken together, whether a monetary authority can maintain price stability depends crucially on whether the public believes that inflation will be kept low. In other words, as illustrated by the red dot in Fig. 7.2, it is the task of a modern central bank to set a 'nominal anchor' for the value of money. However, to anchor inflation expectations, the public must be convinced that it is indeed the overriding goal of monetary policy to safeguard the purchasing power of the currency. In this regard, a central-bank mandate emphasising the strategic goal of price stability can be helpful. Furthermore, it is also helpful when this mandate is broadly supported, and when the level of inflation thought to be compatible with price stability is clearly defined. Unlike in a commodity-money system, keeping the inflation expectation under control poses a major challenge in a fiat-money system. In a sense, the nominal anchor, which is supposed to maintain the expectation of low and stable levels of inflation, has replaced the natural constraints that existed when currencies were convertible into a fixed quantity of precious metal (gold or silver).

How is this discussion related to central-bank independence? The key issue is that the value of fiat money cannot be firmly anchored merely by promising low inflation. Owing to the interdependencies between inflation and inflation expectations, the public must also be convinced that this promise will be kept. However, a credibility issue arises. It is exactly when inflation expectations are low when it is most tempting to exploit this benign situation by loosening monetary policy. After all, in such a scenario, it seems possible to create jobs by stimulating aggregate spending at virtually no cost (inflation remains low, because the corresponding expectations are low). Of course, this scenario is too good to be true in the sense that such monetary policy suffers from the drawbacks of any kind of opportunistic behaviour. In particular, announcing low inflation expectations is inconsistent with pursuing a policy of cheap money. Nevertheless, when, for example, an election is around the corner, it is unpopular to raise interest rates, which might be necessary to tame inflation but also temporarily reduces economic activity. Central-bank independence is seen as a solution to this problem by orienting monetary policy toward strategic goals rather than short-term temptations. Then again, only by giving due weight to long-term considerations, such as the neutrality property of money, can central banks build a reputation to keep inflation and the corresponding expectations under control. Against this background, it should be evident that relatively long terms of office which do not overlap with elections, and legally enshrined rules preventing the government from influencing or even overturning monetary-policy decisions are key elements of central-bank independence.[8]

Central-bank independence gives, of course, rise to accountability issues. Throughout its history, central banking has indeed moved from a rather opaque world of privately organised institutions linking the currency to some monetary metal, to more publicly oriented authorities pursuing broad economic goals, such as maintaining price stability. Thus, it has likely become more important to inform the public as to why certain decisions have been made. Under ideal circumstances, a better understanding of monetary policy should also help the public form low inflation expectations. In this regard, challenges arise when, for whatever reason, inflation has spiralled out of control, implying, as illustrated by the bottom panel of Fig. 7.2, that the Phillips-curve needs to be shifted downwards. However, such nominal re-anchoring typically warrants a temporary tightening of monetary policy, which is associated with upsurges in interest-rate levels and unemployment. In a schematic manner, the bottom part of Fig. 6.5 depicts such a 'stabilisation crisis'. The hooked arrow of Fig. 7.2 shows the same relationship by means of the Phillips-curve.[9] Then again, considerable independence from daily politics might be helpful when a central bank has to take unpopular decisions entailing

---

[8]Expectations and credibility issues arise in several economic-policy areas. In macroeconomic textbooks, the corresponding discussion appears under the somewhat clumsy expression of the 'time-inconsistency problem'. For example, before making an investment, firms must also be confident that fiscal and tax policies remain sufficiently stable. However, a credibility problem might arise, because a successful fiscal policy with a modest and stable tax burden offers the greatest scope for opportunistic behaviour such as surprisingly imposing addition taxes on profits from past investments. Then again, such tricks no longer work when firms learn their lessons and react by not investing in the first place. Thus, by avoiding bad outcomes, principles-based approaches to economic policy can be valuable.

[9]The temporary increase in unemployment (in percentage points) that is necessary to lower inflation permanently by one percentage point is called the 'sacrifice ratio'. Depending on the exact circumstances, the value of this ratio has varied considerably. However, rough estimates suggest that typical sacrifice ratios fall in between two and six, that is, unemployment must temporarily climb by around two to six percentage points to permanently reduce inflation by one percentage point (see Ball, Laurence, 1994: What determines the sacrifice ratio, in: Mankiw, N. Gregory, *Monetary Policy*, Chicago University Press, pp. 153–193).

a period of economic misery to achieve the sustainable benefits associated with lower inflation expectations.

7.4   What Are the Limitations of Monetary Policy?

To summarise this chapter and the previous chapter, Fig. 7.4 provides an overview of the possibilities and limitations of central banks to affect broad economic outcomes. In particular, the ways in which monetary policy can travel along the sides of the depicted triangle and impact nominal variables, such as the average price level, as well as real variables, such as employment, are discussed in Chap. 6. The key concepts are the neutrality of money which implies a close long-term connection between money and inflation, and the transmission mechanism which implies that monetary impulses temporarily impact aggregate spending and, in turn, real economic activity.

This chapter has raised several caveats regarding the capacity of central banks to manage broad economic developments. In particular, as depicted in the bottom of Fig. 7.4, the broad effects of money are subject to well-known policy conflicts between, for example, inflation and unemployment. Above all, owing to the unstable behaviour of inflation expectations, it is impossible to permanently exploit the corresponding trade-offs. Other perils arise from political opportunism, which inconspicuously shifts the focus of monetary

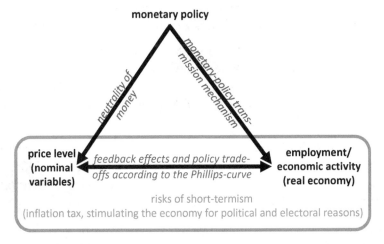

Fig. 7.4   Synoptic overview of the effects of monetary policy

policy towards short-term goals, such as maximising employment, financing public debt, and directly funding public projects. However, pursuing such fiscal or electoral motives warrants a loose monetary policy with relatively low interest rates, which may have instantaneous benefits, but creates long-term collateral damage by generating unnecessarily high levels of inflation and entrenched doubts regarding the future purchasing power of the currency.

Taken together, there are good reasons to make sure that the central bank never loses sight of the long-term effects of monetary policy. Over the last few decades, central-bank independence has turned out to be a successful institutional ingredient to uphold the kind of monetary-policy stance, which is necessary to maintain price stability. However, in a system with fiat money, a large degree of central-bank independence raises a tricky follow up question. Who guards the guardians of the currency? Voters are probably only willing to tolerate the delegation of key monetary-policy responsibilities to a body of unelected technocrats when this arrangement indeed results in stable monetary conditions.

Further Reading

The macroeconomic relationships among money, the average price level, and economic activity are discussed in every introductory textbook on macroeconomics. A popular example is Mankiw, N. Gregory, 2015: *Macroeconomics*, Macmillan Learning, Ch. 14 and 18.

A well-written chapter on central bank independence can be found in Blinder, Alan, 1998: *Central Banking in Theory and Practice*, The MIT Press, Ch. 3.

For a discussion on central-bank mandates and independence see Fischer, Stanley, Modern central banking. In: Capie, Forrest, Charles Goodhart, Stanley Fischer, and Norbert Schnadt, 1994: *The Future of Central Banking - The Tercentenary Symposium of the Bank of England*. Cambridge University Press.

A nontechnical discussion and a list of key references on the time-inconsistency problem in monetary policy can be found in Taylor, Herb, 1985: Time inconsistency: A potential problem for policymakers, *Federal Reserve Bank of Philadelphia Business Review*, pp. 3–12.

At the advanced level, a thorough but still concise treatment of the complex interrelationship between monetary policy and inflation can be found in Romer, David, 2012: *Advanced Macroeconomics*, McGraw-Hill, Ch. 11.

A monograph dedicated to macroeconomic models of monetary policy, inflation, and the business cycle is Gali, Jordi, 2015: *Monetary Policy, Inflation and the Business Cycle - An introduction to the New Keynesian Framework*, Princeton University Press.

8

International Monetary Policy

So much barbarism, however, still remains in the transactions of most civilised
nations, that almost all independent countries choose to assert their nationality
by having, to their inconvenience and that of their neighbours, a peculiar
currency of their own. John Stuart Mill (British economist, 1806–1873)[1]

8.1 The International Financial System

Large volumes of cross-border transactions and highly interrelated financial
systems are potent symbols of economic globalisation. As such, international
payments are not a recent phenomenon but rather have existed since ancient
societies began to trade goods over long distances, which required some
kind of settlement in the form of an exchange between local and foreign
money.[2] However, large-scale international monetary and capital flows, which
have by far outgrown the volume of trade in goods and services, represent a more recent phenomenon.[3] An increasingly internationalised financial

---

[1]Mill, John Stuart, 1848: *Principles of Political Economy*, John W. Parker, p. 414.

[2]For a more extensive discussion of the joint development of international trade and finance see
Baltensperger, Ernst, and Nils Herger, 2010: The nexus between trade and finance, in: Cottier, Thomas
and Panagiotis Delimatsis, *The Prospects of International Trade Regulation - From Fragmentation to
Coherence*, Cambridge University Press.

[3]The globalisation of the financial system occurred in two waves, with a first peak reached during the
classical gold standard around 1900. Two world wars, the Great Depression, and the Cold War resulted
in a relative downturn in international financial activity during most of the twentieth century. A second
peak in global integration of the financial system was reached before the outbreak of the Global Financial

© Springer Nature Switzerland AG 2019
N. Herger, *Understanding Central Banks*, https://doi.org/10.1007/978-3-030-05162-4_8

system has manifested itself not only in growing volumes of foreign direct investment, through which multinational firms establish affiliate production and distribution networks abroad, but also in an improved access to foreign securities, through which investors can earn financial returns outside of their national constituencies and better diversify their portfolios.[4] Finally, since the collapse of the Bretton Woods System, the desire to speculate on foreign-exchange markets to exploit international differences in asset returns has provided another impetus for the growth in global capital flows. Altogether, the current international financial system comprises a set of closely interrelated markets providing commercial banks, nonbank financial firms, internationally operating companies, governments, and, last but not least, central banks with a forum to trade large amounts of money, capital, and other assets denominated in different currencies. By and large, trading and the associated activities take place within a network of financial centres (including London, New York, Tokyo, Hong Kong, Singapore, Frankfurt, and Zurich), which are connected via advanced communication and information-technology systems that provide the physical setup for the global payment system and the financial-market infrastructure.

To this day, most countries have continued to 'assert their nationality by having a peculiar currency of their own'. However, although it is tempting to lament this situation, it should not be overlooked that the organisation of the international monetary system touches on several policy conflicts which are comparable to the far-reaching issues that arose regarding the specification of the mandate of the central bank or its degree of independence. One such issue is whether the exchange rate, that is, the external price of a currency, should be allowed to move freely to meet the demand and supply on the foreign-exchange market, or should be managed, or even be fixed, by the central bank? Other questions include whether countries want to impose restrictions on the international flow of capital, or have their own currency? These are only some of the questions addressed by international monetary policy, which refers to all measures and institutional arrangements affecting

---

Crisis in 2008. See Obstfeld, Maurice, and Allan M. Taylor, 2004: *Global Capital Markets - Integration, Crisis, and Growth*, Cambridge University Press.

[4]Data about cross-border transactions are reported in the balance of payments of a given country. The balance of payments distinguishes transactions involving the exchange of goods, services, and factor income (which are summarised in the so-called 'current account') and transactions resulting from financial settlements and investments (which are summarised in the so-called 'financial account'). Good introductions to the balance of payments can be found in chapter 2 of Harms, Philipp, 2016: *International Macroeconomics*, Mohr-Siebeck, and in chapter 13 of Krugman, Paul, Maurice Obstfeld, and Marc Melitz, 2018: *International Economics—Theory and Policy*, Pearson.

a currency beyond its national borders. Despite the long history of the debate, as illustrated by the introductory quote, the corresponding issues have not resolved, which bears witness to the entrenched trade-offs between internal (domestic price, financial, and output stability) and the corresponding external monetary-policy goals, including exchange-rate (or external-price) stability, a stable international monetary system (external financial stability), and sustainable levels of imports and exports (external output stability). In this regard, the design of the exchange-rate regime imposes important limitations on the conduct of monetary policy by a given central bank. Against this background, the connections between the national and international aspects of various currency systems, the advantages and disadvantages of different foreign-exchange regimes, the role of international reserves, and the benefits and costs of common currencies are some of the topics discussed in this chapter.

8.2   You Cannot Have It All: The Trilemma of International Finance

The thorny conflicts between internal and external goals pose, perhaps, the biggest challenge to designing a suitable international monetary framework. It has become popular to discuss the corresponding constraints by means of the trilemma of international finance, which is illustrated in Fig. 8.1 by a triangle

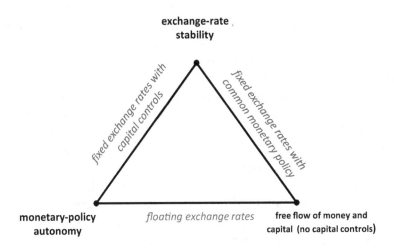

Fig. 8.1 Constraints in international monetary policy. The trilemma of international finance

whose corners represent three desirable properties of the monetary system. First, stable exchange rates offer clear advantages. Because several months can pass between the delivery and payment of merchandise goods, erratic exchange-rate fluctuations are widely seen as an impediment to international business, as well as to investments in foreign assets, which may yield a return only after several years and, hence, are subject to the uncertainty regarding the future rate at which currencies can be exchanged. Taken together, unstable exchange rates undermine international trade and finance and typically result in a lack of global economic integration (to understand why a lack of global economic integration poses a problem, consider how many goods you have recently consumed that were produced abroad). Second, an autonomous monetary policy focusing on internal goals might be useful, insofar as the corresponding central-bank interventions help to maintain domestic price, financial, or output stability. In this case, it can be useful to pursue a monetary policy tailored to domestic conditions. Third, free capital flows have several advantages. Clearly, a sufficiently free exchange of money and capital across borders is a precondition for settling transactions that involve foreign goods and services. Furthermore, open money and capital markets expand the investment opportunities and allow financial risks to be spread across a larger number of assets. Small countries, in particular, face substantial constraints when foreign capital is unavailable for domestic investments.

The main message of Fig. 8.1 is that no monetary system can simultaneously fulfil the three desirable properties mentioned in the previous paragraph. Instead, depending on the choice of exchange-rate regime, a central bank must sacrifice one internal or external policy goal. To understand the rationale, first consider a system with freely floating exchange rates, which, according to Sect. 2.6, has been the norm for the most important currencies around the world since the collapse of the Bretton Woods System. As represented by the triangle's base, major restrictions arising from foreign monetary-policy spill overs or from impediments to international capital flows are absent, when exchange rates float freely. Drawbacks of preserving monetary policy flexibility and the freedom to invest abroad arise, of course, in the form of potentially large fluctuations on the foreign-exchange market (see Fig. 2.8).

Erratic fluctuations can simply be eliminated by fixing the exchange rate. However, doing so typically warrants foreign-exchange interventions, which go hand in hand with a loss of monetary-policy autonomy. In particular, a central bank committed to fix the exchange rate at some predefined level can no longer freely adjust domestic interest rates. To understand this idea, consider a central bank, which increases domestic interest rates above the foreign level. Investing in assets denominated in the domestic currency therefore becomes very attractive. The prospect of high returns, in turn, results in large capital inflows. However, this outcome is incompatible with a fixed exchange rate, because an ongoing high demand for the home currency eventually leads to an appreciation (or a strengthening) of the exchange rate. Of course, the converse situation arises when domestic interest rates are relatively low. To overcome attempts of interest arbitrage—that is, the exploitation of international differences in interest rates—countries sharing a fixed exchange rate must choose similar interest-rate levels and, hence, pursue similar monetary policies.[5] Thus, as illustrated by the right leg of the triangle in Fig. 8.1, countries with fixed exchange rates typically give up monetary-policy autonomy (represented in the example above by the freedom to set a base interest rate).

Restricting the free flow of money and capital across borders, by imposing so-called 'capital controls', is another way to defeat interest arbitrage. As long as fees, quotas, or other government restrictions regulate cross-border trans-actions, currency speculators lack the freedom to move capital across borders and, hence, an instrument to exploit interest-rate differences between curren-cies. By imposing capital controls, fixed exchange rates can be combined with monetary-policy autonomy. The left leg of the triangle showing the trilemma of international finance depicts this scenario. Of course, an international mon-etary system that combines fixed exchange rates with capital controls sacrifices most of the benefits of an internationally integrated financial system. Although this sacrifice may not seem to be important, limitations on international payments narrow investment opportunities and restrict possibilities to manage financial risks. Furthermore, only providing local households and firms with access to domestic capital constitutes a financial form of protectionism, which creates the usual adverse effects. For example, domestic banks might welcome the repression of foreign competition insofar as they can impose higher interest rates on bank loans. Another practical, and often overlooked, problem with capital controls is red tape from enforcing rules and restrictions including

---

[5]In contrast to purchasing-power parity, which is discussed in footnote 16 of Chap. 6, interest arbitrage is closely associated with the short-term movement of the exchange rate. In the simplest case, the corresponding formula equilibrates the returns to a domestic and foreign asset, that is,

$$\underbrace{\text{domestic interest rate}}_{\text{return on domestic assets}} \approx \underbrace{\text{foreign interest rate} + \text{exchange rate change}}_{\text{return on foreign assets}}.$$

With floating exchange rates, domestic and foreign interest rates can deviate from each other, as the corresponding discrepancy can be offset by subsequent exchange-rate changes. Conversely, under a credible fixed exchange rate, no exchange-rate changes can occur. Hence, the domestic interest rate must equal the foreign interest rate.

paper trails, outsized bureaucracies, and possibilities for self-enrichment. To regulate cross-border flows of money and capital, governments typically establish a network of foreign-exchange branches (typically under the auspices of the central bank), where international financial transactions can officially take place. However, in practice, the exchange of currencies subject to capital controls also partly occurs on unofficial markets. In a world with a freely convertible currency, this practice may seem odd. However, especially within modern financial systems, it has become almost impossible to fully control international transactions and, hence, to permanently and successfully enforce capital controls without inviting some form of black-market activity. It is therefore, perhaps, not surprising that many capital controls can sooner or later be circumvented.[6]

8.3   Fixed and Floating Exchange-Rate Regimes

Perhaps, the most important task of the international monetary system is providing pecuniary links between the domestic economy and the wider world. Owing to changes in the composition of international trade, the growth and subsequent decline of exporting firms and even entire industries, and demographic developments, a country's relationship with foreign economies is typically subject to an ongoing adjustment process. The corresponding monetary side is manifested in cross-border flows of cash, capital, and financial securities denominated in different currencies. In particular, a net inflow of money and capital implies that a country's currency is in high demand, which usually results in a price increase, or a 'nominal appreciation', of the domestic currency. The opposite effect results in a depreciation, or a relative decline in the value of the domestic currency, relative to foreign currencies. Because such appreciations and depreciations transmit monetary policy into the domestic

---

[6]An example of the creative responses to capital controls is the historical development of the so called 'euromarkets' (which refer to certain offshore markets and have nothing to do with the common European currency, the euro). Euromarkets encompass bank deposits and other assets that are not denominated in the currency of the local financial centre. For example, dollar deposits held outside the US are called 'eurodollars'. The creation of eurocurrency provided a clever way to avoid the capital controls and strict US banking regulations during the era of the Bretton Woods System. However, since the development of euromarkets, globally important currencies, such as the US dollar, can be traded at almost anytime somewhere around the world. Oddly, Soviet Bloc banks were among the keenest holders of eurodollars, which were useful for financing imports from Western countries and provided a certain degree of protection against a US confiscation in a time of crisis. Ironically, the former planned economies have inconspicuously fostered the worldwide integration of the foreign-exchange markets, which have turned into the most capitalistic markets the world has ever seen.

economy via the exchange-rate channel (see Sect. 6.3), the exchange rate represents a key economic variable.

A central bank can let the interaction between private demand and supply determine the exchange rate, or can become active on the foreign-exchange market to influence the relative prices of the domestic and foreign currency. In principle, standard monetary-policy instruments affecting the level of interest rates can be used to impact the foreign-exchange market insofar as, for example, relatively high domestic asset returns tend to attract foreign money and capital resulting in an appreciation. Clearly, foreign-exchange interventions, that is, purchases and sales of domestic and foreign currency by the central bank, provide a suitable instrument for directly influencing the exchange rate (see Sect. 4.5). Depending on the exchange-rate regime, central banks intervene more or less regularly in the foreign-exchange market. In particular, to enforce a fixed exchange rate, the central bank must stand ready to trade its own currency against a foreign anchor currency at a preannounced price. In this scenario, foreign-exchange interventions typically occur on a regular basis to keep the exchange rate at the official parity.

Owing to the above-mentioned caveats related to capital-control enforcements, the arrangement of the international monetary system deals primarily with the question as to whether the exchange rate should be more or less freely floating to preserve monetary-policy flexibility, or the central bank should give up monetary-policy autonomy in exchange for a more stable exchange rate.[7] However, it would be wrong to believe that there are only two, fundamentally opposed, exchange-rate regimes. As summarised in Table 8.1, a whole range of regimes exists. Moreover, a pure free-floating regime represents a theoretical ideal, which has never existed and probably will never exist outside economic textbooks. Even if the demand and supply on the foreign-exchange market had always determined the price of foreign currency, central banks retain the option to undertake sporadic foreign-exchange interventions, and consider the international effects of specific monetary-policy decisions. Every exchange rate is managed to some degree by reflecting the overall monetary conditions set by the central bank. Likewise, at the opposite end of the spectrum, no exchange rate can be unconditionally fixed (or pegged) forever. Aside from the practical detail of foreign-exchange trading giving rise to small

---

[7]Of course, examples of capital controls still exist. However, in developed countries, capital controls are typically only used to prevent capital flight in times of severe financial turmoil. Recent examples include Iceland during the Global Financial Crisis and Cyprus during the European Debt Crisis. Furthermore, capital controls are still widely used in emerging markets and developing countries. However, the corresponding countries often lack sophisticated financial systems that are closely integrated with the international money and capital market, which facilitates the enforcement of capital controls.

Table 8.1 Exchange-rate regimes (ranked according to a decrease in flexibility and increase in control over the exchanges rate)

Exchange-rate regime	Brief description	Examples
Floating exchange rate	The exchange rate is freely determined by private demand and supply on the foreign-exchange market	Rather a theoretical ideal that has never been implemented in practice
Managed floating	In principle, the exchange rate is determined by private demand and supply on the foreign-exchange market. However, sporadic foreign-exchange interventions by the central bank are possible	USA
Target zone	The exchange rate can move freely within a band (target zone). At the edge of the band, the central bank is supposed to intervene in the foreign-exchange market	European Monetary System
Adjustable peg	The exchange rate is fixed, but can be adjusted according to some predefined process	Bretton Woods System
Fixed exchange rate	The exchange rate is fixed and adjustments should not happen	Gold standard
Currency board	A country's currency is completely backed with an anchor currency to which a fixed rate is defined	Hong Kong (anchor US dollar); Bulgaria (euro)
Currency union with common monetary policy	Several countries share a common currency and a common central bank	Members of the euro area

deviations from the official parity (Fig. 2.2 illustrates this relationship for the gold standard), central banks always retain the option to devalue or revalue (i.e. realign the fixed exchange rate to weaken or strengthen the domestic currency, respectively). Indeed, the historical experiences with the gold standard, the Bretton Woods System, and with the European Monetary System suggest that major shifts in the international economic and political environment can undermine any currency peg. Historically, most fixed exchange rates have eventually undergone a currency crisis, which typically arises when a country's international reserves are being depleted. It is obviously easier to avoid such crises when each domestic currency unit is fully backed by the anchor currency, in terms of which the parity is defined. In the central bank's balance sheet of Fig. 4.1, this so-called 'currency board' manifests itself in an asset-side, which includes mainly one position, namely, international reserves. Like this, the central bank finds itself in a position to trade an arbitrary amount of anchor currency against its own monetary unit, which gives a fixed exchange-rate regime a high degree of credibility. An even more radical situation occurs when a country abandons its own currency to become a member of a currency union. In this case, the member states have no longer the option to devalue or revalue their own currencies. Section 8.7 includes a detailed discussion of common currencies.

Mixed regimes combining elements of fixed and floating exchange rates are quite common and include target zones and adjustable currency pegs. Under a target zone, the exchange rate can move freely within a specified band, which is typically defined in terms of a percentage deviation from an official parity. For example, within the European Monetary System, deviations from the targeted central rates of up to $\pm 2.25\%$ were tolerated (see Sect. 2.7), and central banks were only obliged to intervene in the foreign-exchange market to prevent the exchange rate from moving outside the band. Of course, it is also possible to define a one-sided band, such as an exchange-rate floor or ceiling. The characteristic feature of an adjustable peg is that realignments of the exchange-rate parity are an inherent feature of the regime. Perhaps, the most famous example is the Bretton Woods System, under which realignments could be made in consultation with the IMF to correct a fundamental disequilibrium in the balance of payments. However, the corresponding experiences were rather disappointing. Although realignments were possible, the Bretton Woods System did not prevent countries from building up substantial economic disequilibria, which led to the destruction of the system in the 1970s (see Sect. 2.5).

Table 8.1 lists some well-known examples of each exchange-rate regime. Of course, countries can, and regularly do, reorganise their exchange-rate regimes. Movements from and to regimes with fixed and floating exchange rates are a hallmark of monetary history. For example, many European countries have recently made the transition from a target zone or currency board towards membership in the euro area.[8]

What are the advantages and disadvantages of fixed and floating exchange-rate regimes? As suggested by the discussion of the trilemma of international finance, floating exchange rates give monetary policy freedom to pursue internal goals. In essence, the central bank does not have to consider the effect of changes in, for example, the base interest rate on the exchange rate, but rather can freely employ monetary-policy instruments to tame inflation at home

---

[8]A more refined and regularly updated classification of countries according to their exchange-rate regimes can be found in the IMF's *Annual Report on Exchange Arrangements and Exchange Restrictions.*

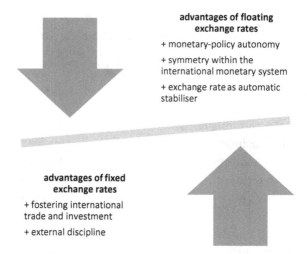

**advantages of floating
exchange rates**

+ monetary-policy autonomy

+ symmetry within the
international monetary system

+ exchange rate as automatic
stabiliser

**advantages of fixed
exchange rates**

+ fostering international
trade and investment

+ external discipline

Fig. 8.2 Advantages and disadvantages of floating and fixed exchange rates

or stimulate domestic employment. Furthermore, regarding the arrangement of the international monetary system, floating exchange rates also exhibit a certain symmetry in the sense that no country occupies a central position by providing the nominal anchor, with respect to which currency pegs are defined.[9] Hence, political tensions, such as those resulting from the 'exorbitant privilege' of the US dollar under the Bretton Woods System, can be avoided (see Sect. 2.5). Finally, floating exchanges rates can absorb economic shocks in an instantaneous manner and, hence, provide a stabilising effect on the domestic economy. A case in point is severe recessions, which typically lower the demand for imports, and, hence, that for foreign exchange. The result is a depreciation of the domestic currency. At the same time, this depreciation boosts economic activity in the export sector and, thus, contributes to the country's economic recovery. In other words, by cushioning the recession without taking economic-policy measures, the exchange rate adopts the role of an automatic stabiliser. The upper part of Fig. 8.2 summarises the key advantages of a floating exchange-rate regime. Of course, they are also the disadvantages of fixed exchange rates, which suffer from a lack of monetary-policy autonomy, asymmetries within the international monetary system, and the lack of an adjustable exchange rate as an automatic stabiliser.

---

[9]The theoretical reason that a country can adopt a privileged position within a fixed exchange-rate regime is that, among n currencies, only $n - 1$ exchange rates are defined. The last, or nth, currency is free, and the monetary policy of the corresponding country is not subject to international obligations to enforce an exchange-rate peg.

The bottom part of Fig. 8.2 lists the advantages of fixed exchange rates (which, in turn, constitute the disadvantages of a floating exchange-rate regime). Recall from the trilemma of international finance that international business benefits from eliminating exchange-rate risk. Indeed, low uncertainty as regards future exchange-rate movements fosters international trade and finance and, hence, promotes cross-border economic integration. Of course, this advantage only arises when a fixed exchange rate is credible (see Sect. 8.6 below). Furthermore, currency pegs can impose discipline on a central bank, because their enforcement is typically incompatible with a massive money and credit expansion. Imposing external discipline can be very useful when a central bank lacks the reputation to tame inflation. Then, pegging the domestic currency to a stable foreign currency, in particular when organised around a currency board, can send a strong signal to lower inflation expectations.

Due to the many trade-offs between these advantages and disadvantages of the various exchange-rate regimes, the corresponding choice has far-reaching implications regarding the flexibility and power of a country's monetary authority. Reflecting the move towards greater central-bank independence, most large and developed countries have adopted floating exchange rates. However, fixed-exchange rate regimes were the norm before the 1970s. Even today, various forms of pegged currencies have remained popular with small open economies and developing countries. When, due to large trading volumes and similar economic backgrounds, the business cycle is synchronised between closely integrated countries, the lack of an autonomous monetary policy is not a big deal. Indeed, small countries often favour a fixed exchange rate, because they would regardless pursue a monetary policy that is similar to that of their larger neighbour. Moreover, the economic conditions of developing countries often depend on commodity exports, such as oil, mineral resources, or agricultural products, which are typically traded in US dollars. Hence, a dollar peg can dampen the impact of volatile commodity prices on the domestic economy. Finally, the discipline and simplification of importing a foreign monetary policy can also be a key consideration for adopting a fixed exchange rate.

8.4   The Role of International Reserves

Foreign-exchange interventions entail transactions between domestic and foreign currencies made by the central bank (see Sect. 4.5). These interventions alter the stock of foreign assets on the central bank's balance sheet, which are also called (official) international reserves (see Fig. 4.1).[10] In particular, a purchase of foreign against domestic currency by the central bank increases its international-reserves position. Conversely, to support the domestic currency, the sale of foreign currency is warranted, resulting in a decrease in the international-reserves position.

To this day, there is a widely held belief that international reserves represent an outstanding form of national wealth. If this belief were true, however, the stockpiling of foreign assets would be an important monetary-policy goal, and a loss of international reserves would be a worrying sign of economic decline. Despite the long tradition of turning the amount of international reserves into a matter of national prestige, the corresponding views suffer from several well-known flaws. The debate on this issue can be traced to at least the seventeenth century, that is, to the era of absolutism, in which economic questions were usually analysed within the framework of mercantilist theories. In France, the corresponding policies were most developed under Jean-Baptiste Colbert (1619–1683), who was finance minister and wielded great influence during the reign of Louis XIV. In general, mercantilism touched on a large number of economic and social issues. However, for monetary economics, the accumulation of international reserves was thought to be of pivotal importance. At a time of metallic currency systems, this principle essentially implied that countries should try to attract as much gold and silver as possible. To increase the domestic stock of precious metals, a trade surplus was of course warranted; only when a country's exports exceeded its imports could it receive more payments in the form of metallic currency than it had to make to the rest of the world. Following the monarch's absolute claim to authority, under a mercantilist system, rigid government interventions in cross-border economic transactions were deemed necessary to push a country towards a trade surplus and, hence, to expand its international power. In particular, as illustrated in a stylised manner by Fig. 8.3, the export of finished products was promoted, whereas their import was suppressed through tariffs and other protectionist measures. In contrast, low-value commodities could be freely imported, whereas their export was subject to government-imposed constraints.

Early classical economic thought was essentially a response to mercantilism and gave rise to convincing arguments as to why the 'wealth of nations'—to

---

[10]The definition of 'international reserves' is slightly broader than that of 'foreign-exchange (or forex or FX) reserves'. The latter includes only foreign banknotes and assets, such as government bonds and money-market paper, that are denominated in foreign currency. In addition, the former includes, for example, gold reserves, and special drawing rights (SDRs) issued by the International Monetary Fund (IMF).

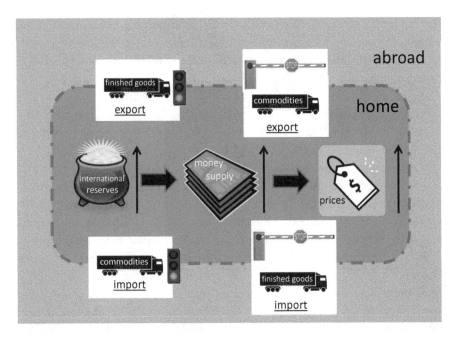

Fig. 8.3 The mechanism of mercantilism

quote the title of a comprehensive critique by Adam Smith (1723–1790)—is neither increased through international-trade restrictions nor reflected by the holdings of gold or other forms of international reserves. Rather, protectionism in trade and finance typically undermines economic development. Regarding the official management of international trade, a problem arises, because not all countries can simultaneously achieve a surplus of exports over imports. Absent trade with aliens from Mars, for example, the global economy is a closed system, meaning that every export surplus must somewhere be matched by an equivalent import surplus. Furthermore, and probably more importantly, free trade does not just benefit countries which manage to export many goods and services. The advantages of free trade are more comprehensive and include the efficiency gains resulting from an international division of labour, the specialisation of countries in relatively productive industries, faster technology transfers, and access to a much broader range of products than a closed economy could ever produce.[11] By developing the theory of 'comparative advantage', British economist David Ricardo (1772–1823), above all, has demonstrated that even relatively poor countries without

---

[11]A brief discussion on popular misconceptions regarding international trade can be found in Krugman, Paul, 1993: What do undergraduates need to know about trade?, *American Economic Review*, pp. 23–26.

sophisticated industries can benefit from international trade and finance. Instead of providing a lengthy theoretical discussion, I quote the memorable words of Benjamin Franklin (1706–1790), one of the founding fathers of the United States, that 'no nation was ever ruined by trade, even seemingly the most disadvantageous'.[12] This statement has remained true until this day. Note that during Benjamin Franklin's lifetime, the United States had not yet reached the status of an economic superpower, but rather were a relatively backward agricultural country.

In the context of international trade, it is undesirable to keep accumulating international reserves, because exports are not good per se, but rather are only valuable insofar as they can be exchanged for current or future imports, which expand the consumption possibilities of the local population. In the very long-term, exports to the world must be counterbalanced by corresponding imports from the world. Of course, international reserves, and in general also other forms of foreign wealth, allow a country to sustain trade surpluses across many years or even decades. An export surplus typically results in the export of capital, which simply establishes a claim on future imports of goods and services. These claims may be very useful to offset the effects of future recessions or deal with an aging population. However, a country that hoards foreign assets (including international reserves) also exposes itself to defaults when foreign debtors are no longer able or willing to fulfil their financial obligations. Because countries generate exports to finance imports and because of the long-term correspondence between trade outflows and inflows, it is not sensible to stockpile arbitrarily large amounts of international reserves.

In the context of international finance, an unconditional quest for international reserves also has monetary side-effects by impacting the money supply which could, in turn, initiate an economic adjustment process undermining the desired increase in, for example, holdings of gold. The corresponding connection was previously observed by the Scottish scholar David Hume (1711–1776). His 'price-specie-flow mechanism' suggests indeed that the fear of losing international reserves might be overblown, and the following famous thought-experiment illustrates the key insight:

> Suppose four-fifths of all the money [...] to be annihilated in one night, and the nation reduced to the same condition, with regard to specie, [...] what would be the consequence? Must not the price of all labour and commodities sink in proportion [...]? What nation could then dispute with us in any foreign market [...], which to us would afford sufficient profit? In how little time, therefore,

---

[12] This quote appears in a pamphlet on the 'principles of trade' published in 1774.

must this bring back the money which we had lost, and raise us to the level of all the neighbouring nations? Where [...] we immediately lose the advantage of the cheapness of labour and commodities; and the farther flowing in of money is stopped [...].. (Hume, David, 1741: *Essays: Moral, Political, and Literary*.)

In a modern world with fiat money, similar mechanisms are at work. In particular, a massive increase in a country's international reserves does not necessarily enhance long-term welfare, because they can map to a corresponding expansion in the money supply and, eventually, an upsurge in inflation due to the neutrality property of money. The centre of Fig. 8.3 illustrates this relationship in a stylised manner. In the end, a policy geared towards the accumulation of international reserves may end up at an unstable price level, which will also affect the prices of exported goods and, hence, undermine a country's international competitiveness. Furthermore, high levels of domestic inflation make foreign goods relatively cheaper, which may result in increasing imports. Thus, the price-specie-flow type of mechanism eventually reverses the trade surplus, which originally stood behind the inflow of international reserves.

That the inconsistencies of mercantilism are not a mere economic phantasm is, perhaps, best illustrated by the rivalry between Spain and Britain to become the dominant global power between the sixteenth and eighteenth century. Initially, Spain was in the lead by gaining control over large parts of Central and South America. The colonies in what is today Latin America provided ample opportunities to extract large amounts of gold, as during the conquest of the Incan empire. However, rather than expanding Spain's economic power, the corresponding massive influx of gold and silver money into the Old World merely gave rise to the so-called 'price revolution', that is, a marked upsurge in inflation in Europe around 1600.[13] Conversely, 200 years later, it was the industrial revolution which expanded Britain's economic power and gave rise to unprecedented increases in welfare as well as dramatic reductions in poverty.

Taken together, the belief that international-reserve holdings are of paramount importance reflects, yet again, the mistake of confounding nominal, or monetary, values with real aspects of economic welfare. Recall that economic welfare ultimately depends on a country's productivity and, hence, the quality of its public and private infrastructure, the freedom of enterprise, whether entrepreneurs develop innovative ideas and technologies, and whether the political and legal system proliferates stable economic

---

[13] For a discussion of this example see Ferguson, Niall, 2009: *The Ascent of Money: A Financial History of the World*, Penguin Books, Ch. 2.

conditions. Conversely, international reserves represent a small aspect of the monetary framework, which primarily enhances welfare by maintaining the purchasing power of the currency and safeguarding a stable financial system.

The discussion thus far does not, however, imply that international reserves are completely irrelevant. First, in times of national crisis, they can be used as emergency funds to finance imports. Although private banks are today largely responsible for the provision of trade finance, and many companies even export on open accounts,[14] these methods of finance could be disrupted in case a severe international crisis, or even a war, breaks out. During such extreme events, perhaps, only the central bank remains to finance trade. From this angle, international-reserve holdings can be seen as a kind of insurance policy against international crises and conflicts. To quantify this notion, the amount of international reserves is typically expressed relative to the volume of imports, which indicates how long a country could sustain its demand for foreign goods without having normal access to the international-financial system. Second, and much more importantly in peace times, an adequate stock of international reserves is required when a country wishes to manage its exchange rate.

8.5   From International Reserves to International-Reserve Currencies

When shifting the focus from international reserves to the current section dealing, among other things, with international-reserve currencies, there are not only semantic connections. The term 'international-reserve currency' refers to a form of money that is widely held outside the borders of the issuing country. The terms 'international-transaction currency' and 'international-anchor currency' refer to further international functions of money. In particular, the degree of internationalisation depends on the extent to which a certain currency fulfils the functions of money across countries. An international-transaction currency is commonly used to settle cross-border trade and financial transactions. Furthermore, money's function as a unit of account can also have an international dimension. For example, at the centre of any fixed exchange-rate regime, a so-called 'anchor currency' is warranted to serve as point of reference with respect to which the official parities are defined. Although this issue is absent within a floating exchange-rate regime, it still

---

[14]A survey on the issues of trade finance can be found in Herger, Nils, 2011: Trade, Trade Finance, and Financial Crises, in: Delimatsis, Panagiotis, und Nils Herger, *Financial Regulation at the Crossroads*, Wolter Kluwer.

matters in which currency the prices of internationally traded goods, services, or commodities are denominated. Finally, as regards the function of store of value, an 'international-reserve currency' is commonly used by central banks to hold international reserves (of course, a currency can also be a popular means of savings for foreign households and companies). Currently, the prime example of a form of money with an international status is, of course, the US dollar, whereas the euro, the Japanese yen, sterling, the Swiss franc, and increasingly the Chinese yuan are of international importance.

Like the properties of money in general, the functions of international-transaction, anchor, and reserve currency are interdependent and tend to reinforce each other. For example, when a country, such as the United States with the dollar during the Bretton Woods System (see Sect. 2.5) and Germany with the mark during the European Monetary System (see Sect. 2.7), has officially or unofficially adopted the role of nominal anchor within a fixed exchange-rate system, the central banks of the participating countries are forced to hold substantial international-reserve positions of the corresponding currency. Otherwise, an official parity would be an empty commitment. Owing to these interdependencies, at any given point in time, typically only a small number of currencies achieve an internationally important status. Often, the currency of a global power dominates in international economic and financial affairs. For example, during the gold standard, sterling reigned supreme as the international-transaction and reserve currency (whereas gold adopted the role of nominal anchor and ultimate means of payment and reserve). At least since the establishment of the Bretton Woods System, the US dollar has replaced sterling as the leading currency, and has also retained this position after the worldwide transition toward floating exchange rates in the 1970s. In recent decades, the dollar was involved in around 80% of cross-border transactions and accounted for about half of the official international reserves held at central banks.[15] Even the Global Financial Crisis has not reversed the dollarisation of the global economy, although the increasing economic and political importance of emerging economies in general, and of China in particular, could challenge the dominant position of the United States in international monetary affairs at some point in the future.

---

[15] Data on the denominations of international-financial transactions can be found in the 'Triennial Central Bank Survey' of the Bank for International Settlements (BIS). The database 'Currency Composition of Official Foreign Exchange Reserves (COFER)' of the International Monetary Fund (IMF) provides a statistical account of the composition of international reserves.

Aside from functional interdependencies, other factors explain why only a handful of currencies are important within the global financial system. In general, the requirements on a currency to achieve an international status are high and, therefore, typically only a small number of countries meet all of them. Above all, a certain economic size and political as well as military clout are warranted to underpin international monetary ambitions. However, size alone is not enough. The United States have never accounted for more than 50% of worldwide economic output and this share has currently dropped below 20%. As mentioned above, the weight of the US dollar within the international financial system is far greater. Furthermore, during the last few decades, the Swiss Franc was among the five most important international currencies, even though Switzerland is not a large country. Conversely, the currencies of major powers, such as Russia and India, have, hitherto, never played a major role abroad, likely because of capital controls which imply that a currency is not freely convertible across borders and, hence, does not lend itself to being an international means of payment or store of value. Furthermore, a large and well-developed financial sector offering a wide range of financial products and sophisticated payment systems is warranted to underpin international-currency status. Finally, the quality and stability of the political and legal systems matter to ensure that financial claims are backed by property rights, which are easy to enforce when private contracting parties do not honour their financial obligations and, more importantly, provide safeguards against erratic government interventions aimed at expropriating financiers. Despite their increasing economic importance, many emerging countries still struggle with relatively high levels of corruption and suffer from malfunctioning political and legal authorities failing to protect financial claims. As a result, these countries' currencies are of relatively low quality. Taken together, economic prosperity, stable monetary and financial conditions, and trustworthy political and legal institutions foster the international status of a currency. By holding foreign exchange, foreign households and companies can, at least to some degree, take part in this stability.

Several benefits can be derived from the status of an international-transaction and reserve currency. In fiscal terms, foreigners holding large amounts of a given national currency contributes to a country's seigniorage revenue. Furthermore, a widely used currency reduces the costs and risks associated with trade finance as well as cross-border financial transactions when local companies can settle and invoice exports and imports in their own monetary units. Last but not least, an internationally important currency is also a source of political power and prestige. Regarding the globally dominant currency, these advantages represent, of course, the 'exorbitant privilege' which used to be invoked against the US dollar during the Bretton Woods System (see Sect. 2.5). However, the status of international currency also has disadvantages. For example, a country's economic and financial problems might be transmitted more rapidly through international-transaction and reserve currencies and, hence, might expose the issuing countries. In a similar vein, a country whose currency has obtained international status, also holds special responsibilities for the stability of the global financial system and might—especially in times of crisis—be expected to put foreign concerns ahead of national interests.

8.6 Causes and Consequences of Currency Crises

Freely floating exchange rates are inherently unstable and can, in times of aggravated economic and political uncertainty, fluctuate in a highly erratic manner. Indeed, the so-called 'volatility' of an exchange rate represents a closely watched indicator of the level of uncertainty within a given country. It would, however, be misleading to believe that the vagaries of the foreign-exchange markets only beset regimes with floating exchange rates. Interestingly, some of the most spectacular collapses in international monetary history have occurred in the form of massive uncertainties, and eventual devaluations, of supposedly fixed exchange rates. Typically, such currency crises involve a first phase during which the loss of international reserves, unsustainable government deficits, the stockpiling of public and private debt, and other forms of economic inconsistencies gradually undermine a currency peg. During the second phase—which only occurs when these problems remain unaddressed—a country is eventually forced to abandon a fixed parity by either devaluing its currency or letting it float on the foreign-exchange market. Initially, such a devaluation may be beneficial in terms of conserving the international-reserve holdings of the central bank and providing a boost to the export sector. In particular, because currency and public-debt crises tend to be intertwined, it is often highly tempting to simply devalue the currency, rather than increasing taxes, lowering public spending, or presiding over an explicit sovereign default. Of course, abandoning a fixed exchange rate is not without costs. First, the destruction of a fixed exchange rate almost always reduces, or even suddenly stops, capital inflows, as foreign investors are uncertain about future monetary and fiscal conditions. Moreover, when large amounts of money and capital leave the country, a currency crisis can, in turn, destabilise the domestic financial and banking system. Taken together, crises in the foreign-exchange market, in public finances, and in the financial system occur often simultaneously and, hence, result in a twin or even a triple crisis. Typically, these crises are associated with marked economic downturns with massive increases in unemployment and painful reductions in prosperity. South East Asia (1997), Russia (1998), Argentina (2001), Turkey (2001), and Iceland (2008) provide some recent examples of such episodes of economic and financial havoc.

All currency crises are essentially artefacts of the finite amount of international reserves required to support a weak currency. In particular, as long as a currency tends to depreciate, the central bank standing behind it must constantly resort to its international-reserve holdings to intervene in the foreign-exchange market and maintain the fixed rate. However, this type of support cannot go on forever. At latest when a central bank runs out of international reserves, a devaluation is inevitable (see Fig. 8.4). Hence, to explain why currency crises occur, the economic forces weakening a currency must be understood. Recall from the above discussion that, in the short-term, differences in returns on domestic and foreign assets, as reflected by the

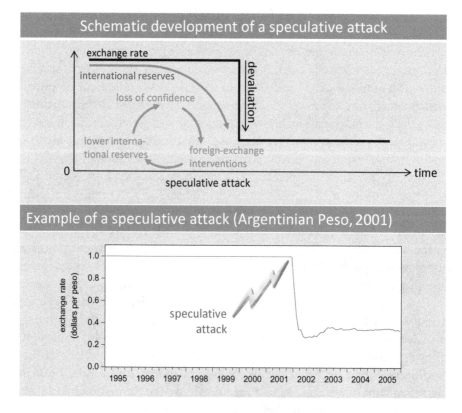

Fig. 8.4   Currency crisis: when currency values come down

level of interest rates, are the main determinant of the exchange rate. More specifically, when a country's level of interest rates is relatively low, its currency tends to depreciate, because domestic assets provide relatively unattractive investment opportunities. Of course, under a regime with fixed exchange rates, the central bank can prevent any type of interest arbitrage from happening by simply adopting the foreign interest-rate level or, in other words, importing the foreign monetary policy (see Sect. 8.2). Conversely, long-term economic developments, which depend on many factors besides monetary policy, can give rise to exchange-rate trends that are much harder to control. Although the corresponding details are again hard to understand without economic models, it can be said that currencies of countries with relatively weak economic growth and high levels of inflation tend to weaken across time. In this regard, any inconsistency between overall economic conditions and a fixed exchange rate can undermine the latter, possibly to the point that a currency crisis erupts. Perhaps the most notorious example of such a development is the case of incompatible monetary and fiscal policies in the sense that a central bank must defend a fixed exchange rate, but the government runs unsustainably large deficits. Insofar as these deficits are partly funded by a policy of cheap money, an upsurge in inflation will eventually result. In turn, the relative loss of purchasing power renders domestic investments relatively less attractive. The result is capital outflows that must be matched by the central bank resorting to its international-reserve holdings to keep the exchange rate stable. In the end, if a government does not depart from its profligate fiscal policy, the pervasive effects of inflation and the ongoing deterioration in the country's international-reserve position will eventually destroy the currency peg.

Sudden devaluations virtually always occur well before the central bank's international reserves are fully depleted. Although this notion might seem odd, it highlights the incompatibility between monetary and economic policies as a driving force behind a currency crisis, whereas the decline in international reserves merely represents a symptom of wider, underlying problems. In particular, as soon as it is more or less obvious that, for example, a given fiscal policy is incompatible with maintaining a currency peg, foreign-exchange traders will begin to worry when the central bank will no longer be able to avert a devaluation. However, the more uncertain the future of a fixed exchange rate is, the greater the incentives are to buy foreign assets and, hence, avoid losses when the domestic currency loses much of its value amid a devaluation. The resulting capital outflows warrant, in turn, more aggressive foreign-exchange interventions at the expense of the international-reserves position. This process may set in motion a vicious cycle, in which the fear of a devaluation reinforces itself by giving rise to an increasingly rapid decline in international-reserves, which further undermines the trust in a fixed exchange-rate regime. In the worst case scenario, a currency peg can fall victim to a so-called 'speculative attack'.[16] The top panel of Fig. 8.4 illustrates this development in a stylised manner, whereas the bottom panel shows a famous example of a speculative attack on the Argentinean peso, which was held on par with the US dollar for years before quickly losing two-thirds of its value at the beginning of 2001.[17] When a fixed exchange rate falls victim to a currency crisis, it is tempting to place the blame entirely on the evil actions of speculators. However, doing so again implies blaming problems on someone else by, essentially, confounding the causes and consequences of a currency crisis. Although speculation does determine when a speculative attack occurs, untenable combinations of monetary and other economic policies have always been the deeper cause for the collapse of fixed exchange-rate regimes.

Given the chaotic nature of a speculative attack, one may wonder why central banks do not simply devalue the currency in an orderly manner as soon as it is clear that a fixed exchange rate is on a collision course with economic reality. Of course, the corresponding debate cannot be made in public, because questioning an exchange-rate peg would send an open invitation to speculators to bet against the domestic currency. Still, in many cases, central banks have missed the right moment for a devaluation, because it could be interpreted as an admission that the country's economic policy has failed. Moreover, a devaluation gives also rise to tangible disadvantages, including an upsurge in inflation, because imported goods and services become more expensive when more domestic currency is suddenly required in exchange for foreign currency.

How can a country protect itself against a currency crisis? Accumulating large buffers of international reserves constitutes a straightforward measure to better guarantee a fixed exchange rate. Several countries hit by a currency crisis during the 1990s (e.g. Thailand, South Korea, China, and Russia) have, thereafter, indeed bolstered their foreign-currency holdings. To repeal an imminent speculative attack, another possibility is to raise foreign credit to replace shortfall left by private investors abandoning a given currency.

---

[16]In 1931, a speculative attack forced the Bank of England to abandon the gold standard (see Sect. 2.4). Furthermore, the Bretton Woods System (see Sect. 2.5) and the European Monetary System (see Sect. 2.7) witnessed several episodes of severe turmoil in the foreign-exchange market.

[17]During the second half of the 1990s, Argentina was on a currency board linking the peso with the US dollar via a one-to-one parity. This parity was installed after hyperinflation at the end of the 1980s to rebuild trust in the Argentinean currency. Despite of the positive experiences with this arrangement in the 1990s, a marked appreciation of the US dollar and, hence, the peso, paired with increasing public deficits and high rates of unemployment in Argentina eventually began to undermine this regained trust. At the end of 2001, this situation led to a speculative attack and, subsequently, a sharp devaluation of the peso.

Such emergency credit lines are nowadays often officially arranged under the auspices of the International Monetary Fund (IMF), which, among other tasks, acts as the international lender of last resort. Because any international financial rescue is only a temporary solution, which would be unsuccessful when the underlying causes of a currency collapse remained unaddressed, IMF loans are almost always subject to certain conditions (in IMF parlour, the so-called 'conditionality'). For the affected countries, these conditions manifest themselves in programs calling for such things as painful public-spending cuts and tax increases to reconcile fiscal and monetary policies, and labour-market reforms that can lead to a reduction in jobs in run-down industries, but gradually strengthen the growth potential in other parts of the economy. Finally, a country can also impose capital controls to stem capital flight during a speculative attack. The downside of restrictions on cross-border financial transactions lies in their direct and indirect economic and bureaucratic costs (see Sect. 8.2).

In principle, speculative attacks may also force a country to revalue its currency. Nevertheless, there is a certain asymmetry in defending the fixed exchange rate of a strong and a weak currency. Because modern central banks have obtained a monopoly over issuing publicly-backed fiat money, in principle, they can deal with an arbitrarily large foreign currency demand without having to resort to a revaluation by simply accumulating more and more international reserves. In contrast to the finite amount of international reserves, creating domestic fiat money has no clear limit. Nevertheless, insofar as such a development is associated with an expansion of the domestic money supply, which could undermine the goal of price stability, a country could decide to revalue its currency for internal economic reasons.[18]

8.7 Common Currency and Monetary Union

When countries share a currency such as the euro (see Sect. 2.7), in daily life, this manifests itself primarily in terms of common banknotes, coins, and harmonised units of account to quote prices. Otherwise, it is perhaps tempting to conclude that an abolishment of national currencies represents just a small step toward completing a fixed exchange-rate regime. However, upon closer inspection, it turns out that common currencies have rather

---

[18]An example for this is Germany after World War II. In particular, to tame inflation, the German mark was revalued on several occasions during the Bretton Woods era as well as within the European Monetary System.

profound implications for the conduct of various kinds of economic policy. Above all, countries that share an officially recognised means of payment have also locked their monetary policies together, as is potently symbolised by the establishment of joint central bank. Sharing a currency necessitates other, and potentially far-reaching, harmonisations of monetary institutions, including banking supervision, the payment system, and even fiscal policy. Furthermore, compared with a currency peg, a complete integration of monetary affairs is much harder to reverse. Recall that even with a currency board, which represents the purest form of a fixed exchange-rate regime, the external value of the currency can be changed simply by decree. As long as a national currency remains in circulation, abandoning a given monetary policy or moving to a different exchange-rate regime remain viable options. In contrast, it is much harder to leave a currency union, as such a step would involve a monetary and financial overhaul that cannot be accomplished overnight.[19]

Similar to fixed exchange rates, a common currency facilitates international trade and investment and, hence, fosters economic integration between the participating countries. These advantages receive a further impetus from abolishing national currencies, as it is then no longer necessary to make costly conversions of money across borders. Furthermore, because there are no exchange rates within a monetary union, uncertainties associated with speculative attacks and forced devaluations no longer exist. As discussed in Sect. 2.7, before the introduction of the euro, so-called 'currency realignments' were indeed a recurrent feature of the European Monetary System. Finally, an identical unit of account also facilitates the comparison of prices across borders and, hence, can foster cross-border competition between local and distant product markets. Taken together, rough estimates suggest that these factors have led to an expansion in trade and cross-border capital flows within the euro area of several per cent.[20]

If the advantages of sharing a currency held unconditionally, a global form of money would probably have long prevailed to fully exploit the welfare benefits of free trade. The introductory quote to this chapter essentially entertains this idea. However, common currencies also suffer from several disadvantages. Above all, the freedom to pursue an autonomous monetary policy tailored

---

[19] Despite its name, the Latin Monetary Union—which provided the framework for France, Belgium, Switzerland, and partly of Italy and Greece to share the same bimetallic standard (see Sect. 2.3)—was not a monetary union but only a multilateral agreement, which did not abolish the national currencies of the member countries.

[20] For an assessment of the economic effects of the introduction of the euro, see Baldwin, Richard, Guiseppe Bertola and Paul Seabright, 2003: *EMU: Assessing the Impact of the Euro*, Blackwell Publishing.

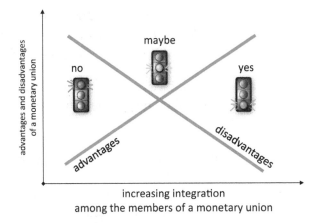

Fig. 8.5 When is it appropriate to have a monetary union?

to national economic goals is eliminated. Furthermore, across the member states, exchange rates are no longer available to stabilise diverging economic developments. As discussed in the previous paragraph, these disadvantages coincide, by and large, with those of fixed exchange-rate regimes. Then again, in the case of a monetary union, the effects of losing monetary-policy autonomy are more severe. Whereas, under a fixed exchange-rate regime, a country retains the option to devalue its currency amid an economic crisis and, hence, provide a boost to the exporting sector (see Sect. 6.3), it is virtually impossible to take similar action with a common currency, which would have to be replaced before a county could walk away from a common central bank. Similarly, being able to revalue a national currency can be helpful to tame inflation, as such a step tends to reduce import prices as the domestic currency suddenly buys more foreign currency units. Remarkably, such considerations played a major role when realignments within the European Monetary System were undertaken (see Sect. 2.7).

When is it appropriate to have a monetary union? It turns out that the trade-offs between the economic advantages and disadvantages of a common currency are essentially a function of the degree of economic and cultural integration between the member countries. As illustrated in Fig. 8.5, the advantages of a common currency tend to increase, whereas the disadvantages tend to decrease, when the involved economies are more interconnected.[21] It

---

[21]This insight results from the 'theory of optimum-currency areas', as proposed by Robert Mundell (*1932), who was awarded the Nobel Prize in Economics in 1999 for, among other things, his analysis of monetary and fiscal policies in common-currency areas.

should be obvious that the gains from an international exchange of economic products are greater between countries with a large potential to trade due to their close geographic or cultural proximity. That the disadvantages of a common currency decrease with the degree of integration is perhaps less clear. An important reason for this view is the synchronous development of the business cycle between highly integrated economies, which implies that similar monetary policies would regardless be warranted to stabilise their macroeconomic development. Conversely, when economic shocks hit some member countries much harder than others, parts of a monetary union could suffer from high levels of inflation, whereas elsewhere average prices are stable or even declining. In this scenario, the lack of a monetary policy tailored to national conditions can become a burden. Similar issues arise when some countries in a monetary union suffer from a recession, but others experience an economic boom. Such situations would call for, respectively, expansionary and contractionary monetary policies. However, under the constraints imposed by a common currency, both policies cannot be simultaneously pursued. Thus, economic imbalances must be offset through other channels, including labour migration from declining to prospering regions. However, people are more likely to move within a monetary union consisting of countries with similar economic and cultural backgrounds.

Overall, Fig. 8.5 suggests that at a certain level of (cultural and economic) integration, a monetary union creates more advantages than disadvantages. Although this result is theoretically compelling, in practice, it is difficult or even impossible to pin down this level (the range of uncertainty reflected by the orange traffic light is, so to speak, rather broad). Certainly, the world economy is currently far from being sufficiently integrated to make a global currency worthwhile. Furthermore, on balance, small territorial units, such as provinces and towns, would suffer from leaving a common-currency framework. Nevertheless, it still remains unclear whether the euro area provides an example of an overall beneficial monetary union.

Thus far, the advantages and disadvantages of a common currency have been framed in purely economic terms as a comparison between cost and benefits. However, it should not be overlooked that some of the main sources of conflict regarding the organisation of a country's monetary system are political in nature. For example, the creation of the euro was widely driven by the desire to deepen economic integration and, thus, overcome the political fragmentation between European nations. Furthermore, political measures can also help to foster the necessary level of integration to hold a monetary union together. In this regard, fiscal transfers, which tend to occur in the opposite direction of labour migration, can be helpful, as they provide an instrument to level economic conditions and, hence, offset the loss of monetary-policy autonomy between heterogeneous member states. Of course, certain political goodwill in all territorial parts of a common currency as well as some degree of central-decision making on government spending and taxation are a precondition for running a public-transfer scheme in an ordinary manner. These observations point yet again to the intimate connections between fiscal and monetary-policy considerations and emphasise that the organisation of the monetary framework has implications for other areas of economic policy. A single currency is more or less equivalent to sharing a common level of inflation, sharing a strategy to stabilise prices and business-cycle fluctuations, and communalising financial risks through lender-of-last-resort interventions. Therefore, successful currencies require political support, which cannot simply be created by government decree. By the same logic, a lack of political support, due to incompatible views on monetary affairs or the unwillingness to make fiscal transfers across the member states, can undermine the stability of a currency.

The previous paragraphs may invoke the experiences of the euro area, which, 10 years after its establishment around 2000, began to suffer from aggravated levels of financial, monetary, and fiscal instability (see Sect. 2.7). It is perhaps surprising to hear that these events are not without historical parallels. For example, the early monetary history of United States was also characterised by political conflicts regarding the adequate level of monetary and fiscal centralisation.[22] In a nutshell, the United States emerged from the war of independence (1775–1783) against the British Empire with high levels of public debt. At the same time, the Articles of Confederation, which provided a first constitutional agreement within the United States and were ratified in 1781, set up a highly decentralised system of government. In particular, the federal government's power to raise taxes was severely restricted. This restriction led to an ongoing public-debt crisis throughout the 1780s reflecting entrenched uncertainties as to whether the United States would be able to honour their financial obligations. By writing a constitution in 1788, this issue was addressed by giving the federal government the prerogative to collect customs and duties—at the time one of the most important sources of government revenue. In exchange, the states could pass on large parts of their debt accumulated during the war of independence to the federal level. However, a monetary union with a central bank emerged only gradually and

---

[22]For a comparison between the US experience and the recent tensions within the euro area see Sargent, Thomas, 2011: *United States then, Europe now*. Lecture given upon receiving the Nobel Prize in Economics.

with several setbacks during the nineteenth and the beginning of the twentieth century, which was long after the move towards fiscal-policy centralisation had begun. Reflecting this discrepancy, nineteenth-century American financial history is marked by a power struggle between the states and the federal government on monetary affairs. Although the ratification of the constitution paved the way for the Bank of the United States, which was founded to serve as a central note-issuing bank, in 1830, its charter was not renewed by Congress, mainly for fear of concentrating too much power at the federal level. Across the subsequent decades, American monetary integration remained incomplete with a common currency (i.e. the dollar) which lacked a single monetary authority providing government-backed reserves in a flexible manner, or acting as the lender of last resort. The absence of a single note-issuing bank was, arguably, one reason for the endemic instability of the US banking system before 1900 (see Sect. 2.2). It was only in 1913 that long-lasting political struggles regarding monetary policy gave way to the establishment of the Federal Reserve System. Owing to the major changes in monetary policy and the economic role of governments since the nineteenth century, the overlaps between the early experiences of the United States and the much more recent tensions within the euro area are, of course, far from complete. However, both episodes underscore that steps towards monetary centralisation are inherently interrelated with fiscal-policy considerations and raise the question of to what extent public-debt obligations are shared. Because the fiscal side of government always forces some groups to pay for the financial privileges of others, the corresponding political controversy is bound to be protracted and ugly.

Further Reading

A popular textbook on international trade and finance is Krugman, Paul, Maurice Obstfeld, and Marc Melitz, 2018: *International Economics—Theory and Policy*, Pearson. Parts 3 and 4 of this book are devoted to issues on the exchange rate and international monetary economics.

A more intuitive introduction to the international monetary system, exchange rates, and international capital flows can be found in textbooks on international financial management. A good text is Eun, Cheol S., and Bruce G. Resnick, 2015: *International Financial Management*, McGraw Hill.

For a long-term perspective on the development of the international financial system, see Obstfeld, Maurice, and Alan M. Taylor, 2004: *Global Capital Markets: Integration, Crisis, and Growth*, Cambridge University Press.

The most comprehensive economic treatment of mercantilism is still Heckscher, Eli, 1955: *Mercantilism*, 2 volumes, George Allen and Unwin. Part 4 of the second volume is devoted to mercantilism as monetary system.

A detailed economic analysis of the currency union, including the challenges to European monetary integration, can be found in De Grauwe, Paul, 2012: *Economics of Monetary Union*, Oxford University Press.

9

Final Chapter: The Past, Present, and Future of Central Banking

Money is like language—an instrument of communication. Money and language have both emerged spontaneously, where human beings wanted to exchange something—ideas on the one hand, and property rights or financial claims on the other hand. Similar to the meaning of the words and sentences of a language, the value of money should not quickly change much if communication is not to suffer from misunderstandings. Herbert Giersch (German economist, 1921–2010)[1]

Against the background of the eventful German monetary history during the last century, it is maybe appropriate to end this book with a quote from Herbert Giersch, who witnessed not one, but two complete collapses of the monetary system (in 1923 and 1945), before becoming an influential economist for the German federal government. However, it is easy to extent Giersch's marvellous comparison between money and language to matters of central banking. The privilege to issue currency, that is, officially recognised forms of money, empowers the central bank to influence the monetary, financial, and economic conditions of a given country. Similar to the way in which official rules on grammar, syntax, or spelling simplify reading and writing, some degree of government regulation to standardise money can facilitate economic transactions. Of course, governments should not, and probably cannot, manage every aspect of money and language, as many developments are simply the result of a spontaneous historical process resulting in many informal norms

---

[1]Origin of quote unknown.

© Springer Nature Switzerland AG 2019
N. Herger, *Understanding Central Banks*, https://doi.org/10.1007/978-3-030-05162-4_9

and unofficial conventions. With language, this spontaneous order—which some might call chaos—manifests itself in such things as dialects, the current buzzwords, and the many peculiarities of the spoken language, which often deviates substantially from the official standard. With money, the central bank is only directly involved in the provision of cash and bank reserves, whereas commercial banks and other financial firms offer, for example, bank deposits as close substitutes to legal tender and, furthermore, have often been the driving force behind innovations within the payment system. Hence, governments may propose their favourite forms of money, but, at the end of the day, the economic interaction between ordinary people determines the prevailing means of payment (an analogy can again be made to language). In any case, as the guardian of the currency, the central bank has the key responsibility of maintaining the purchasing power of money and, hence, of providing a certain degree of stability within the monetary system. A failure to do so typically results in unhealthy levels of inflation, which hinders economic activity as the confusion of tongues undermined the construction of the Tower of Babel.

In more concrete terms, central banks are today primarily responsible for the conduct of monetary policy, which encompasses a range of measures, including setting the base interest rate, intervening in money and foreign-exchange markets, managing and supervising the payment system, holding the ultimate reserve from commercial banks, and managing the international-reserve position. Originally, these monetary-policy measures were intended to ensure that an adequate supply of officially recognised forms of money circulates within a given economy. However, at least since the Great Depression of the 1930s, central banks have adopted much broader mandates, in the sense of taking responsibility for stabilising the macroeconomic environment, whereby the adjustment of the money supply and other monetary variables is only a means to an end. Of note, macroeconomic management is any-thing but trivial, as money exhibits fundamentally different relationships with other economic variables across different time horizons. In particular, because prices and wages do not immediately absorb changes in the monetary environment—including the money supply, the level of interest rates, and the nominal exchange rate—the policy pursued by a central bank can temporarily affect the real-side of the economy. Whereas additional central-bank money may stimulate aggregate spending on consumption and investment in the short-term, different relationships hold in the long-term, when all economic adjustment processes have occurred and, above all, prices and wages have had enough time to react in a completely flexible manner. In this scenario, real economic growth can no longer be boosted via monetary policy, whereas increases in the money supply exhibit directly proportional effects on nominal variables, such as the average price level. This neutrality result is intuitive when bearing in mind that money is simply a convenient means to settle economic transactions. Unfortunately, an economic paradise, in which profits or wages can be increased by printing more money does not seem to exist in this world. All these considerations are of crucial importance for the strategic orientation of monetary policy. Because inflation is a monetary phenomenon in the long-term, it is a logical step to instruct the central bank to keep current and future changes in the average price level in check. Doing so is an important public task. In fact, by undermining the functions of money as a means of payment, unit of account, and store of value, inflation is costly. Furthermore, aggregate price 'shocks' tend to give rise to an antisocial wealth redistribution, because the less well-off are often disproportionately affected by inflation.

To maintain the purchasing power of the currency, the overriding goal of central banks for centuries was to link the value of money to the value of precious metals, such as gold or silver. Under a metallic monetary system, violations of the 'rules of the game' were plainly obvious when, for example, the convertibility of banknotes was suspended. However, the lack of monetary flexibility to deal with severe recessions or banking crises introduced a severe caveat to any form of precious-metal-based money. To address this issue, the history of central banking has been characterised by a gradual move towards a more flexible fiat system, in which the necessary amount of money can be supplied to settle current economic transactions at the current level of prices. However, by severing the link to precious metals, it has become much harder to preserve the public's trust that the purchasing power of the currency will be kept stable. In this regard, clear and widely backed mandates defining the ultimate goals and principles of monetary policy have become crucial ingredients to ensure that central banks do not get embroiled in economic fine-tuning or profligate fiscal-policy adventures.

Due to the Global Financial Crisis, the past decade has been particularly challenging for central banks. Although it is too early to draw conclusions regarding the large number of measures that have been taken, it can be said that the monetary interventions have at least prevented a complete collapse of the financial and economic system. An economic depression comparable to the 1930s thankfully did not occur. Still, the recent experiences with conventional and unconventional measures, including unprecedented experiments with slightly negative nominal interest rates, are likely to influence the monetary-policy discussion during the next years, or even decades.

Although central-bank issues will probably always be discussed along ideo-logical lines, historical experience suggests that it is dangerous to believe that monetary policy provides a panacea against all kinds of economic problems.

Of course, the monopoly over issuing currency is a potent instrument to shape the economic environment. Furthermore, central banks are doubtless important institutions to safeguard the stability of the financial system. Nevertheless, monetary policy has many limitations, which result from the trade-offs between the short and long-term effects of monetary-policies and the limited choices between safeguarding the internal and external stability of the currency across various international monetary systems. Despite the success of many central banks in fighting inflation since the 1990s, there is no guarantee that marked increases in the average price level will not return. The temptation to raise an inflation tax or abuse monetary policy for short-term economic or fiscal gains is an endemic feature of any monetary system.

Given these complex considerations, I conclude with the following observation. As shown in various parts of this book, any potential reorganisation in monetary affairs can have far-reaching economic and social effects. Hence, the definition of the central bank's mandate is not a mere triviality, implying that any reform should be thought through and broadly supported. In this regard, it is important to realise that modern central banks are macroeconomic institutions that can guarantee an adequate supply of fiat money and, in doing so, keep average prices stable. Conversely, economic challenges, such as high levels of unemployment and public debt, cannot be solved via monetary policy. Hence, in the past as well as in the future, probably the biggest danger lies in expecting central banks to suddenly be able to run some kind of monetary perpetuum mobile, or, in other words, holding the erroneous belief that the monopoly over issuing currency 'out of nothing' allows to create prosperity 'out of nothing'.

Glossary

Anchor currency (See international currency).

Appreciation An appreciation reflects an increase in the value of the domestic currency relative to foreign currency. In this situation, the value of the exchange rate can fall or increase, depending on whether the price of the foreign currency unit is defined per domestic currency unit or vice versa. An appreciation can result from changes in private demand and supply on the foreign-exchange market, or central-bank interventions. In case the central bank changes the exchange-rate parity, such that the value of the domestic currency increases, this is called a revaluation.

Arbitrage Arbitrage refers to the exploitation of price differences of substitutable goods or assets across time or regions to make risk-free profits. In particular, the purchase occurs at the lower price, to sell the good or asset at a higher price in another market. Under certain conditions (such as low transaction costs), arbitrage transactions adjust the prices in markets with sufficiently substitutable goods and assets. Arbitrage is a key mechanism behind the purchasing-power-parity theory and the interest-parity condition.

Asset transformation Asset transformation refers to the simultaneous holding of assets and liabilities that differ in terms of their liquidity, maturity, risk, or denomination within a financial firm.

Automatic stabiliser An automatic stabiliser smooths economic fluctuations without requiring policy-makers to make discrete decisions. An example of an automatic stabiliser is the exchange rate. When the currency of a country depreciates amid a severe recession, the exchange rate provides a boost to exports and, thus, improves economic conditions.

Balance of payments The balance of payments records the international (or cross-border) transactions of a country during a specific period (e.g. a year). In particular, the current account mainly provides a statistical summary of international trade,

© Springer Nature Switzerland AG 2019
N. Herger, *Understanding Central Banks*, https://doi.org/10.1007/978-3-030-05162-4

whereas the financial account records the international flow of money and capital with the rest of the world.

Balance sheet A balance sheet is a list of the financial assets (or claims) and liabilities of an economic unit (typically a firm).

Bank reserves Bank reserves (sometimes also called ultimate reserves) encompass deposits held by commercial banks at the central bank, as well as currency that is physically held in their vaults (vault cash).

Base interest rate The base interest rate is an interest rate determined by the central bank to affect the refinancing conditions of commercial banks. The base interest rate is one of the most powerful instruments of monetary policy and adopts a key role in the communication of changes in monetary policy. Originally, the base interest rate referred to the discount rate. Depending on the monetary-policy strategy, today, the base interest rate often relates to an interbank rate (e.g. Libor, federal funds rate) or directly to the refinancing rate (e.g. bank rate, repo rate, etc.) of the corresponding central bank.

Bill of exchange A bill of exchange is a financial security, with which cashless payments in international trade and finance used to be made. In particular, a bill of exchange was a written order by an issuer, called the drawer, instructing a counterparty, called the drawee, to pay a certain amount of money at a specific place. Bills of exchange could be sold before their due date to a third party, called the acceptor, who took over the responsibility to make the final payment, but charged an interest rate called the discount rate. Because central banks mainly accepted bills of exchange as collateral for central-bank money, the discount rate was long the key interest rate for conducting monetary policy. Today, bills of exchange have no important role in international payments. However, in some countries, the base interest rate is still called 'discount rate' for historical reasons.

Business cycle The joint fluctuations of macroeconomic variables (consumption, investment, employment, etc.) are called the business cycle. Typically, economies do not grow steadily, but rather witness periods of marked upsurges, or booms, and downturns, or recessions, in general economic activity and employment.

Capital controls Capital controls are administrative measures and constraints limiting the cross-border exchange of money and capital.

Capital market The capital market encompasses financial markets on which securities (and other assets) with terms to maturity of more than 1 year are traded (See also money market).

Capital requirements Capital requirements reflect the mandatory ratio of equity to assets at a commercial bank. Capital requirements are an important instrument of banking regulation.

Cash Cash refers to physical forms of money, that is, banknotes and coins.

Central bank The central bank (also called the national or reserve bank) is a financial institute—nowadays usually under the public law—responsible for setting monetary policy. Central banks wield influence over the economy, because they have been granted the monopoly over the issuance of currency. Among other things, this monopoly gives them the power to steer interest rates and, hence, determine how much money and credit circulates through the economy. By employing a range of monetary-policy instruments (repurchase agreements, open-market operations, etc.), modern central banks pursue macroeconomic goals such as keeping the price level stable (preserving the purchasing power of a currency) or smoothing the business cycle. Among many other tasks, central banks play also a leading role within the financial system in the sense that they traditionally act as the lender of last resort to the banking sector in times of financial crisis. Additional activities can include, acting as a banker for the government and other banks, supervising individual commercial banks and determining their minimum-reserve requirements, supervising and managing parts of the payment system and financial-market infrastructure, issuing banknotes, raising money for the government, managing a country's international reserves, or providing consumer protection in monetary and financial matters.

Central-bank money (See monetary base).

Commercial banks Commercial banks are financial intermediaries that accept deposits but can also be refinanced through other sources, such as debt and equity, and at the same time provide loans on their own accounts to firms and households.

Commodity money (See fiat money).

Currency Currency refers to forms of money that are officially recognised by the government.

Currency parity (See parity).

Deflation Deflation refers to a sustained reduction in average prices (See also inflation).

Denominated The adjective denominated means 'expressed in terms of a given currency'.

Deposits Deposits are highly liquid assets held by the public (households and firms) on their bank accounts.

Depreciation A depreciation reflects a decline in the value of the domestic currency relative to foreign currency. In this situation, the value of the exchange rate can increase or fall, depending on whether the price of the foreign currency unit is defined per domestic currency unit or vice versa. A depreciation can result from changes in private demand and supply on the foreign-exchange market or central-bank interventions. In case the central bank changes the exchange-rate parity such that the value of the domestic currency decreases, this is called a devaluation.

Devaluation (See depreciation).

Discount and discount rate (See base interest rate and bill of exchange).

Eurocurrency Eurocurrency encompasses bank deposits and other assets that are not denominated in the currency of the local financial centre. For example, dollar-denominated assets held outside the United States (say, in London or Tokyo) are called eurodollars.

Exchange rate The exchange rate reflects the rate at which domestic currency can be converted into foreign currency. In particular, the nominal exchange rate reflects the relative price of domestic and foreign currency in terms of monetary units. A change in this price that decreases the value of the domestic currency is a nominal depreciation, and a corresponding increase is a nominal appreciation. The real exchange rate reflects the ratio of the purchasing power of currencies and, thus, accounts for international differences in average prices. A relative reduction in foreign prices also increases the purchasing power of the domestic currency and, hence, causes a real appreciation. Conversely, a relative increase in foreign prices causes a real depreciation (See also appreciation, depreciation, and purchasing-power parity).

Exchange-rate parity (See parity).

Exchange-rate regime The exchange-rate regime refers to the institutional framework, within which the exchange rate is determined. In general, a distinction can be made between a fixed exchange-rate regime, in which the exchange rate is primarily determined by interventions of the central bank, and a floating exchange-rate regime, in which the exchange rate reacts freely to demand and supply in the foreign-exchange market. In addition to pure fixed and floating exchange-rate regimes, there are numerous intermediate systems.

Fiat money Fiat money is a form of money in which the direct link to precious metals or other commodities has been severed. Alternatively, it can be called 'money created by decree' or, formerly, 'paper money' (which is becoming rapidly outdated due to the massive growth in electronic payments). The opposite of fiat money is commodity money, whose value is directly defined in terms of some commodity (gold, silver, copper, precious stones, etc.). Commodity money has largely disappeared.

Fiscal policy Fiscal policy encompasses all government efforts and actions aimed at affecting macroeconomic outcomes (economic output, employment, etc.) through fiscal variables, that is, the way in which public funds are used, managed, or raised. The prime objective of fiscal policy is typically to stabilise the business cycle, whereas the main measures are changes in the levels of taxes and public expenditures.

Fisher equation According to the Fisher equation, the real interest rate is approximately given by the difference between the nominal interest rate and the inflation rate, that is

$$\text{real interest rate} \approx \text{nominal interest rate} - \text{inflation rate}$$

For example, with a nominal interest rate of 5% and an inflation rate of 3%, the real interest rate equals 2%. In the ex-ante version of the Fisher equation, which is relevant for investment decisions, the inflation rate is measured by its expectation. The actual return of a fixed-income security depends, however, on the ex-post version, where the inflation rate is measured by its actual value, which is of course only known with hindsight (or ex-post) (See also interest rate).

Federal-funds rate The federal-funds rate is the interest rate against which banks can lend and borrow short-term loans on the United States' interbank market (See also interbank market).

Foreign direct investment Foreign direct investment encompasses the part of international capital flows through which multinational firms establish ownership control over foreign firms or plants. In contrast, portfolio investments occur when a foreign investor establishes only a minority stake in a foreign firm/plant. Foreign direct and portfolio investments are reported in the financial account of the balance of payments.

Foreign-exchange interventions Foreign-exchange interventions involve the buying and selling of foreign currency against domestic currency by the central bank.

Government bonds Government bonds are debt-instruments issued by the state (allowing the government to raise debt). In different countries, government bonds have different names, including Treasury bills and Treasury bonds (USA), Gilts (United Kingdom), and Bundesanleihen or 'Bunds' (Germany).

Gross domestic product The gross domestic product (GDP) reflects the value—measured at market prices—of all goods and services produced within an economy during a specific period (e.g. a year). Using the market prices in the current year yields nominal GDP. When the market prices in a specific base year are used instead, the result is real GDP. The ratio of nominal to real GDP is the so-called GDP deflator, which provides a possible measure for inflation.

High-powered money (See monetary base).

Hyperinflation By definition, a monthly increase in the average price level of 50% or more is called a hyperinflation. The corresponding annual inflation rate is around 13,000%.

Illiquidity Illiquidity refers to a situation, in which an economic unit, such as a bank, does not have enough liquid funds (money) to honour its current financial obligations. In that sense, illiquidity represents an inability to pay.

Inflation Inflation refers to a sustained increase in the average price level. Usually, inflation is measured according to the percentage increase in a consumer-price index referring to a fixed basket of goods and services, or the GDP deflator. The corresponding per-cent change is called the inflation rate. Inflation can have vastly different economic effects depending on whether it has been expected or unexpected (See also deflation and gross domestic product).

Inflation tax The inflation tax is connected to the notion of seigniorage. The inflation tax emphasises that the monopoly profit from issuing currency results from an increase in the money supply and, due to the neutrality property, inflation. Part of seigniorage therefore arises from the loss in purchasing power when firms and households hold money. The counterpart to this loss is the inflation tax accruing to the government (See also seigniorage).

Insolvency Insolvency refers to a situation, in which the financial liabilities of an economic unit exceed its assets (or claims). In other words, over-indebtedness has occurred.

Interbank market On the interbank market, commercial banks grant each other short-term loans. Hence, the interbank market is a part of the money market.

Interest-parity condition The interest-parity condition is a theory to explain the short-term behaviour of the exchange rate. In particular, a connection is made between the domestic and foreign interest rate and exchange-rate changes. The formula of interest parity reflects primarily a no-arbitrage condition between the return on a domestic and a foreign asset, that is

$$\underbrace{\text{domestic interest rate}}_{\text{return on a domestic asset}} \approx \underbrace{\text{foreign interest rate} + \text{exchange rate change}}_{\text{return on a foreign asset}}.$$

The interest-parity condition suggests that an increase in domestic interest rates is typically associated with an immediate appreciation of the domestic currency.

Interest rate An interest rate reflects the monetary compensation, typically expressed as a percentage, for loaning out various forms of money, capital, and other economic resources. The corresponding percentage rate is called the interest rate and is usually expressed in monetary units (nominal interest rate), but can also be adjusted for the effect of inflation (real interest rate). Across the economy, a whole range of time-varying interest rates reflect, for example, different terms to maturity or probabilities of default. The broad average of these interest rates is called the level of interest rates.

International currency An international currency is widely used outside the borders of the issuing country and, hence, fulfils the functions of money in an international context. In particular, an international transaction currency is a broadly used means to pay for exports and imports or to make cross-border capital flows. An international anchor currency is used as a reference point (or unit of account) within a fixed exchange-rate regime. An international reserve currency is used abroad as a store of value and, in particular, for foreign central banks, to hold international reserves.

International monetary policy International monetary policy refers to all efforts and actions by the government to influence the state of the economy by determining the external value of the currency. Particularly relevant is the definition of the exchange-rate regime.

International (official) reserves (See reserves).

Investment banks Investment banks raise money for businesses and government and act as brokers or dealers in financial markets. Investment banking used to be limited to the subscription of shares and bonds and the trading of financial assets on secondary markets. Today, investment banking is thought to include participation in mergers and acquisitions and consulting, among other activities.

Lender of last resort As the lender of last resort, the central bank provides emergency liquidity assistance to commercial banks in times of crisis. Thereby, the aim is to safeguard the aggregate supply of money and credit to prevent a full blown banking and financial crisis. Crisis-hit countries can also be supported by international organisations, such as the International Monetary Fund (IMF), which can act as the international lender of last resort.

Libor Libor is an acronym referring to the London interbank offered rate, which is the (indicative) interest rate against which commercial banks are willing to provide short-term loans in the London interbank market. The corresponding interest rates are fixed daily for various currencies and terms to maturity. The Libor provides an important reference rate for the international financial system. There are currently attempts to replace the Libor with a benchmark based on money-market interest rates on actual financial transactions (See also interbank market).

Liquidity Liquidity refers to the ease with which an asset can be used as a means of payment. Cash, for example, is highly liquid.

Minimum-reserve requirements Minimum-reserve requirements determine the mandatory fraction of bank reserves relative to the reservable deposits of commercial banks (See also bank reserves).

Monetary The adjective monetary means 'pertaining to money or currency'.

Monetary aggregates Monetary aggregates measure the empirical amount of money in circulation. Depending on how strictly the features of money are defined, monetary aggregates encompass only cash or additional items such as sight deposits (M1), savings deposits (M2), and time deposits (M3).

Monetary base The monetary base is composed of cash and the sight deposits (bank reserves) held at the central bank. The corresponding values appear on the liability-side of the central bank's balance sheet. Another expression for the monetary base is central-bank, or high-powered, money (See also bank reserves and cash).

Monetary policy Monetary policy refers to all efforts and actions by the central bank and the government to influence macroeconomic outcomes (economic output, employment, inflation, etc.) by manipulating monetary variables, such as interest rates, the supply of money, credit conditions, and exchange rates.

Monetary-policy-transition mechanism The monetary-policy-transition mechanism describes the way in which monetary interventions affect the various parts of the economy in the short-term. The most prominent example is the interest-rate channel, through which changes in the base interest rate shift the average level of interest rates entailing further investment and consumption effects. Other transmission mechanisms occur via asset prices, the amounts of loans issued by banks, and the exchange rate.

Money Money encompasses all assets that are generally accepted to settle economic transactions. Hence, money fulfils primarily the function of a means of payment. Derived from this function, money almost always serves as a unit of account (to measure prices) and a store of value. The best (but by far not the only) example of an asset that can readily be used to make transactions is cash.

Money market The money market encompasses financial markets, on which securities (and other assets) with terms to maturity of less than 1 year are traded (See also capital market).

National bank (See central bank).

Neutrality property The neutrality property of money suggests that changes in monetary conditions impact only nominal variables, such as prices, and not real variables. In the long-term, there is indeed a more or less proportional relationship between the growth of money and inflation as well as the nominal interest rates and inflation expectations.

Nominal Nominal is a measure in terms of monetary units (See also real).

Note-issuing bank The expression note-issuing bank originally referred to financial institutions having the right to issue their own banknotes. Owing to the public monopolisation of the note-issuing business, the term 'note-issuing bank' is often used synonymously with 'central bank'.

Open-market operations Open-market operations are the direct purchase and sale of securities by the central bank on the open market to influence the monetary base. Open-market operations are an instrument of monetary policy.

Parity Parity refers to fundamentally equal prices of domestic and foreign currency. In a broad sense, parity is achieved when the market exchange rate coincides with the fixed (also called pegged or official) exchange rate set by the central bank. In a narrower sense, parity can also refer to a situation in which the nominal exchange rate or the purchasing power between currencies is one-to-one (See also purchasing-power parity).

Phillips-curve The Phillips-curve depicts the joint behaviour of inflation and unemployment. In the short-term, the corresponding relationship tends to be negative (more inflation is associated with less unemployment). Owing to time-varying inflation expectations, this negative relationship is unstable. Over the long-term, the developments of inflation and unemployment are largely unrelated.

Purchasing-power-parity theory According to the purchasing-power-parity theory, the exchange rate reflects long-term, international differences in inflation. In particular, the relative version of this theory is given by

$$\text{exchange rate change} = \text{domestic inflation rate} - \text{foreign inflation rate},$$

whereby the exchange rate is defined in terms of domestic currency units per foreign currency unit. Hence, a relatively high level of domestic inflation results in a depreciation of the domestic currency. This makes sure that the international purchasing power of the involved currencies does not diverge.

Real Real refers to measures in terms of goods, services, and other economically useful items. By avoiding a direct reference to monetary units, real values are invariant to the effect of inflation, that is changes in the value of money (See also nominal).

Repurchase agreements Repurchase agreements (in short **repos**) are an important instrument to implement monetary policy. Thereby, a central bank issues a short-term credit to a commercial bank, which in turn must provide collateral for receiving central-bank money. At the outset, the terms and conditions of the repurchase are also defined. The term to maturity is typically short (several days or weeks). The interest charged by the central bank for such short-term credits is the repo rate.

Reserves Reserves is a notion referring to the international reserves of the central bank as well as the bank reserves. International reserves (including foreign-exchange reserves) are the stocks of foreign currency held as claims by the central bank. International reserves provide a basis for making foreign-exchange interventions. Conversely, bank reserves are liabilities on the central bank's balance sheet and encompass the sight deposits held by commercial banks on their accounts at the central bank.

Reserve bank (See central bank).

Reserve currency (See international currency).

Revaluation (See appreciation).

Seigniorage Seigniorage is the government's profit resulting from the publicly backed monopoly to issue currency. This profit accrues from several sources that lend themselves neither to straightforward economic measurement, nor a direct comparison with accounting profits. Fiscal seigniorage, that is, the actual financial transfer from the central bank to the ministry of finance, is relevant to the budget process (See also inflation tax).

Sight deposits Sight deposits include deposits that can be withdrawn on demand and, hence, are almost always available to make payments (See also deposits).

Stagflation A stagflation refers to the combined occurrence of economic stagnation (or a recession) and high inflation.

Too big to fail Too big to fail refers to the problem that an economic unit (typically a bank) has become so large (or systemically relevant) that a bankruptcy would have massive negative effects on virtually all parts of the economy.

Zero-lower bound The zero-lower bound suggests that nominal interest rates cannot fall below (or at least not far below) the value of zero.

Index

© Springer Nature Switzerland AG 2019
N. Herger, *Understanding Central Banks*, https://doi.org/10.1007/978-3-030-05162-4

CPSIA information can be obtained
at www.ICGtesting.com
Printed in the USA
BVHW011011010522
635836BV00002B/29

9 783030 051617